The Making of Social Policy
in Britain 1830–1990

The Making of Social Policy in Britain 1830–1990

Kathleen Jones

ATHLONE
London and Atlantic Highlands, NJ

First published 1991 by The Athlone Press Ltd
1 Park Drive, London NW11 7SG and
171 First Avenue, Atlantic Highlands, NJ 07716

© Kathleen Jones 1991

British Library Cataloguing in Publication Data
Jones, Kathleen *1922–*
    The making of social policy in Britain 1830–1990.
    1. Great Britain. Social policies
    I. Title
361.610941

    ISBN 0–485–11392–9
    ISBN 0–485–12077–1 pbk

Library of Congress Cataloging in Publication data
Jones, Kathleen, *1922–*
    The making of social policy in Britain, 1830–1990 / Kathleen
    Jones.
        p.   cm.
    Includes bibliographical references and index.
    ISBN 0–485–11392–9. — ISBN 0–485–12077–1 (pbk.)
    1. Great Britain—Social policy.   2. Great Britain—Social
conditions—19th century.   3. Great Britain—Social conditions—20th
century.   I. Title.
HN383.5.J66   1991
361.6′1′0941—dc20

Typeset by J&L Composition Ltd, Filey, North Yorkshire
Printed in Great Britain by Billings, Worcester

Contents

List of Figures		vii
List of Tables		viii
Introduction		ix
Chapter One	Old Problems and New Economics	1
Chapter Two	The Poor and the Poor Law	13
Chapter Three	Dirt, Disease and Danger	25
Chapter Four	Voluntary Action	42
Chapter Five	Darkest England and the Poverty Surveys	57
Chapter Six	Bypassing the Poor Law	69
Chapter Seven	Victorian Values or Socialist Visions?	82
Chapter Eight	The Liberal Answer	95
Chapter Nine	The Hungry Thirties	104
Chapter Ten	War, Peace and the Beveridge Plan	120
Chapter Eleven	Setting up the 'Welfare State'	134
Chapter Twelve	Problems of Expansion	149
Chapter Thirteen	Problems of Contraction	166
Chapter Fourteen	Social Policy in the 1980s	188
Epilogue		209
Appendix I	Political Parties in Power, 1830–1990	212
Appendix II	Biographical Notes	214
Bibliography		222
Notes and Sources		235
Index		261

In memory of Brian Rodgers
Words have ancestors

List of Figures

Figure I   Population, United Kingdom, 1821–1901   5
Figure II   Live births per 1000 population, United
               Kingdom, 1870–1940   78
Figure III   Infant mortality, England and Wales, 1881–1987   81
Figure IV   Unemployment, United Kingdom, 1900–1945   106
Figure V   Beveridge's economic and social indices, 1930   113
Figure VI   Live births per 1000 population, United
               Kingdom, 1939–51   135
Figure VII   The Six Classes of the Population in the Social
               Insurance proposals of 1944   137
Figure VIII   Age-structure of the population, 1901 and 1981   170
Figure IX   Structure of the National Health Service in 1948
               and 1975   176
Figure X   Local Government areas, England, before
               1 April 1974   178
Figure XI   Local Government areas, England, since
               1 April 1974   179
Figure XII   Unemployment, United Kingdom, 1977–87   191

List of Tables

Table 5.1   Charles Booth's classification of the distribution
            of poverty   61
Table 9.1   Unemployment Insurance: contributions and
            benefits 1920–31   105
Table 9.2   Persons in receipt of Public Assistance,
            1 January 1936   117
Table 10.1 Beveridge's proposals for meeting the Eight
            Primary Causes of Need   127
Table 14.1 Responses to survey questions on paying for the
            social services, 1983–1987   203

Introduction

History, as A. J. P. Taylor reminds us, gets thicker as it approaches modern times. 'There are more people, more events, and more is written about them'.[1] Social history gets particularly thick, because more attention is paid to the lives of ordinary citizens, more of them are literate, and more join in the debate. As a result, any attempt to chronicle social history in the nineteenth and twentieth centuries must be largely a matter of précis: there is a flood of information – reports, blue books, surveys, memoranda, diaries, books. No modern publisher would consider the seventeen volumes of Charles Booth's *Life and Labour of the People of London*, and Her Majesty's Stationery Office would now be unlikely to publish all the evidence of the Royal Commission on the Poor Laws of 1909, which ran to thirty-seven volumes.

Condensing the story of a hundred and sixty years of social policy into a single introductory text is a fairly rash enterprise. Much has to be omitted. Some writers have concentrated on economic change, heavily weighting the text with statistics about coal production, shipping and the price of corn. Some have focused on outstanding individuals – politicians, social reformers. Fabian writers like the Webbs and the Coles have concentrated on collective movements – the rise of the Labour Party, the development of trade unions, the Co-operative movement.

After the Second World War, the focus of interest switched to the 'Welfare State'. Titles like Maurice Bruce's *The Coming of the Welfare State*, Derek Fraser's *The Evolution of the British Welfare State* or Pat Thane's *The Foundation of the Welfare State* suggested a belief in (or at least a desire for) linear progress. For forty years, there was a public consensus about welfare, supported by both Labour and Conservative governments. It was taken for granted that a civilized society should provide two kinds of social services: universal services, ranging from environmental health care to income maintenance and education, which affected all the population; and special services for people who could not be self-supporting – neglected and deprived children, poor families, sick, handicapped and disabled people, the infirm or isolated elderly. Though there were problems in how this could best be done, the debates about *whether* it should be done seemed to belong to the remote past. It was assumed that the framework of welfare, organized through the structures of central and local government, was basically sound, and that it could be steadily improved by means of more surveys, more blue books and more acts of Parliament.

In the 1980s, these placid assumptions were sharply challenged. A new Conservative Government rejected consensus, introduced stringent financial controls, and brought the values and methods of the business world into the area of welfare. Some very old arguments about the nature of poverty, the evils of state intervention and the virtues of standing on one's own feet have been revived, and presented with a new conviction.

Nearly forty years had passed since the Beveridge Plan caught the public imagination with its promise of 'social security from the cradle to the grave'. (The phrase was not Beveridge's own – it came from the popular Press.) The vision of a 'Welfare State' developed in the war-torn 1940s had begun to lose its power – there were too many complaints about bureaucracy, about the way individuals got lost in the administrative machine, about the untargeted use of public funds, about the controlling tendencies of experts and professionals. And there had to be limits to service expansion. Public expectations of what the state could provide had outrun the capacity of any government to finance. England, no longer an imperial power, edging towards membership of a European bloc, in fierce competition for overseas markets, could no longer rely on continuous economic growth to finance increasing demands; but the question of what demands could and should be met was still a matter for heated political debate.

The story has to start before 1834 – the date of the Poor Law

Amendment Act – because so many of the problems of that generation are with us again: the stigmatization of poverty, the battle over public and private control of essential utilities, the hope that voluntary social services can provide from charity what the state will not provide by right, the battle over centralization. Though the context has changed, there are many lessons to be learned from studying the nineteenth-century controversies, and the nineteenth-century discoveries. Some of these lessons are in danger of being forgotten.

I have tried to steer a middle course between the history of individual social thinkers and reformers, and the history of more broad-based social movements; to put in something of the clash of ideas and personalities at the top of the social system, while not forgetting the effect on people at the bottom – Seebohm Rowntree's 'mass of stunted human life'. I have also tried to keep a sense of political balance – for which I may well be blamed by those with stronger convictions either to the political Right or the political Left. But my own strong conviction is that, while no writer can be fully objective, it is not academically respectable to distort the past in order to make a political point in the present.

Inevitably, this is 'topic' history rather than 'line' history. Given seventeen volumes, it would have been possible to follow particular themes – Education, Child Care, Social Insurance and so on – in some detail through the period. A single volume can only go hedge-hopping through the years, picking out the major controversies and the major developments. The specialist histories in many cases already exist, and have been noted in the footnotes and the bibliography.

There are so many sources for this story that reference to all of them would be tedious, and take up most of the available space. Footnotes have been kept to a minimum in the earlier chapters, where the material has been well worked over by social historians and other specialists. More footnotes are necessary in the later chapters – particularly the last two, which are too recent to be 'history'. Each chapter is followed by a note on sources for further reading, and there are brief bibliographies of the main characters at the end of the book.

A familiar apology is due to readers from Scotland, Wales and Northern Ireland. I have written primarily about social policy in England. Sometimes that also applies to other parts of the United

Kingdom, and sometimes not. Scotland and Northern Ireland in particular tend to have slightly different forms of provision. Another dimension which has had to be omitted is that of welfare services in other parts of the EEC, and the current work on harmonizing social legislation. The British (or English) 'Welfare State' has not been a unique development. Other European countries have their own stories to tell, and services which in some respects are superior to ours. In the future, these may have considerable influence on what happens in England (Britain). But comparative social policy is still very limited, and there is a great deal more work to be done before we can make broad comparisons in space as well as in time.

I should like to thank two colleagues, Barbara Rodgers, formerly of the University of Manchester, and Tony Fowles of the University of York, for their assistance in reading and commenting on the manuscript. I am also grateful to my undergraduate Development of Social Policy class in the University of York, to whom I fed it, chapter by chapter, through the academic year 1989–90. It was very useful to know what they liked and disliked, which parts they found exciting and what was boring or incomprehensible. I profited from the experience, and I hope they did. On this occasion, any errors or omissions are mine and not theirs.

K. J.
University of York

ONE

Old Problems and New Economics

In 1830, a Whig Government took office after forty-six years in Opposition, broken only briefly by Fox's short-lived 'Ministry of All the Talents' in 1806. One of their first responsibilities was to pilot the Reform Act of 1832 through Parliament, abolishing the rotten boroughs and pocket boroughs which powerful landowners regarded as their personal patronage, and substituting a modest degree of democracy by giving the vote to small property owners. The '40 shilling freeholders' and '£10 copyholders' who then voted in another Whig Government in 1832 expected more reform to follow, and they were not to be disappointed. Social reform had been held back by a long succession of Tory governments, fearful of revolution, since before the storming of the Bastille in 1789. But change was no longer to be denied. Now the aristocratic Whigs, allied to the new Liberals,* had achieved power at last, and they were concerned to bring a new humanity and a new efficiency into government.

Between 1832 and 1834, Lord Melbourne's government introduced factory reform, prison reform, the abolition of slavery and the setting up of the great municipal corporations which were to be the foundation of modern local government; and while these enlightened measures were going through Parliament, they set about reforming the Poor Laws. The younger Pitt in 1797 had

* The term Liberal was certainly extant in 1832 but there was no Liberal Party as we understand the term. Technically, the first Liberal administration, as such, was Gladstone's of 1868–74.

tried, and failed. A Select Committee of the House of Commons had considered the issues in 1816, but had not come up with workable recommendations. Now the matter was urgent.

Up to 1834, the consolidating Poor Law Act of 1601 (43 Eliz. I c. 2) was still in force. The Old Poor Law provided a set of arrangements – hardly a system – designed for a predominantly rural society. Most parishes had almshouses for the old and infirm (some of which still exist in rural areas). There were small relief payments for the sick and unemployed of working age, and apprenticeship schemes for orphans. Some 15,000 parishes, some of them very small, were responsible for dealing with their own poor.[1] Overseers carried out the work of poor relief. Some were humane, some harsh; some were efficient, some muddled and amateurish; some were honest, some corrupt. Most parishes did not even bother to keep accounts, and the only appeal from vestry decisions was to the local magistrates, who were likely to be the major landowners of the district. Before the development of modern local government, the magistrates were responsible for many aspects of local administration in addition to the work of the lower courts, and their position was a powerful one.

Methods of relief and standards of relief inevitably varied from parish to parish; but any attempt by the poor to move from a harsh district to a more generous one was frustrated by the Acts of Settlement. From the 1660s, when the major movement of population from the rural areas to the towns threatened to overwhelm the town parishes, the law required that paupers should only be relieved in their parish of settlement – usually the parish in which they were born. The vagrancy laws were older – designed to deal with such undesirables as tramps, poachers and gypsies, who were often consigned to the local gaol for the crime of 'wandering without visible means of support'; but by the eighteenth century, people who were genuinely seeking work might find themselves confined in the local Bridewell, forced to work for a month, often on the treadmill, to cover the cost of their keep, and then sent back where they came from. Though there was a need for labour in the new manufacturing areas – Birmingham, Leeds, Manchester, Liverpool – the risks of moving in search of work were high. When economic hardship forced families to move in from the country in desperation, there was near-panic in the city vestries. Harassed overseers spent much of their time in argument about which parish was responsible for particular paupers, and moving groups of paupers from place to place.

Probably most parishes were more lax in their treatment of the poor in times of prosperity, when the ratepayers were better off and paupers were fewer in number, and harsher in times of economic depression, when the need was greatest; but in good times or ill, the problems were accelerating dramatically by the last years of the eighteenth century.

The traditional patterns of village organization in England were no longer adequate (if they ever had been) to cope with the problems. Rural distress was nothing new; the effects of the Enclosure Movement were already apparent in Tudor times. As the price of wool rose, wealthy and powerful landowners took over farms and common land, and devoted them to sheep-farming. The financial returns were good, and sheep required only a shepherd or two, while mixed farming or corn-growing was labour-intensive. In the early sixteenth century, Sir Thomas More wrote in *Utopia* of the effects when 'each greedy individual preys on his native land like a malignant growth, absorbing field after field, and enclosing thousands of acres in a single fence'. So the farmers and their families were evicted:

> They're either cheated or bullied into giving up their property, or systematically ill-treated until they're forced to sell. Whichever way it's done, out the poor creatures have to go, men and women, husbands and wives, widows and orphans, mothers and tiny children, together with all their employees – whose great numbers are not a sign of wealth, but simply of the fact that you can't run a farm without plenty of manpower. Out they have to go from the homes they know so well, and they can't find anywhere else to live.[2]

More was a man of integrity and understanding; but the problems continued, and intensified in the next three hundred years. Enclosures by private Act of Parliament became increasingly frequent, and the life of the rural poor became increasingly harsh. J. L. and Barbara Hammond quote evidence[3] which suggests that between 1761 and 1844, nearly 4,000 private Acts were passed, enclosing some six million acres of land.

The original petition could be made by one big landowner.

From 1774, it was the practice to affix a notice to the church door
in each of the parishes affected for three Sundays in August or
September before the Act was passed; but many villagers could
not read, and those who could had no means of appeal – except to
the magistrates; and if they took action in protest, the magistrates
could charge them with a criminal offence:

> They could tear down the notices from the church doors; they
> could break up a parish meeting if one were held; but the only
> way they could protest was by violent and disorderly proceedings
> which made no impression at all upon Parliament, and which the
> forces of law and order could if necessary be summoned to
> quell.[4]

In Parliament before the Reform Act of 1832, the landed gentry
were very heavily represented. Usually the first and second
reading of an enclosure Bill would go through unopposed, and
there would be no objection in Parliament at the Committee stage
unless some powerful person in the House of Commons was
persuaded to intervene. The small proprietors and cottagers had
no voice, and no way of making their plight known. 'The anchorage
of the poor was gone.'[5]

The Agricultural Revolution of the first half of the eighteenth
century increased the problems, for new techniques and new crops
decreased the need for labour even where the farms survived. The
drift to the newly industrializing areas grew more marked, and the
massive disruption of the Industrial Revolution replaced much
quiet rural poverty by the bitter and more visible squalor of the
crowded towns.

The population was rising rapidly: in 1801, the first national
census listed the population of England and Wales as 8,893
thousand; by 1851, it had more than doubled to 17,928 thousand.
Vagrancy and destitution were not new factors. What was new was
the sheer volume of distress, and the total inadequacy of traditional
methods to meet it. For people desperately seeking a means of
livelihood were flocking to the towns in spite of the Acts of
Settlement, which punished them for moving if they could not
support themselves.

'The men, women, country and houses are *all black*' marvelled
the future Queen Victoria when she toured the Midlands in 1832 at

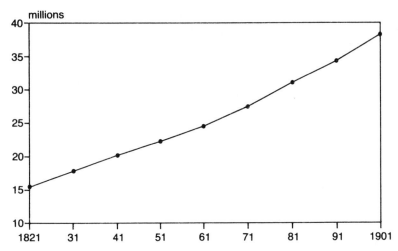

Figure I Population, United Kingdom, 1821–1901
Source: Annual Abstract of Statistics, 1935, table 6.

the age of thirteen.[6] They lived in hovels or cellars among the belching fumes of the factories, filthy and hungry and disease-ridden, helpless in the face of a new industrial system which exploited their labour. And they died young.

Even after the Reform Act, Parliament had little understanding of the new industrial middle class or its labour force. 'Blackguardly manufacturers' said Lord Melbourne – not objecting to the way they treated their workforces, but merely indicating that they were not gentlemen. The main problems as the new Whig Government of 1832 saw them were chronic under-employment in the rural areas, largely due to enclosures, and the effects of bad harvests. British corn-growers were protected by the Corn Laws, which prohibited the import of foreign corn when the price of corn was low; but bread was the staple diet of the poor, and a poor harvest could mean a winter of near starvation.

In the late eighteenth century, different parishes tried a number of expedients to deal with unemployment. None of them worked very well. A commonly employed device was the 'labour rate' – or 'rate in aid of wages', by which employers were encouraged to take men on for less than a living wage, and a supplement was paid from Poor Law funds. This increased the number of jobs available, but at the cost of depressing wages, and the poor rates soared.

Much parliamentary time was spent in the 1820s and early 1830s in discussing the effects of the labour rate, which was both expensive and inefficient.

The Speenhamland system, introduced by the magistrates of Berkshire in 1795, was one of many attempts to introduce a fairly primitive cost-of-living index, by tying the level of relief to the price of bread and the size of the family. This provided some protection against the fluctuations in the price of corn; but if the rate of relief went up, the farmers, also suffering from the bad harvest, were less able to pay what was demanded of them.

Some parishes tried to overcome the apparent circularity of Poor Law problems by use of the Roundsman system, collecting the able-bodied male paupers together and marching them from farm to farm or factory to factory to hire them out at low wages. This led to frequent conflicts: the labourers often reacted violently to the orders of overseers and the demand that they work for less than they and their families could live on, and the farmers resisted taking on gangs of sullen and angry men.

Some parishes invented parish labour as an alternative, setting the able-bodied paupers to work on the roads, or in gravel-pits. Some found it less intimidating to develop schemes of 'relief without labour', enclosing the resentful and humiliated paupers in a stockade during the hours of daylight, or making them walk long distances to claim their relief, or summoning them to frequent and arbitrary roll-calls to establish their availability.

The theme of 'setting the poor to work' had been debated again and again in Parliament ever since Tudor times, for it seemed that this surplus labour ought to be capable of being turned to profit. The term 'workhouse' has acquired such strong connotations of a different kind since 1834 that it is necessary to recall that it was originally a place where able-bodied paupers were set to work to keep themselves and their families, and not a place for the 'impotent poor' – those who were unable to work. Carey's workhouse in Bristol, set up in 1697, was the prototype; but this was only part of an enlightened scheme which provided separate and classified accommodation for the 'impotent poor'. The Bristol Corporation of the Poor developed a hospital for the sick and women in childbirth, a lunatic hospital, an orphanage;[7] but when other parishes copied the workhouse system, the needs of the 'impotent poor' were often forgotten in the anxiety to make paupers industrious.

A permissive Workhouse Test Act of 1722 allowed any Poor Law authority to set up a workhouse; but because many parishes were small, and administration was haphazard, there was often no attempt at real employment or classification on the lines developed in Bristol. Often there would only be room for the sick and aged, the orphans and a few pregnant girls. All would be housed together, and attempts would be made to force them all to work. Gilbert's Act of 1782 was designed to overcome the problem of small-scale relief. It made it possible for parishes to form Unions, which could develop a joint policy for poor relief and spread the cost. But the Labour Rate Acts, the Workhouse Test Act and Gilbert's Act were permissive measures, adopted in one parish and not in the next. Expedients were tried and abandoned, but nothing improved the situation. There were Select Committees on the Poor Laws in 1816–1817 and 1824, but no action was taken – the problems seemed insoluble. The numbers of paupers rose, the cost of relief rose, and the frustration and the anger rose through long years of Tory repression. When a Whig Government took power in 1830 and achieved the passing of the Parliamentary Reform Act, there was a new mandate for a radical solution. The brave new science of economics was invoked to provide scientific and rational answers to old problems.

The Liberal Economists

Progressive economic thinking of the period was based on Adam Smith's doctrine of *laissez-faire* and the untrammelled operation of market forces.[8] The confused expedients of Poor Law policy were held to be mistaken not because they failed to solve the problem of poverty, but because they involved intervention in the market. The future prosperity of rich and poor alike depended on a free market in labour. Labour was held to be subject to the laws of supply and demand, and wages had to find their natural level.

Nassau Senior, who was to become a major figure on the fact-finding Poor Law Commission of 1832–1834, wrote to Lord Brougham, the Lord Chancellor, in 1832 to explain the new doctrines. He was horrified to discover that the labourers believed that they were entitled to a living wage – that wages were 'not a matter of contract, but of right'. These 'monstrous and anarchical doctrines' were supported 'not only by the rioters themselves, but by the farmers, the clergy, the magistrates, in short by all the ignorant and timid throughout the country.'[9]

A major impediment to the existence of a free labour market was the operation of the Laws of Settlement. In a *laissez-faire* economy, unemployed men would be free to go where they chose in search of work – and employers would be free to take them on for the lowest wage they would work for. A proper wage, in Senior's view, depended on what the employer was ready to pay, not on the wants or expectations of the labourer.[10]

This bracing doctrine was reinforced by Malthusian thinking. T. R. Malthus' *An Essay on the Principle of Population*[11] was a curious combination of the new science of economics, the old science of mathematics, and the even older art of theology. Malthus was an Oxford lecturer in mathematics, and like most Oxford dons of his period, a clergyman. He started his analysis as follows:

> I think I may fairly make two postulata:
> First, that food is necessary to the existence of man.
> Secondly, that the passion between the sexes is necessary, and will remain nearly in its present state.
> I do not know that any writer has supposed that on this earth man will ultimately be able to live without food ... Assuming then, my postulata is [sic] granted, I say that the power of population is infinitely greater than the power of the earth to provide subsistence for man.

Since he was a mathematician, Malthus expressed this proposition in mathematical terms:

> Population, when unchecked, increases in a geometrical ratio. Subsistence increases only in an arithmetical ratio. A slight acquaintance with numbers will show the immensity of the first power in comparison with the second ... the effects of these two powers must be kept equal.

Arithmetical ratio, as Malthus explained, proceeds by addition (i.e., $2 + 2 = 4, 4 + 2 = 6, 6 + 2 = 8 \ldots$) while geometrical ratio proceeds by multiplication (i.e., $2 \times 2 = 4$, $4 \times 2 = 8$, $8 \times 2 = 16 \ldots$). Since, as Malthus noted, 'the passion between the sexes' was unlikely to decrease, it followed that many children would be born who could not possibly be fed. Starvation was the inevitable fate of many human beings:

> It has appeared that, from the inevitable laws of our nature, some human beings must suffer from want. These are the unhappy persons who, in the great lottery of life, have drawn a blank.

Malthus saw a terrible vision of the inevitable fate of the poor if they were allowed to breed unchecked:

> Premature death must in some shape or other visit the human race. The vices of mankind are active and able ministers of depopulation. They are the precursors in the great army of destruction; and often finish off the dreadful work themselves. But should they fail in this war of extermination, sickly seasons, epidemics, pestilence and plague advance in terrific array, and sweep off their thousands and ten thousands. Should success still be incomplete: gigantic, inevitable famine stalks in the rear, and with one mighty blow, levels the population with the food of the world.

His conclusion was that the poor were responsible for their own condition by breeding irresponsibly, and that poor relief only encouraged them in irresponsibility. Harriet Martineau, the fashionable and formidable bluestocking who visited him in 1832, commented that 'a more simple-minded, virtuous man, full of domestic affections, than Mr. Malthus could not be found in all England' and that 'Prudence as to the time of marriage, and making provision for it, was, one would think, a harmless enough recommendation under the circumstances.'[12] Miss Martineau enquired of Malthus whether the storm of controversy which his pamphlet had aroused had worried him, and caused him to lose sleep. 'Never after the first fortnight' was the cheerful reply.

In the context of his own day, it can be argued that Malthus was right. Before the days of modern methods of birth control, and with the limited means of agricultural production at the time, population did outstrip the food supply. At the end of the eighteenth century, the problems must have seemed – and indeed were – insoluble. Any attempt to relieve the condition of the poor would only result in the birth of more children, who in turn would inevitably die as the grim agents of population control took their toll.

Malthus worked closely with David Ricardo, economist and Member of Parliament. Ricardo took up the analysis, and translated it into economic terms in the form of the Iron Law of Wages. Basically, his thesis was that labour, like other commodities, was subject to the simple laws of supply and demand. If the supply of labour was less than demand, wages would go up. If the supply of labour exceeded demand, wages would go down. But the supply of labour was dependent on the numbers of children reared to working age. If the ordinary labourer starved, his family would starve with him, and the children would not live long enough to join the labour force – so wages would increase; but when wages increased, more children would be able to survive – which would in time increase the labour force, depress wages and bring labourers down to starvation level again:

> Like all other contracts, wages should be left to the fair and free competition of the market, and should never be controlled by the interference of the legislature. The clear and direct tendency of the Poor Laws is in direct opposition to these obvious principles ... the nature of the evil points out the remedy. By gradually contracting the sphere of the Poor Laws; by impressing on the poor the value of independence, by teaching them that they must not look to systematic or casual charity, but to their own exertions for support ... we shall by degrees approach a sounder and more healthful state.[13]

Such were the basic ideas which lay behind a new appraisal of the Poor Laws. It is important to note that they were not particularly new even in the early 1830s: there is much in this mechanistic view of the operation of the laws of the universe which belongs to the late eighteenth century rather than to the nineteenth; but they were to be given a new twist by the constitutional and philosophical thinking of Jeremy Benthan, the founder of Utilitarianism.

Bentham devoted his life to the search for rational principles to replace the 'hot-bed of uncertainty' in English government and administration. He looked for a new guiding principle. He was 'in a mizmaze' until he discovered the doctrine of 'the greatest happiness of the greatest number'. He found it in a pamphlet by Dr Priestley which he picked up in a London coffee-house. It was an overwhelming revelation, and he recorded that he 'cried out as it were with an inward ecstacy'.[14]

Bentham's doctrine of 'the greatest happiness of the greatest number' needs careful interpretation. It is ironic that the scholar who wanted to reorganize the entire system of law and government in England could not organize his own work. His vast and unmanageable corpus of writing contains many fragments, endlessly revised and annotated, which are often difficult to name and date; but his biographer, Mary Mack, makes it clear that in his more considered versions of the doctrine, he was not advocating the greatest sum total of pleasure regardless of the numbers involved; nor did he look for the greatest happiness of a simple majority of the people. He meant 'the greatest pleasure and the least pain of all the people involved';[15] and towards the end of his life, he moved (characteristically in a footnote) to the view that 'the greatest happiness of *all*, not of the greatest number only, would in the end be aimed at'.[16]

But the damage had been done. The 'greatest happiness' principle was taken to mean that the poor must suffer for the rest of society; and Bentham's exposition of the pleasure-pain principle or 'hedonistic calculus' was used to provide the means.

Bentham observed that human beings sought pleasure and avoided pain. The best and the least interventionist form of government therefore involved the utilization of 'the logic of the will' – framing laws and organizing government so that good actions were pleasurable to the individual, and evil or anti-social actions were painful. By this means, social problems could be not merely tackled, but virtually eliminated. It could be argued that to make poor relief painful was good for the poor, since it would lead them to be self-supporting; and indeed, in the long run, it would increase their pleasure as well as that of the rest of society. The poor would no longer be parasites. They were being given back their dignity.

In his plans for the new Millbank Penitentiary, Bentham developed an ingenious architectural device for dealing with that small proportion of the population who were unable or unwilling to follow 'the logic of the will' and to take responsibility for their own independent lives. This was the Panopticon – a circular building like a wheel, where the inmates were distributed along the spokes, and the staff concentrated in the hub or centre. Thus the inmates were always under surveillance, and unable to take joint action, while a small staff could supervise and quell any disturbances. This pattern formed the architectural plan of the Millbank Penitentiary, and a number of other prisons, some of which are still in use, were built on the same model. Some lunatic asylums adopted a similar architectural design, and Bentham's remorseless logic led him to propose its extension to other kinds of institution, such as hospitals, schools and universities.

But the main application of the 'Panopticon' concept was less as an architectural plan than as an administrative device for the government of England. While *laissez-faire* was the popular Whig philosophy, Bentham's thinking represented another and contradictory strand in Whig policy: the need for strong, responsible central government. The idea of central government as the all-seeing eye, controlling and setting standards for local authorities, was fundamental to Bentham's view of constitutional order, and it is not difficult to see this as an extension of the principles of the Panopticon. As early as 1813, he proposed a 'Ministry of Indigence' to deal nationally with the problems of poverty.

David Roberts, in *The Victorian Origins of the British Welfare State*[17] provides an insight into how the institution of a powerful central government agency with an inspectorate was used repeatedly in the 1830s and 1840s – and how unpopular it was among the country squires and justices who, in days of poorer roads and slower travel, had been left very much to their own devices; but Telford and Macadam were building the bridges and laying the foundations of the best roads since Roman times, and as communications improved, so the prospects of central planning and control became more feasible.

A new Whig government in 1832 provided a legislative platform for the new ideas about how to deal with poverty; but how were they to be translated into law?

TWO
The Poor and the Poor Law

The Poor Law Amendment Act of 1834 is one of the great watersheds in English social policy: before and after are two different worlds. It marked a shift from muddle to order; from half-hearted benevolence to whole-hearted deterrence; from exasperation with the perennial problem of poverty to a ruthless determination to eliminate it for all time.

One of the major puzzles of social history in this period is why a political party (soon to be renamed the Liberal Party) which stood for all that was enlightened and progressive at the time introduced a Poor Law system which has become a byword for inhumanity. Some explanations can be found in the economic and constitutional ideas which were current at the time. The arguments of the economic theorists were forcefully put, and appeared irresistible; but another set of explanations lies in the continuing fear of revolution and the breakdown of public order. In 1832, when the Poor Law Commission was appointed, England was in a turmoil of civil unrest. Strikes, riots and machine breaking occurred in at least eighty different parts of the country.

Hobsbawm and Rudé, who describe the Swing Riots in detail,[1] tell how at demonstrations in the cities, the banners often bore the slogan 'Bread or Blood', and the trade unions, then regarded as subversive organizations, were rumoured to be drilling ready for the revolution. In the rural areas, hayricks blazed, land agents were manhandled, and the clergy, the traditional supporters of the aristocracy, were threatened. Derby gaol was broken into, Nottingham castle was destroyed, and the Bishop's palace at

Bristol went up in flames. There was panic in the London clubs and drawing-rooms. William Cobbett, who was to become one of the leaders of the radical anti-Corn Law and anti-Poor Law movements, travelled the country on horseback, and what he observed in the North was 'just the state of things that existed in France on the eve of the Revolution'.[2] The riots were a threatening background to the work of those trying to remedy the deficiencies of the Poor Laws.

The newly appointed Commissioners therefore undertook their investigations in conditions of some urgency. One of them was Nassau Senior, then Oxford's first Professor of Economics, and on Senior's advice, Edwin Chadwick, a lawyer from Longsight in Manchester who had been Jeremy Bentham's secretary, was promoted from Assistant Commissioner to full Commissioner. Chadwick was a man of ideas, and the ideas were derived from his understanding of Bentham's work. Though there were other Commissioners, including Bishop Blomfield of London, who was to become one of Chadwick's main supporters, the main work of the Commission was undertaken by Nassau Senior and Chadwick.

It was, by any standards, a remarkable exercise, and the first of its kind. Questionnaires, carefully constructed and detailed in character, went out to something like 10 per cent of all the 15,000 parishes. The Assistant Commissioners followed, asking supplementary questions of those magistrates, parish clergy and overseers who had responded, and securing returns from those who had not. They wrote and sent back to London weekly diaries, and they compiled exhaustive reports on their findings.[3] The diaries were unfortunately subsequently destroyed – they might have provided many useful insights into the Commissioners' experiences – and all that remains in the Sessional Papers are the formal reports; but this flood of information both documented the situation and suggested Draconian remedies for the problems. When the reports had been received, Professor Senior concentrated on the analysis of the existing system, and Chadwick on the recommendations. These were precise and far-reaching:–

1. *Centralization*: there would be a Central Board of Control in London, with Assistant Commissioners who would act as inspectors. Local administration would be caried out by paid overseers.

2. *The Workhouse Test*: The condition of relief for the able-bodied would be 'the offer of the house'. Outdoor relief (payment

to people living in their own homes) would be abolished, so that entry to the workhouse would be the only alternative to self-maintenance.

   3. *Uniformity*: the Laws of Settlement would be abolished. Conditions in all workhouses would be prescribed by the central Commission, so that there would be no advantage to the pauper in moving from one parish to another.

   4. *'Less eligibility'*: the condition of the pauper in the workhouse should be 'in no case so eligible as the condition of persons of the lowest class subsisting on the fruits of their own industry', so that there was no incentive to idleness.

   5. *Classification*: general mixed workhouses would be replaced by well regulated classified workhouses.

   Historians have debated whether this scheme could be described as 'Benthamite' or not. Certainly Chadwick was a Benthamite. So was Nassau Senior, and there was a powerful Utilitarian lobby which thought as they did. Brundage,[4] takes the view that the scheme 'owed little to Benthamism', being largely a systematization of the principles of the Workhouse Test and the amalgamation of Unions, for which permissive Acts already existed. Bentham, as he points out, developed quite a different scheme for 'setting the poor to work', proposing a Joint Stock Company to run 250 workhouses at a profit; but Bentham's prolific mind generated many schemes, including the scheme for a 'Ministry of Indigence'. The administrative device of a central Commission and local administration was distinctly Benthamite – Finer points out that 'the debt to the Panopticon was profound' while the 'less eligibility principle' was a direct application of Bentham's hedonistic calculus.[5] But the Act was to be put into force by harsher minds than Bentham's.

Implementing the Act

The analysis was accepted by Melbourne's government. It displeased the Tories by its radical nature, and it equally displeased the radicals like Cobbett and Oastler, who were aware of problems in the industrial north which had been totally ignored in this recipe for the agricultural south. Lord Melbourne himself was not enthusiastic about the Poor Law Bill which followed. According to Lord David Cecil, he 'was repelled by the idea of dragooning the poor into thrift and industry ... The consequence was that he defended it in lukewarm tones, and was heard swearing in a loud, angry undertone as he gave his vote for it'.[6]

But the situation was desperate. Only a few months earlier Melbourne, as Home Secretary, had been responsible for confirming the sentence of transportation on the Dorchester labourers or Tolpuddle Martyrs, who had dared to band together to ask for a small increase in their wages, and some 30,000 trade unionists had marched on London. Something had to be done to avert revolution.

The new economic philosophy seemed to offer a way out of a crisis situation – the investigation had been exhaustive, and ran to sixteen volumes of evidence, and the conclusions were closely argued, and seemed inescapable. Many reservations were expressed in heated debate. The House of Commons vote on the second reading of the Bill was 319 in favour and 20 against, but by the third reading, there were only 187 ayes and 50 noes – a strong indication of diminishing enthusiasm.[7] The doubts about the wisdom of centralization were such that the new Poor Law Commission was not created on a permanent basis – its first term of office was only five years. But the Bill passed into law, despite Lord Melbourne's loud, angry undertones and the many reservations expressed by other members of Parliament, because it was the only solution available.

The Poor Law Amendment Act of 1834 followed all the main points of the Commission's recommendations. Immediate reaction in political circles seems to have centred not on the effects on paupers, but on who would be appointed to the three powerful and lucrative new posts of Poor Law Commissioners. The salary was £2,000 a year. Nassau Senior, who had no desire to be appointed as a Commissioner himself, had assumed that Chadwick would be in charge to put the report into practice; but it was decided in Cabinet that Chadwick's 'station in society' did not warrant an appointment at this level, and he was offered only the post of Secretary to the Commission. Senior was dismayed. Chadwick himself, precise, unimaginative, and quite unable to understand a system of government which preferred to make appointments on the grounds of social status rather than of merit, wrote twenty-six foolscap pages of meticulous and carefully argued protest. Lord Althorp, who was Chancellor of the Exchequer, was called in to ease a difficult situation, and Chadwick, at first reluctant to take the lowly post of secretary, finally accepted on the promise that he would be able virtually to act as a fourth Commissioner with the prospect of promotion to Commissioner when a post became vacant.[8]

The three men appointed as Commissioners were Thomas Frankland Lewis, George Nicholls and J. G. Shaw-Lefèvre – a choice dictated by immediate political interests. All three were people of some public status. Frankland Lewis had been a member of a previous enquiry into the Poor Laws. He was a Tory, and his appointment saved the Whigs from charges of political bias. Nicholls had been concerned with Poor Law reform in Southwark, and was manager of the Birmingham branch of the Bank of England. Shaw-Lefèvre was Lord Althorp's personal protégé.

These three became the 'Uncrowned Kings of Somerset House'. Lord Althorp's flustered promises to Chadwick were not kept. When the offices of the Commission at Somerset House were furnished, there was luxurious provision in the shape of mahogany tables and plush chairs for the Commissioners, but their secretary found his office equipped with deal tables and cane-seated chairs.[9]

Chadwick, convinced that he was the only man who could implement the system which he had devised, and still smarting from the insult of being passed over, attempted to take charge. He found that he could work with Nicholls, and he was dismissive about Shaw-Lefèvre – writing to Bishop Blomfield that he was 'about as fit to act for the Poor Law Administration as a delicate girl would be to assist in performing an amputation'; but in Frankland Lewis, he met an immovable obstacle. Frankland Lewis was a Malthusian, determined that 'less eligibility' should be translated into wholehearted deterrence for all the poor, including the sick, the old and the children. Chadwick was not a Malthusian. Benthamism was an ameliorating philosophy, destined to induce the poor to become useful and productive citizens, not a system of punishment.

Differences of purpose and an impossible administrative situation soon led to open conflict and personal animosity between two intransigent personalities. Frankland Lewis attempted to dismiss Chadwick – only to find that, by the terms of his office, he was irremovable. Further Chadwick had his own supporters in the Government, and did not hesitate to keep them informed of his disapproval of Commission proceedings. Discovering that he could not dismiss Chadwick, Lewis retaliated by barring him from

Commissioners' meetings at which decisions were made, permitting only the presence of a minutes clerk.

In 1838, Frankland Lewis retired – but Chadwick was not named as his successor. The post went to Frankland Lewis's son, George Cornewall Lewis, who was to describe Chadwick to a Select Committee of the House of Commons as being 'as unscrupulous and dangerous an officer as ever I saw within the walls of an office'.[10] The situation between Chadwick and both Lewises seems to have been one of total confrontation.

In this atmosphere of acrimony and administrative stalemate, the Commissioners and their secretary had begun to reorganize the entire Poor Law system. Chadwick, with his mind on the main object of freeing the labour market, advised that they should move swiftly in banning outdoor relief. He knew that the move would be unpopular, and his strategy was that it should be introduced while the harvests were good – there was 'perfect Poor Law weather', as he called it, in 1834 and 1835. He also proposed that they should begin with the less pauperized parishes, where opposition to centralization would be strongest, leaving the really poor parishes, where he thought it would be welcome, until last.

The Commissioners ignored this advice. They started to ban outdoor relief slowly, and they started with the parishes where implementation was easiest. In this respect, the first two years of their operations were relatively uneventful. The majority of parishes were agricultural, the harvests were good, and the poor were cowed by the fate of the Dorchester labourers. The Commissioners assumed that work was available if men would go and find it. Chadwick knew that this was not always the case, and succeeded in setting up an emigration agency to supervise the shift of surplus labour from the rural areas of the south to the manufacturing areas of the north. This received little support from the Commissioners, and collapsed when the severe trade depression of the late 1830s followed a bad harvest in 1836. By the time the Commissioners got round to trying to ban outdoor relief in the north, slump had replaced boom, and poverty was acute, while the opposition had had time to organize.

But the Commissioners' interest in the early period focussed less on the relief of poverty than on the bureaucratic tasks of creating Unions and setting up Boards of Guardians to administer them. On this front, they moved with speed. In two years, they had combined 7,915 parishes with a total of 6,221,940 people into 365 Unions.[11] King William IV, who appears to have supported the implementation of the New Poor Law at every stage, was given a coloured map showing the results, and expressed his approval.

Chadwick's original intention had been to utilize the existing parish poorhouses and workhouses for different groups in need rather than housing all the paupers under one roof; but a survey of the existing buildings indicated that they were inadequate. Many dated from Tudor times, and substantial rebuilding was necessary. Frankland Lewis expressed the view that there was 'no doubt that a Central workhouse is if it can be obtained at a Moderate Cost a better Thing than a Collection of Houses'.[12]

This decision had three main consequences: the new Union workhouses were more amenable to central control than small parish workhouses (and this no doubt pleased the Commissioners); they were large, which meant that they were formal and bureaucratic in administration – as the Hammonds note, the larger the institution, 'the more detailed and exact the regulations that are necessary to keep order and arrangement';[13] and they had to be run very cheaply, because the Commissioners had justified the capital expense of rebuilding on the grounds that running costs would be low.

'Less eligibility' might have made sense if the jobs had been available and the labourer in work had received a living wage, for it was reasonable to argue, as Chadwick had done, that those who worked should be better off than those who did not; but in practice, this proved difficult. Chadwick noted that 'The diet of the workhouse almost always exceeds that of the cottage, and the diet of the gaol is generally more profuse than that of the workhouse'.[14] When wages were down to starvation level, 'less eligibility' became difficult to enforce.

But the Commissioners tried. Malthusian theory suggested that paupers were the unhappy people who had 'drawn a blank in the great lottery of life', and nothing should be done to better their condition. Classification by need might be impossible: classification by age and sex were rigidly enforced. Men and women were separated, children over the age of seven separated from their mothers, and the aged from their younger relatives. Until 1847, eldery couples who entered the workhouse as a last resort were housed in separate blocks, and might never be allowed to meet.

The breakup of families came as a surprise to Lord Brougham, who categorically stated in the House of Lords in 1835 that there was no intention of separating members of the same family – 'the idea never entered the head of any person, even in a dream'; but his Lordship was mistaken. One of the Assistant Poor Law Commissioners, Sir Charles A'Court, expressed the Commissioners' conviction that 'such separation must be *entire* and *absolute*'.[15] The Commissioners had no intention of building expensive accommodation for separate families – paupers were to be housed in dormitories, not dwellings.

Minimal diets were drawn up in great detail. The Commissioners boasted that they knew what every pauper in England had for breakfast; and the requirement of meagre and unpalatable food was supplemented by other measures to reinforce the lessons of 'less eligibility'. Paupers had to wear workhouse dress, a badge of shame. From 1836 to 1842, silence was enforced at meals. Chadwick had wanted schools for the children, but the idea was waved away on the grounds of expense. Pauper children were to be drilled into obedience, but not educated. Most bitter of all were the conditions of a pauper funeral: the plain deal coffin, the forbidding of the tolling of the bell which let the neighbourhood know of the passing of a human life. The workhouse became not only the 'uninviting place of wholesome restraint' which Chadwick had envisaged for the idle able-bodied, but an object of dread to every working class family.

Opposition to the New Poor Law

> Britons! . . . if you love your country – if you value your liberty – if you regard equal laws – if you abhor tyranny and delight in justice . . . if you regard your aged parents and love your children – if you hate the Devil and all his works – join hand, heart, voice and unwearied exertions, to rid your degraded, afflicted country of this hell-concocted New Poor Law.[16]

Mr Sam Roberts of Sheffield was one of many campaigners who poured invective on the Poor Law Amendment Act of 1834 – the Act which set up the dreaded Union workhouse, and refused the unemployed, the aged and the sick any public relief unless they entered it. The 'odious Act', the 'injurious Act', the 'unjust law' was widely opposed and widely hated – and not only by radicals like Sam Roberts. Lord Eldon, a former Tory Lord Chancellor of extreme right-wing views, called it 'the most execrable law that ever was enacted in any Christian country'. *The Times* described it as 'an insult to our common sense'. The *Metropolitan Conservative Journal* thundered 'Peasants of England! Be not trodden under like Russian serfs or African slaves!' But a writer with no less indignation and more literary skill personalized the activities of the Boards of Guardians in the story of a small hungry boy:

> The members of this board were very sage, deep philosophical men; and when they came to turn their attention to the workhouse, they found out at once, what ordinary folks would nemer have discovered – the poor people liked it! . . . 'Oho', said the board, looking very knowing; 'we are the fellows to set this to rights; we'll stop it all, in no time'. So, they established the rule, that all poor people should have the alternative (for they would compel nobody, no, not they) of being starved by a gradual process in the house, or a quick one out of it . . . The relief was inseparable from the workhouse and the gruel; and that frightened people . . . It was rather expensive at first, in consequence of the increase in the undertaker's bill . . . but the number of workhouse inmates got thin as well as the paupers, and the board were in ecstacies.[17]

Charles Dickens's first instalment of *Oliver Twist*, published in Bentley's *Miscellany* in February 1837, included this savage description of the background to the 'parish boy's progress'. Oliver, born in a workhouse of an unmarried mother who died at his birth, challenged the whole structure of the New Poor Law:

> 'That boy will be hung,' said the gentleman in the white waistcoat. 'I have never been so convinced of anything in my life than I am, that that boy will be hung'.[18]

Both the radical Press and the Tory Press fought against the Poor Law Commissioners and their system, for very different reasons. While Dickens was writing for the weeklies, the daily newspapers helped to spread the story of the cruelties and inhumanities of the New Poor Law from end to end of England. John Walter II of *The Times*, a Tory of Tories, thundered against

the power of the centralizers in his editorials. Other newspapers
took up the theme from different political perspectives. It was the
Bradford Argus – a radical paper in an area of strong opposition –
which reported the attack of a Conservative Parliamentary candi-
date in 1837, who called the Poor Law Amendment Act:

> That Act which separated those whom God had joined together,
> gave a premium to murder, made poverty a crime, starved the
> poor man, and tried to prove whether he could not live on bread
> and water.[19]

A more measured but equally telling protest came from the
young radical Benjamin Disraeli in the House of Commons:

> It is impossible to conceive a revolution which exercised a
> greater influence upon the people at large . . . if they had not, in
> passing the Poor Law, outraged the constitution and violated
> the law, they had done that which he conceived was of greater
> importance: they had outraged the manners of the people.[20]

Opposition was strongest in the north, where the wholesale
introduction of Unions was commenced in late 1836, coinciding
with a severe trade recession caused by the failure of American
banks which had speculated in frontier enterprises.[21] The radical
leaders, Oastler and Cobbett, addressed huge protest meetings in
violent and denunciatory terms, such as Cobbett's description of
the Act as 'the damnable, the devilish, the Anti-God New Poor
Law', 'infernal, anti-Christian, unsocial, the catechism of hell . . .
the Devil's own Book'. Wythen Baxter's *The Book of the Bastiles*
(1841) provides a rich collection of the anti-Poor Law literature of
the time, mixing invective with considered protest, drawing dark
parallels between the French Revolution and the turmoil created
in England:

> Had there been no *lettre de cachet*, the revolutionary *Marseillaise*
> would never have been tuned in retribution, and Louis XVI
> would have died in his bed and not on the block. Had there been
> no New Poor Law, the name of Chartist would never have been
> heard; nor would Birmingham have been heated with fire and
> fury, or Newport have run red with the gore of Britons from the
> hills.[22]

Baxter's compendium of New Poor Law literature contained 'descriptive accounts of the Bastiles, Bastile food, Bastile treatment and tyranny, mortality in the Bastiles and the wretched paupers' dread of those houses of death and bondage'. Though his spelling was shaky, and his style somewhat florid, he knew his subject. 'The Steel' was a common name for the workhouse in the 1830s and 1840s.

The workhouse system, designed for individual long-term unemployed labourers in the rural areas, was no answer to the problems of the manufacturing towns, where the experience was of short-term mass unemployment when mills or factories closed. In these circumstances, attempts to impose the workhouse test brought great hardship, the workhouses overflowed, and eventually the attempt to ban outdoor relief had to be abandoned. Significantly, the worst problems were encountered in the smaller cotton and wool towns – Huddersfield, Todmorden, Bradford, Bury, Keighley, Preston, Oldham – rather than in the larger cities, where there was some possibility of alternative employment when disaster struck a particular industry.

The Assistant Commissioners (charged with the duty of enforcing the Workhouse Test and banning outdoor relief in the north) went literally in fear of their lives. Chadwick wrote to Lord John Russell in 1838 that one had been 'pursued by wild persons intent on assassinating him', another 'had been shot at, a third manhandled, while others had been driven out of the towns by threats'. Outdoor relief was never fully abolished in the north, though the agitation died down early in the 1840s, when the anti-Poor Law movement merged with the other radical movements in Chartism. The hope was that all social wrongs could be redressed through the medium of the ballot box and manhood suffrage.

In Parliament, criticism of the New Poor Law continued. In 1837, a Select Committee of the House of Commons was set up on a motion from John Walter II to study the subject in detail. The Government packed the committee – seventeen of its twenty-one members were known to be supporters of the Poor Law Amendment Act, and no action resulted; but the committee's hearings recorded faithfully the cruelties, the confusion throughout the country, and the political struggles in Somerset House.

The Commission's first term of office expired in 1839. It was cautiously extended for a single year, but at the end of that time, it was extended again because there was still no viable alternative. The Andover scandal in 1846, when hungry paupers in the Andover Workhouse were found to be eating the gristle and sucking the marrow from horse-bones they had been given for sorting, led to such public revulsion that some change had to be made; and in 1848, the Commissioners' arbitrary power ended when they were replaced with a Poor Law Board whose President was a member of the Government, and thus answerable to Parliament.

It is possible to view these events fom a variety of perspectives: as the vain attempt of politicians with an eighteenth-century cast of mind to deal with a nineteenth-century situation; as the failure of economic dogma to solve the problems of human distress; as a tragedy of Benthamism distorted to purposes which Bentham himself would never have countenanced; as the story of Chadwick defeated by snobbery and jobbery; as a study in class conflict and social control; as a clash between north and south, or industry and agriculture; as a resurgence of a puritan and punitive streak in the English character; as the inevitable result of major social change too long delayed and then too harshly implemented; or as a case study in social policy, illustrating the twists and turns which can occur between the recognition of a problem and the framing of a law to meet it, between the law and the policy which is subsequently implemented. The story will bear all these interpretations; but the truth is that the issues were very complicated, and of an unprecedented kind. There was no experience to draw on. In the last resort, the rigours of the New Poor Law may have been due more to muddle than to malevolence.

The Whigs of the 1830s got some things right: they initiated new social survey methods, they recognized the need for bold innovation, they realized that new communications led to a need for new administrative patterns; but though the Poor Law was to become somewhat more humane after 1848, the basic principles and structure remained untouched for many decades simply because no-one could think of an alternative.

THREE
Dirt, Disease and Danger

Initially, Chadwick appears to have attached little importance to sickness as a cause of poverty. His formidable mind was engaged with the application of Benthamite principles to the problem of able-bodied paupers, who had to be made to work; but by 1838, after four years of frustration at Somerset House, his interest was caught by the views of three medical colleagues on the Poor Law Commission: that much poverty and misery was caused by sickness, and that much of the sickness could be prevented.

Dr James Kay (later Sir James Kay-Shuttleworth and better known as an educational reformer), was an Assistant Poor Law Commissioner who had been a physician in a poor area of Manchester – Ardwick and Ancoats. His work on *The Moral and Physical Condition of the Working Classes*[1] was already well known. Dr Neil Arnott had worked with Kay on the incidence and causes of fever in London.[2] Dr Southwood Smith was physician to the London Fever Hospital, and like Chadwick, had worked closely with Jeremy Bentham, and absorbed many of his ideas and principles. Southwood Smith delivered the funeral oration over Bentham's body before it was handed, as Bentham directed, to the anatomists. (Bentham's skeleton, dressed in his clothes and installed in his sedan chair, sits in the entrance hall of University College, London, and is regularly carried in procession by the students of that Utilitarian institution.)

All three doctors were concerned at the toll which cholera, typhus, tuberculosis and other diseases took of the population in the poorer districts of the crowded towns. Britain had been a safer place to live in when the population was spread thinly over the country, but the move to the towns had brought new dangers. Between 1821 and 1831, West Bromwich increased its population by 60 per cent, Manchester and Salford by 47 per cent, Bradford by 78 per cent, Glasgow by 37 per cent;[3] and as the poor congregated and multiplied, so endemic, epidemic and contagious disease spread.

In 1834, although bubonic plague had not returned, outbreaks of cholera, typhus, typhoid and 'consumption', created spasmodic attacks of public panic reminiscent of the terrible plague year of 1665, when the death carts had toured the London streets with the cry, 'Bring out your dead'. Cholera first occurred in Britain in 1831–1832. There were recurrences in 1848–1849, 1854 and 1867. Cholera attacked all social classes. It 'struck swiftly and sharply, raising local death rates dramatically, if ephemerally. Cholera frightened people'.[4]

Typhus and typhoid fever were largely diseases of the poor. There were epidemic outbreaks in 1826–1827, 1831–1832, 1837 and 1846–1847, and these coincided, as Dr Southwood Smith had noted,[5] with periods of economic recession and high unemployment. But both were endemic – that is, the incidence rate was high even in the periods between epidemics; and many doctors had reported that it was highest in the poorest quarters of the towns, where people lived in overcrowded conditions in insanitary hovels surrounded by mounds of rubbish.

Tuberculosis, then known as 'consumption' (there was little diagnostic accuracy, and 'consumption' may have included other wasting diseases and even malnutrition) was also a disease of the poor. In 1796, according to the London Bills of Mortality, it accounted for nearly one-third of all deaths in the Metropolis.

Here was a set of problems which seized Chadwick's attention while he brooded over his exclusion from the decisions of the Poor Law Commission. While the Poor Law Report had concentrated on the problems of the able-bodied poor, he seems to have been increasingly convinced by his medical colleagues that sickness and the early death of the breadwinner were major causes of poverty. He was tough-minded, and often high-handed, but he respected evidence, and he was capable of shifting his position if the evidence warranted it. He became convinced that there were new skills available which could be utilized to provide remedies.

There was the new science of 'vital statistics'. The British Association was founded in 1831. Three years later, its President deprecated the application of statistics to social problems on the grounds that statistical enquiries would 'touch on the mainsprings of feeling and passion'.[6] There was a sense in which he was right, for few subjects were to raise so much feeling and passion in the next two decades. The Statistical Society of London was formed as a breakaway movement from the British Association, and Chadwick became a member and a regular attender.

Through the Statistical Society, he was already in contact with a number of these enquiries, and had had some influence on the framing of the Registration of Birth, Deaths and Marriages Act of 1836. The main purpose of this Act was not to collect social statistics, but to end the monopoly of registration held by the clergy of the Church of England, whose religious services were unacceptable to Roman Catholics and Nonconformists, and who charged fees for marriages and funerals. Local registrars were appointed, who would make returns to the General Register Office in London.

Chadwick was not responsible for the main provisions of the Act, though the general public blamed him for the new bureaucratic procedures, and the notification process was commonly referred to as 'being Chadwicked'.[7] But he was quick to see its potential for providing information about the causes of death for different age-groups and in different areas. It was on his suggestion that a clause was included to the effect that, when a death was notified, it should be accompanied by a medical certificate stating the cause. Thus the registration of death became more than a simple notification procedure. It became a diagnostic tool.

Chadwick had a fruitful partnership with Dr William Farr, who was appointed Compiler of Abstracts in the new office of the Registrar-General in 1837. There was a sense in which they were two of a kind. Both were technically civil servants. They shared a sense of outrage at the waste of human life involved in urban squalor; and both were prepared to appeal to anyone who would help their cause – ministers of state, members of the nobility, bishops, academics – over the heads of their immediate superiors. Farr's Annual Reports from the General Register Office were vehement by modern Civil Service standards. For instance, his tenth report states:

This disease-mist, arising from the breaths of two millions of people, from open sewers and cess-pools, graves and slaughter-houses, is continually kept up and undergoing changes. In one season, it is pervaded by cholera; in another, by influenza; at one time, it bears smallpox, scarlatina and whooping-cough among our children. Like an Angel of Death, it has hovered for centuries over London. But it may be driven away by legislation.[8]

Another new development which offered a promise of improvement was the developing science of civil engineering. Sewers in the big cities were commonly fed from open drains, and constructed on medieval lines. With the huge increase in population, they were becoming choked, and there were engineers with new ideas on how they might be constructed and kept clean. Chadwick's chief adviser on this subject was John Roe, engineer to the Holborn and Finsbury Commission of Sewers. Roe's technical advice was that drains should be in closed pipes, not open; and sewers should be capable of being easily flushed with water, so that they did not silt up. This would involve a major reconstruction of the metropolitan sewage system: sewers would be built to curve rather than having right-angled bends; they would have steep gradients down which the water might run; and they would be 'egg-shaped' with 'a pinched-in base' through which the water would flow with a stronger pressure.[9]

Though Chadwick's public image was that of an aloof and bureaucratic official, he was not alone in his work. He was at the centre of the new Utilitarian movement, with many fellow workers who shared and contributed to his innovatory ideas; and if he was cold and abrasive in his relationships with the Poor Law Commissioners, he could show warmth to people who shared his furious distaste for squalor and muddle and incompetence, and who were prepared to match him in industry. Fired with the new ideas of Farr and Roe and their supporters, he turned all his considerable energies to this fresh cause.

The first step was to systematize the evidence. The opportunity came when London suffered an epidemic of influenza and typhoid fever in 1837–1838. In the following year, on a motion from Bishop Blomfield, the House of Lords instituted an enquiry in the Sanitary Condition of the Labouring Population of Great Britain. Technically, the enquiry was under the auspices of the Poor Law

Commission. Chadwick, Kay, Arnott and Southwood Smith were relieved from their Poor Law duties, and given a fresh sphere of operation, unhampered by the tensions and frustrations of daily battles with the Commissioners.

The Sanitary Report

Chadwick, in charge at last, organized the field. He used the Poor Law machinery to obtain evidence and written reports from Assistant Commissioners, Poor Law Guardians, Relieving Officers and Medical Officers, and approached a wide variety of other individuals with knowledge of the problems of squalor and disease in the towns. In all, he approached over 2,000 possible informants, and most of them replied with detailed evidence. There was 'a flood of written evidence'[10] which he ploughed through with characteristic thoroughness. He read widely, studying reports from other European countries, and paying particular attention to the work of Quetelet, a Belgian statistician who had published a pioneer study comparing population statistics for countries in western Europe in 1827. Chadwick used statistical evidence from countries as far apart as Mexico and Egypt, though he may have been somewhat optimistic about the accuracy of the figures.[11]

But despite all this labour, he was not office-bound. He visited Manchester, Leeds, Macclesfield, Leicester, Edinburgh and Glasgow to see for himself, and proved to have a stronger stomach than some of his companions. At one point he noted:

My vacation has been absorbed in visiting with Mr. Smith and Dr. Playfair some of the worst parts of the worst towns. Dr. Playfair has been knocked up by it, and has been seriously ill. Mr. Smith has had a little dysentery. Sir Henry de la Beche was obliged at Bristol to stand at the end of alleys and vomit while Dr. Playfair was investigating overflowing privies. Sir Henry was obliged to give it up.[12]

When Chadwick sent the draft of his report to John Stuart Mill, the acknowledged leader of the Benthamites, he received devastating criticism in return. Mill wrote back acidly to point out 'defects of arrangement', 'numerous typographical errors' and 'occasional ungrammatical sentences'. Chadwick evidently had the humility to profit from this critique, and the self-discipline to revise his work. The final version is cogent, lucid and impressive, and Mill expressed his satisfaction with it.[13]

The report, published in 1842, consists of three volumes – one written by Chadwick, and two consisting of an edited version of the detailed reports on which his conclusions were based. Chadwick starts with an analysis of the deaths in one year, 1838. Two points stand out: there were 56,461 deaths from epidemic, endemic and contagious diseases, 'the great proportion of which are proved to be preventible [sic]'. This was equivalent to the entire population of the county of Westmorland (now the southern half of Cumbria). It was as if the entire population of one such county were wiped out annually. Further, the 'annual slaughter' in England and Wales from typhus alone, 'which attacks persons in the vigour of life', was twice that of the Allied casualties in the Battle of Waterloo.

Chadwick goes on to give a catalogue of the problems, drawn from the detailed reports of his many correspondents. It is an unpleasant record, but Chadwick was prepared to make the public face facts without euphemism or evasion. He recorded in blunt terms the problems of 'human refuse' (few houses had water-closets, and some lacked even earth privies); the accumulation of rubbish, which rotted and stank in heaps; the blockage of drains, silted up with excrement; the filthy, fly-infested slaughter-houses; the pale and sickly people, living their short lives surrounded by disease and death before they too succumbed; the young widows, left without a breadwinner, and the abandoned orphans. He estimates that 'nearly 27,000 cases of premature widowhood and more than 100,000 cases of orphanage may be ascribed to removable causes'.[14]

In Wigan, the Poor Law medical officer reported on 'the filthy condition of the town':

> Many of the streets are unpaved, and almost covered with stagnant water, which lodges in numerous large holes which exist upon their surface, and into which the inhabitants throw all kinds of rejected animal and vegetable matters which then undergo decay and emit the most poisonous exhalations.[15]

A number of correspondents reported on poor families living in 'damp, dark cellars'. A medical officer from West Derby wrote of 'a family of 13, twelve of whom had typhus fever', lying on the floor without even straw or wood shavings (common substitutes for bedding). In the Axbridge Union in Somerset (which might have been thought to be relatively healthy), the Poor Law Medical Officer described circumstances in which 'filth and poverty go hand in hand without any restriction or control'. In Windsor, under the shadow of the young Queen Victoria's castle, 'a double line of deep, open, black and stagnant ditches' scored the poorer areas of the town, and 'an intolerable stench is perpetually arising, and produces fever of a severe character . . . cases of typhus fever are frequent in the neighbourhood'. The Prince Consort was to die prematurely of typhoid, and the drains of Windsor Castle were blamed for his death.

In Macclesfield 'in a part of the town called The Orchard', one of Chadwick's informants found:

> a most foul and putrid mass, disgusting to the sight and offensive to the smell: the fumes of contagion . . . produces different types of fever and disorders of the stomach and bowels. The people inhabiting these abodes are pale and unhealthy.[16]

He described the 'filthy, putrid gutters' of Carlisle; the insanitary habits of the population of Gateshead, where chamber pots were still emptied out of the window; the condition of the poor of Edinburgh – 'worse off than wild animals'; the agonizing cold and damp in winter, causing rheumatism and chest infections, and the more dreaded heat of summer, when the stench became overpowering, and disease multiplied.

A largely neglected section of the report deals with 'Comparative Chances of Life in Different Classes of the Community'. Chadwick was struggling with imperfect statistics and a lack of statistical technique, and he realized this, complaining of the 'very dangerous errors' which could arise from crude statistical returns. But he initiated the first analysis of mortality by social class, and he provided some disturbing statistics on death-rates, comparing those for urban areas with those for rural areas.

These showed that the average age of death for mechanics, labourers and their families in Manchester was 17. In Leeds, it was 19, in Bethnal Green, 16, in Liverpool, 15, but in rural Rutland, it was 38. Though infant mortality statistics had not yet been evolved, Chadwick recognized that the figures for infant deaths pulled down the average. The techniques were rudimentary, but the case for action was proved. Chadwick ended his report with an argument for state intervention. He was aware that many members of the Whig Government were supporters of a *laissez-faire* philosophy; but he was at pains to demonstrate that both Benthamite theory and practical experience supported the case for state action. He argued that 'the physical evils by which the health, strength and morals of the labouring classes are depressed' could not be remedied by 'private and voluntary exertions'. He pointed out that Parliament had already sanctioned 'legislative interference' for factory reform, reform of conditions in the mines, and the relief of the 'climbing boys', or young chimney-sweeps (all issues which his ally Lord Ashley, later the seventh Earl of Shaftesbury, had brought before the House of Commons). Chadwick was prepared to be unashamedly interventionist. Efficient drainage, sewerage and town cleansing were matters for government action, and came 'within the acknowledged province of the legislature'.[17]

Chadwick made his summary with relative brevity and unanswerable logic. Epidemic and endemic diseases in the towns were spread by four factors: refuse, damp, dirt, and bad housing. 'These adverse circumstances tend to produce an adult population short-lived, improvident, reckless and intemperate, and with habitual avidity for sensual gratifications'.[18] This passage has been much quoted and misunderstood. Chadwick writes of 'pestilence and moral disorder' made 'fearfully manifest', but on the whole he shows a remarkable avoidance of moral condemnation for his time. He takes the view that the environment degrades the poor, and understands that they snatch the few pleasures they can get: 'Discomfort comes before intemperance ... workpeople are generally found to have few or no rival pleasures to wean them from intemperance'.[19] He was not judging the poor. He was making an intellectual point on population growth. Malthus had assumed that disease and early death would level the indigent population; but it seemed that the poor bred faster than they died. Chadwick had already noted that though the poorest districts had the highest death-rates, they also had the highest birth-rates; and he cited the city of Alexandria, 'a seat of pestilence', where, despite a horrific death-rate, the population had more than doubled in twenty-five years.

The conclusions of the report were both clear and coherent. The answer lay in water supply. Pure water could clean the people, the houses and the streets, and flush the sewers. Nor was this all; for sewage suspended in water might be 'most cheaply and innoxiously conveyed to any distance out of towns' and used for liquid manure on the land.

Here was the perfect Benthamite solution – the perfect self-eliminating mechanism. The effluvia of the towns would increase the productivity of the rural areas. The result would be an improvement in the moral condition of the population, a decrease in sickness and suffering, and a remarkable saving in public expenditure. No longer would it be necessary for rubbish to be shovelled up and taken away in stinking carts, for sewers to be scoured by hand. Water would do the task, once the drains and sewers were properly constructed.

But the scope of the project was awesome. Reservoirs would have to be constructed to hold the huge quantities of water necessary. It would be necessary to tunnel under every street in every town, laying mile upon mile of pipes; and every house would eventually be connected to them. For this massive undertaking, legislative action was necessary, and all new public works should be 'devised and conducted by responsible officers qualified by the possession of the science and skill of civil engineers'.[20]

The Health of Towns Movement

Chadwick's vision of a more hygienic England impressed the House of Lords, and in 1844, a Health of Towns Commission was set up under the chairmanship of the Duke of Buccleuch. Since all the members were peers, Chadwick was officially only a witness, but he drafted most of the report, and spelled out the legislative implications of the proposals in the Sanitary Report, devising an administrative framework for a new Public Health service. David Roberts[21] notes that this was basically the same Benthamite device which he and Nassau Senior had employed for the Poor Law Amendment Act: a central board in London with inspectors who would supervise the work of consolidated local bodies.

But Sir Robert Peel's government had other preoccupations.

The Irish Famine occurred in 1845, the Corn Laws were finally repealed, and the Tory Party irretrievably split in 1846. A slogan burned with a hot iron into the wood of a door opposite the Chapter House in Christ Church Oxford, the last ditch of Tory resistance to the Peelites, remains to this day: it reads 'No Peel', and testifies to the violence of extreme right-wing reaction. It is hardly surprising that Chadwick's ambitious scheme was not a priority in this time of violent political upheaval. Parliamentary passions were roused in the mid-1840s, but not by the prospects of civil engineering. So the Government took no action, apart from framing two minor and largely ineffective pieces of legislation in 1846 – the Nuisances Removal and Diseases Prevention Act, and the Baths and Wash-houses Act. Both were permissive Acts. Many local authorities ignored them. Chadwick wanted a firm national framework and mandatory legislation. The next step was a public campaign.

Chadwick was not officially a member of the Health of Towns Association, founded in 1844. As a public servant, and one with a professional interest in the reforms the Association existed to promote, he preferred not to be directly identified with it. However, Southwood Smith was a member, and Chadwick worked behind the scenes, suggesting courses of action, providing information and writing many of its reports. More than that, as the Association grew, he acquired a new and astonishing popularity. Finer notes that 'the Public Health movement was approaching its flood-tide, and Chadwick was its hero'.[22] Health of Towns Associations sprang up in most of the cities – London, Birmingham, Manchester, Liverpool and elsewhere. Speaker after speaker quoted Chadwick's analysis. He was supported, not only by his Benthamite colleagues, the public health doctors and the civil engineers, but by many influential figures in the metropolis and the provinces.

In 1847, the City of Liverpool secured a private Act of Parliament, and appointed the first Medical Officer of Health, Dr Duncan. In 1848, the City of London followed suit, and appointed Dr John Simon (pronounced 'Simone', with the accent on the second syllable). In the same year, Lord John Russell's government brought forward the Public Health Bill to set up the system which Chadwick had designed.

The Public Health Act 1848

A central authority, the General Board of Health, was instituted, with three Commissioners and a secretariat. Municipal corporations were empowered to set up local boards of health to consolidate and extend public health work. They were to appoint staff: a surveyor, an Inspector of Nuisances, a Treasurer, a Clerk and a Medical Officer of Health, this last appointment to be subject to the approval of the General Board of Health in London.

Local boards were given wide powers to deal with sewage and drainage; to ensure that the streets were swept, cleansed, watered, flagged and repaired; to erect public conveniences; to register slaughter-houses and common lodging-houses; to regulate offensive trades such as butchering in slaughter-houses and dangerous chemical trades; to clean and purify 'unwholesome houses'. All new houses constructed after the passing of the Act were to have a water-closet, an ash-pit and drains.

The implementation of the Act must have looked fairly straightforward. It was clear and unambiguous. It introduced much needed measures which would benefit all members of the public. It had a wave of public support behind it. The three members appointed to the General Board of Health were Lord Morpeth, later the Earl of Carlisle, Lord Ashley (who became the Earl of Shaftesbury in 1851) and Chadwick, who was at last given full public recognition. Their enthusiasm and commitment were beyond question. It was a moment of triumph. Yet five years later, the Commissioners were summarily dismissed from office. What went wrong?

Action and opposition

The records read like a Greek tragedy. Everything went wrong. To begin with, the Act itself was defective. It was a permissive Act, which meant that it had to be formally adopted in each area in turn; and while some local authorities, like those for Liverpool and the City of London, saw the necessity only too clearly, there were many vested interests to hold the measure back in others. An element of compulsion was introduced by the ingenious provision that the General Board of Health could enforce action in either of two sets of circumstances: if it received a petition signed by one-tenth of the ratepayers for a particular area, or if the death-rate exceeded 23 per thousand population.

David Roberts takes the view that the Public Health Act 'demanded an exact definition of the relations of central and local government', and that the lack of this exactitude was a major feature in its failure. His analysis of the early Victorian opposition to centralization and national inspectorates forms a valuable background to understanding the opposition which the Act aroused. 'Centralisation?' says Mr. Podsnap in Dickens's *Our Mutual Friend*, 'No, never in my life-time. Not English'.[23]

A newspaper protest was less dismissive but more vehement: 'How much further are we to go with centralising?' it asked. 'Is it to come to the supply of raiment and food? Is there to be cobbling and baking boards at Whitehall?' Local susceptibilities were offended. The local authorities felt that the new measures were an infringement of their powers. The hatred which the centralized Poor Law had raised was easily transferred to this new centralized body which proposed to regulate English streets, English homes and English sewers.

In fact, the General Board of Health had too little power rather than too much. It had the power to infringe local autonomy – but only in the circumstances of public petition or a high mortality rate. But it had little power in other circumstances, and it did not even have a permanent inspectorate. Further, it was poorly funded, and had little money to carry out its intentions. There were constant battles with the Treasury over even minor items of expenditure. The Board thus combined the maximum threat with very limited efficacy.

Despite the financial and administrative problems, Chadwick recruited an enthusiastic team of young civil engineers as temporary inspectors. They toured the country, investigating, advising, recommending, and brought some 200 areas under the operation of the Act. There was a massive investigation into water supply in the metropolis, where sewage, discharged into the Thames, was held up at Teddington Lock, and flowed back again. There were battles to be fought with the water companies, which resisted the introduction of a public service. There were more battles to be fought with the vestries and the private cemetery owners. Chadwick had deliberately left the subject of interment out of the Sanitary Report, but he had completed a separate and supplementary report on the subject,[25] which described in much detail the grisly conditions to be found in many of the cemeteries of the metropolis. An Interment Act of 1850 gave the General Board of Health power to construct and manage public cemeteries, but there was furious opposition, and not enough money.

All this activity commenced during the period of a cholera epidemic. Cholera came from Asia across Europe and flared up in all the big cities – often in the same places as in the previous epidemic of 1831–1832. In the heat of summer in 1849, it hit London. Out of a population of 2.2 million, 14,601 people died before the epidemic waned. In England and Wales as a whole, the total deaths from this epidemic were 72,180. The inspectors toured indefatigably. Chadwick and his colleagues were grossly overworked. Early in 1849, Chadwick told Lord John Russell that one of his colleagues was 'knocked up', another 'overdone with work' one inspector had the first signs of cholera and another had fever. He commented 'Lord Carlisle [Morpeth] excepted, it may be said the Board of Health is very unwell'.[26]

A stream of memoranda went out from the Board's headquarters in London to the municipal authorities, but these were often counter productive, since they served only to increase local resistance. In many areas, there were divided authorities – Poor Law Guardians, Cleansing Boards, Sewage Commissioners, all insisting on their own rights, and failing to work together.

The *Lancet* was quick to point out the anomalies of the situation to the medical profession. Here was a General Board of Health managed by two noblemen and a lawyer, prescribing treatment for an epidemic. Civil engineers spent their time analysing mortality statistics; and the only doctor in the team spent his time in organizing street cleansing and the emptying of privies.[27]

To some extent, medical opposition may have been a matter of professional conflict – the traditional healers of the sick resenting the power and prestige of the sanitary engineers. Chadwick had never concealed his thorough contempt for curative medicine, though he was able to work with members of the medical profession like Southwood Smith and William Farr. But the medical establishment, represented by the Royal College of Physicians, was firmly devoted to curative medicine. It was in relation to curative medicine that Chadwick made his much-quoted remark, 'I always doubt the success of mere medicine'.[28] What made it 'mere' in his eyes was the unwillingness of the medical profession to take any steps which would eliminate the causes of disease.

There was also a substantive issue at stake – the causation of the major epidemic diseases. The Sanitary Report provides ample evidence that Chadwick and his colleagues believed that bad smells were the cause of disease – there are repeated references to 'noxious effluvias', 'poisonous vapours', 'obnoxious atmospheres', 'miasma' and 'stench'. His medical supporters shared this belief: Farr had referred to a 'disease-mist' over London, and Southwood Smith described the process in precise terms:

> Wherever human beings live together in communities, these large masses of animal and vegetable substances, the refuse of food and other matters essential to human existence, must be always decomposing. If provision is not made for the immediate removal of these poisons, they are carried by the air inspired to the air-cells of the lungs, the thin, delicate membranes of which they pierce, and thus pass directly into the current of the circulation. It has been shown that by the natural and ordinary flow of this current, three distinct and fresh portions of these poisons must be transmitted to every nook and corner of the system every eight minutes of time:[29]

Chadwick put it more briefly: 'All smell is, if it be intense, immediate acute disease'. As Finer comments, he often acted as though the reverse were true: all disease is smell.[30]

This 'miasmatic theory' was basic to the formulation of the new preventive ideas. Southwood Smith adhered to it so thoroughly that he took his granddaughter with him through the wards of his fever hospital, convinced that if patients were clean they could not transmit disease.[31]

> They were not even aware that cholera was a specific infection, as distinct in its nature from plague and typhus as the elephant from the giraffe and camel. ... Cholera was no more than a virulent form of those familiar crowd diseases which killed thousands every year in the slums of the great towns.[32]

In the early 1850s, the bacilli of disease had not yet been isolated, though many doctors believed that they existed. The Royal College of Physicians held to the 'germ theory' or 'theory of specific contagion', concluding that dirt and smells were harmless, and rejecting what they regarded as the unscientific views of the sanitary reformers. With hindsight, we can see that both were right. Bacilli do exist, but they breed faster in dirty conditions. At this time, neither theory could be proved, and each appeared to exclude the other.

The opposition to the General Board of Health piled up: the doctors, the municipal authorities, the local office-holders, the private water companies and their shareholders, the private cemetery companies and their shareholders, the Mr Podsnaps: to these powerful groups could be added others who had their own reasons for desiring the failure of the General Board of Health: the tenement landlords who were alarmed at the prospect of having to make costly improvements to their property; the builders, resistant to building working class houses with water-closets and piped water supply because working people would not be able to afford them; the factory owners engaged in dangerous trades; the butchers and other shop owners; the older engineers, not trained in the new methods; the ratepayers (since someone had to pay for all the improvements and Chadwick's financial calculations were distinctly sketchy); and finally the Press and Parliament.

A number of newspapers carried out campaigns against the General Board of Health. They included *The Economist, John Bull*, the *Standard*, and the *Morning Chronicle*; but the Board's most powerful opponent was John Walter III, editor of *The Times*, who carried out a campaign of extraordinary vindictiveness. He continued his father's earlier campaign against Chadwick's centralizing policy, commenting that if the government had considered that Chadwick was the most efficient representative of all the issues which arose, 'the proper course would have been at once to invest him with a sanitary dictatorship. . . . This, however, was not done, and the results have been what we now witness'.[33] His attacks culminated in the statement that 'We prefer to take our chance of cholera rather than being bullied into health'.

Chadwick was essentially a believer in the power of the senior civil servant. Though he was adept at inducing members of both the House of Commons and the House of Lords to promote his policies, he never really understood the parliamentary system. He had little time for politicians, whose interest in his schemes was relatively superficial. Finer quotes him as saying 'By all means have a Minister – but only as the defender of the chief permanent officers'.[34]

By 1851, both his fellow Commissioners on the General Board of Health were in the House of Lords, having succeeded to family titles. Lord Ashley became the Earl of Shaftesbury and Lord Morpeth the Earl of Carlisle. Chadwick had few defenders in the Commons, and a number of powerful adversaries: Sir Benjamin Hall, champion of the select vestries – the old authorities which Chadwick's new local boards of health were supplanting; John Walter III of *The Times*; Thomas Wakley, the editor of the *Lancet*.

In spite of all the sources of opposition, the Board might have survived into a second term (its initial term of office was five years from its formation in 1849) had it not been for one critical occurrence. In 1853, there was a new cholera epidemic which started in Croydon soon after a local board of health had been set up, and new pipes installed. The suspicion arose that *the cholera was water-borne*. The more water was used in cleansing, the more the cholera spread, and the new sanitation was blamed directly on the activities of the General Board of Health. The matter appeared to be settled by the celebrated affair of the Broad Street Pump.

Dr John Snow had already written a treatise in 1849 entitled *On the Mode of Communication of Cholera*. In the epidemic of 1853, he obtained a list from the General Register Office of deaths from cholera in particular districts of London. He found that there had been 89 deaths in a single week from the area served by one pump in the Broad Street area of central London. He called late one night on the vestrymen of St James's, who were responsible for the area, and advised the removal of the pump handle. The deaths from cholera stopped.[35] The miasmatic theory was utterly discredited, and so was the ill-fated General Board of Health.

Chadwick and his colleagues were dismissed. Chadwick, as the salaried member, was given a pension of £1,000 a year. He was then 54 years old, and he lived to the age of 90. Though he continued to investigate a variety of social conditions and to write voluminous reports, he never again achieved public eminence. Finer encapsulates nearly forty years of his subject's life in obscurity in a nine-page chapter headed 'The Spent Prophet'. In Chadwick's old age, a member of the Political Economy Club commented that he babbled 'not of green fields, but of sewage'.[36]

Perhaps the most bitter aspect of his downfall was the constitution of the new General Board of Health: his replacement was Sir Benjamin Hall; but the Board was too generally unpopular for even this administrative somersault to make it palatable. In 1858, it was abolished, and replaced by a Medical Department of the Privy Council under the direction of John Simon. While that body carried on the work of vital statistics, it never attempted the kind of centralized direction which led to the destruction of the General Board of Health. The Sanitary Act of 1866 provided an appropriate epilogue to the story of the Board's activities. This Act placed all the responsibilities which had been laid down in the 1848 Act, plus some others, such as dealing with overcrowding, smoke abatement and infection, squarely on the municipal authorities. It was mandatory, and not permissive. There was no central control, and no inspectorate.

There was no public outcry this time. The medical profession, given an enhanced status under the Medical Qualifications Act of 1858, was possibly more secure, and less threatened by the sanitary engineers. It could afford to admit the value of prevention in public health, and to make preventive medicine a specialism. The municipal authorities were given both the powers and the duties of public health work to exercise without interference; and there was a greater public awareness of public health hazards than in the early 1850s. Local control had achieved what centralization had failed to do.

FOUR
Voluntary Action

While Members of Parliament and civil servants were struggling with the legislation and the apparatus of government necessary for social reform, many other groups and individuals were trying to tackle the worst evils on a voluntary basis. William Beveridge, looking back in 1948 in a survey of voluntary social service, defined three distinct movements: Philanthropy, Mutual Aid and what he called 'Personal Thrift'.[1] Philanthropy was a movement between the social classes, from the haves to the have-nots. Mutual aid was the attempt of working men to support each other against the predictable crises in their lives: unemployment, sickness, disability, old age, and to protect their dependents in the event of their early death. Personal Thrift was a matter of making what provision was possible for oneself.

Philanthropy

Victorian philanthropy is a highly controversial subject. In its own day, and for decades after, it was much admired. Every school history book carried stories of the great pioneers who dedicated their lives to the poor and unfortunate, and fought against great odds. Hospital wards and school houses were named after them, voluntary societies perpetuated their memory. By the middle of the twentieth century, a reaction had set in. There was more awareness of the humiliation often involved for the recipients in being offered (and perhaps having no alternative but to accept) 'charity'; of the way in which psalm-singing and Bible-reading were forced on people with empty stomachs by the well-fed; of the social climbing which often went with charity dinners, charity balls and royal patronage. Derek Fraser expresses this view in a mild but dismissive way:

> The Victorian response to the powerlessness (or, as it was often conceived, the moral weakness) of the individual was an over-liberal dose of charity ... it was small wonder that self-congratulation was so common a theme in contemporary surveys of Victorian philanthropy. So many good causes were catered for – stray dogs, stray children, fallen women and drunken men: there was apparently no subject which could not arouse the philanthropic urge of the Victorian public.[2]

Yet neither cynicism nor hero-worship will fit the complexities of philanthropic activity in the Victorian period. We should not read back our own current debates about individualism and collectivism into so different a context, and any generalization is likely to be superficial. 'Victorian philanthropy' is an umbrella term for many different activities which took place at many different levels and in almost every community, carried out by thousands, possibly tens of thousands, of people with a variety of motives; and the motives, like most human motives, were very often mixed. Those who were attracted by the altruistic element in philanthropy cannot assume that it was always conducted on a high spiritual plane, or that it was always efficient in meeting the needs of the recipients. Those who are repelled by snobbery and moral coercion cannot dismiss it all on that account. To conclude that all philanthropists were virtuous and self-sacrificing, or that all philanthropists were gratifying their own egos, is to do less than justice to a very complex subject.

The Victorian period lasted over six decades, at a time of rapid and disrupting social change; and philanthropy also changed, both in methods and scope, during that period. There were at least four different, though overlapping phases:

1. Small-scale voluntary giving of the kind common in the eighteenth century: a landowner might look after his cottagers, a merchant might bequeath a sum of money for the relief of apprentices or indigent seamen or the aged poor of the parish.

2. Pioneer work by outstanding individuals like Florence

Nightingale, Lord Shaftesbury, Dr Barnardo, General Booth of the Salvation Army, or Octavia Hill, the housing refomer, who brought particular social evils to the public notice.
  3. The work of major national societies and associations, often set up by the pioneers, but sometimes developing out of more widely supported local philanthropic effort.
  4. The activities of the Charity Organisation Society, founded in 1869 as the Society for the Organisation of Charitable Relief and the Repression of Mendicity. The COS attempted to place a mass of unregulated charitable activity on a more constructive basis, but earned a reputation for rigidity and harshness in its approach to poor people. Much of the criticism directed against philanthropy relates to the operations of this organization in the late Victorian period. If any group gave charity a bad name, it was the COS.
  Philanthropy could be patronizing, and humiliating to the recipient; but the quotation which is frequently used to demonstrate the class-ridden nature of Victorian philanthropy is highly misleading. The popular version is:

> The rich man in his castle,
> The poor man at the gate,
> God made them high or lowly,
> And ordered their estate.

This verse from the hymn 'All things bright and beautiful' was written by Mrs Cecil Alexander, wife of the Bishop of Derry, in the 1850s. She was a Greek scholar, and a philanthropist in her own right. What she actually wrote was 'God made them, high or lowly'. The comma changes the sense: this was a statement of social equality (rich and poor are both God's creation) not an acceptance of the existing social order.[3]
  Who were the pioneers, and what motivated them? As Lord Beveridge points out, many of them were neither rich nor aristocratic, though they all had time to spare from the daily grind of earning a living. Lord Shaftesbury was an exception among the landed classes, most of whom confined their charitable instincts to their own tenantry; but despite his title and his family connections, he was a poor man – appalled when he took over his father's estate to find that the cottages were 'filthy, close, indecent, unwholesome'.[4] His debts at that time were over a hundred thousand pounds;

but all his work, even on the General Board of Health, was unpaid.

Many philanthropists came from the comfortable upper middle class. Elizabeth Fry, the prison reformer, was the daughter of a banker and the wife of another. When the Governor of Newgate refused to let her visit the women prisoners, she used the best means of persuasion open to her: she asked her husband to invite him to dinner. William Tuke, who founded the York Retreat, a model for the humane management of asylums, was a grocer, but a prosperous grocer (the family eventually sold out to the Rowntrees). Florence Nightingale was the daughter of a wealthy dilettante, 'W.E.N.', who named his daughter after his favourite city, and found her choice of an occupation distinctly unsuitable.

Some had a more precarious social background. Octavia Hill was a banker's daughter, and the grand-daughter of Dr Southwood Smith, but the family fell on hard times after her father's illness and death, and the girls had to support themselves by some fairly low-level teaching. They had little money to spare for the hospitality they offered to tenement-dwellers. General Booth was the son of a speculative builder who described himself as 'Gentleman' in registering his son's birth, but apprenticed him to a pawnbroker when he was thirteen. The future Dr Barnardo went to work at the age of ten as a clerk in a wine merchant's office.

Most philanthropists were people of religious conviction. Shaftesbury was a leading Evangelical Churchman at the time of the great Evangelical revival, and his work as a social reformer was a logical consequence of his faith. Kathleen Heasman's *Evangelicals in Action*[5] gives a full account of the many philanthropic works undertaken by the Protestant denominations in the nineteenth century: the missions, the relief committees, the ragged schools, the temperance societies, the settlements. The Quaker contribution, characterized by such families as the Frys, Tukes, Cadburys and Rowntrees, was particularly innovative. Roman Catholic, Anglo-Catholic and Jewish groups were to develop their own organizations for social care later, in the second half of the century, but the Evangelicals led the way.

Victorian religiosity is alien to late twentieth-century ways of thought and expression. Were the philanthropists sincere, or were they merely paying lip-service to a dominant ideology? We can only answer this by asking – if they were not sincere, what drove them? For driven they were. They worked tirelessly. They went into appalling slums, risked physical attack and disease, and faced lice, bugs and the contempt of their peers for doing so.

Victorian philanthropy was not summed up in the practice of taking soup and calves' foot jelly to the poor – though that kind of gentle, leisured activity survived in country districts, it bore no relationship to the many socially valuable movements which developed in the towns. Philanthropy may not have been well organized, but it was certainly organized.

Voluntary societies developed from the middle of the eighteenth century on; and as communications improved, local movements became national movements. The Annual Register for successive years shows a lengthy and growing list of societies for the Promotion of This or the Abolition of That which were skilled in what we would now call pressure-group activities. Philanthropy involved public meetings, committees, speeches, memoranda, subscriptions, people who could rival Chadwick in their tireless industry and their ability to influence politicians and members of the cabinet. They lobbied ceaselessly, and without mercy. 'Letters, interviews, chairs, boards, speeches' wrote Lord Shaftesbury in his diary, 'I am worn, worn, worn by them all . . . my nerves are sensitive and harsh as wires'.[6]

Philanthropists have often been charged with using the movements which they founded as a means of social control. Many of them certainly preached respectable middle-class values – cleanliness, sobriety, self-improvement and responsibility; and some at least did not realize the inadequacy of these prescriptions for people who lived in disease-ridden squalor on the edge of starvation; but they protected frightened women from violent and drunken men, sheltered neglected and abandoned children, provided schools, cared for social outcasts, and improved housing, providing the evidence and the experience on which the statutory services could later build.

It has been argued that philanthropy was a way of taking the edge off social revolt, and that the real driving force was fear of the mob.[7] This may well have been one motive up to 1848, when the Chartists marched on Westminster; but when Paris, Milan, Naples, Prague, Vienna, Berlin and Budapest were in the hands of revolutionaries, the English Chartists took cabs across Westminster Bridge to present their petition to Parliament in the politest possible manner – and the petition was found to have many forged signatures, such as 'Victoria Rex', and the names of Sir Robert Peel and the Duke of Wellington.[8] The Chartist movement collapsed in general hilarity, though its purposes were mainly achieved in the Parliamentary Reform Acts of 1867 and 1884. There was no danger of revolt after 1848. Social reform turned to more peaceful means of expression, but the philanthropic movement continued to grow in strength.

The best of the philanthropists were neither sentimentalists nor political die-hards. The mild and self-controlled Lord Shaftesbury exploded into anger when he met a lady who objected to the climbing boys going to school in the afternoons, and called her 'a woman who would cut up a child for dog's meat, or for making manure'.[9] When one of Florence Nightingale's shipboard companions gushed 'Oh, let us get straight to nursing the poor fellows', her reply was 'The strongest will be wanted at the washtub'.[10]

It is an over-generalization to say that 'the whole concept of charity was one that tended to degrade rather than uplift the recipient'.[11] There was nothing very uplifting about starving in a garrett or dying in a military hospital. At a time when the only statutory service was the dreaded Poor Law, there was no alternative to philanthropic action; but philanthropy did not provide a sufficient structure for meeting need. By the late 1880s, the amount of money involved was very large – voluntary societies in London alone were handling between £5.5 million and £7 million a year;[12] but these huge sums of money were often not being properly accounted for, or directed where they would do most good. The Charity Organization Society, set up in 1869, argued that charities should co-operate, that individual claims for assistance should be investigated in depth, and that aid should be constructive rather than merely palliative.

This basic argument was sound enough. Modern international charities like Oxfam and War on Want take a similar view; but the COS propounded its views in a manner which was punitive, moralistic, and highly offensive to other charities.

The foundation of the COS coincided with an important policy statement from the Gladstone Government, known as the Goschen Minute.[13] George Goschen, then President of the Poor Law Board, was concerned to tighten up the Poor Law, which had become comparatively generous (or in his view, lax) in its administration.

Local Boards of Guardians had achieved a considerable measure of independence from central control in the preceding twenty years, and some were again giving outdoor relief on a considerable scale. The Goschen Minute was basically a restatement of the Poor Law principles of 1834, but with the concession that, in view of the rapid growth of voluntary charity, a distinction should be drawn between the 'deserving' and the 'undeserving'. The 'deserving' might be helped back to independence by charitable organizations; the 'undeserving' would go to the workhouse.

It is not clear whether this statement was actually inspired by members of the COS, or whether the statement of Government policy inspired them,[14] but it formed the basis of their activities. Many members of the COS were also members of their local Boards of Guardians. They applied themselves with energy to working on both sides of the newly erected fence, apparently experiencing little difficulty in applying their simple binary division. 'Deserving' people were clean, sober, polite and grateful. They had fallen on hard times, but might be assisted back to independence. 'Undeserving' people were dirty, drunken, and frequently abusive, lacking a respect for their betters.

By the end of the nineteenth century, there were more than 40 COS district offices in London, and some 75 corresponding societies in other parts of the country. Their enquiries into individual cases were detailed, severe and highly judgemental, based on the conviction that poverty was a personal failing, and that the poor needed to be forced back into self-sufficiency. They took the view that the poor were being demoralized – turned into beggars of coal tickets, clothes tickets and cash handed out in a manner which encouraged shiftless and irresponsible attitudes.

The COS came into conflict with Dr Barnardo, claiming that his medical qualifications were false, and that he was misappropriating funds. It was true that Dr Barnardo's original qualifications were somewhat suspect (though he had covered them with a licence from the Royal College of Surgeons by the time the investigation took place), and that he was handling some £30,000 a year without proper accounts, but there was no evidence of malpractice. The COS opposed the Salvation Army with particular bitterness, claiming that its work actually created homelessness.[15] Their approach, both with their clients and with more compassionate relief organizations, was so abrasive that it earned much of the opprobrium which has since been directed against philanthropy in general. Their diagnosis of the problems of large-scale Victorian philanthropy was sound enough; but their proposed cure gave the whole movement a bad name.

Mutual Aid

Mutual aid started spontaneously on a local level. It became the custom for groups of men to meet in the local inn for a drink on pay-day, and to contribute a few pence a week for some common purpose. Dissenters, who did not drink beer, met in the chapel. Such groups served a variety of purposes: good fellowship, exchanging information about available work, providing sickness and burial funds for their members. From these simple beginnings, friendly societies, trade unions, housing associations, people's banks and co-operatives were all to develop.

Some of these groups were trade clubs, having their origins in the craft societies of the middle ages. A union of a number of trade clubs was called a 'trade union'. In the eighteenth century, many trade unions were declared illegal because they defended wage rates. As poverty grew and wages were cut, some of the trade unions showed signs of militancy, and in the years after the French Revolution, employers and magistrates saw them as centres of conspiracy and civil unrest.

Rose's Act of 1793 effectively separated the militants from the non-militants by requiring friendly societies to register, and laying down rules for their operation. A friendly society was defined as:

> a society of good fellowship for the purpose of raising from time to time by voluntary contributions, a stock or fund for the mutual relief and maintenance of all and every the members thereof, in old age, sickness and infirmity, or the relief of widows and children of deceased members.[16]

The Act made provision for a register of such societies, and laid down rules for their operation. From that time on, registered friendly societies confined their activities to protecting working men against the predictable dangers of interruption of earnings. Their numbers ran into thousands, and they were never fully counted and classified, though a number of official bodies attempted the task. The Old Amicable Society of Grantham spent five shillings a month on ale, but prudently ruled that the business should be completed before the ale was consumed. The Manchester Unity of Oddfellows was organized by the landlord of the Rope-makers' Arms in Salford. (Jeremy Bentham commented that to run a friendly society in a public house was 'like choosing a brothel for a school of continence' and preferred the concept of 'frugality banks').

The provision made by friendly societies varied. Some were primarily burial societies, protecting the working classes against the ever-present fear of a pauper funeral. Some provided for widows and children, or for sick or aged members. Some were 'collecting' societies, pre-cursors of the People's Banks. Some were 'dividing' societies, which had a 'share-out' from time to time, often at Christmas. It was almost exclusively a men's movement, though there were three 'female clubs' in the villages of Cheddar, Wrington and Shipham in the 1790s, which may have owed something to the work of the Somerset bluestocking, Hannah More.

Many of them had curious names, and some had their own rituals and ceremonies. There were Rechabites, Foresters, Odd-fellows and Hearts of Oak. There were the Total Abstinence Sons of the Phoenix Society, and the Yorkshire Delight Lodge, and the Halifax Order of the Peaceful Dove. None of them were radical. Radicalism developed in the trade union movement, which had a different and more stormy history.

Trade unions were outlawed altogether by the Combination Acts of 1799 and 180 . Any man found joining with another to demand an increase in wages was liable to a prison sentence of three months, or two months' hard labour. Though the Combina-tion Acts were repealed in 1824, the legal position remained obscure, and any trade union activity – like that of the six Dorchester labourers or 'Tolpuddle Martyrs' – was liable to be treated as a criminal conspiracy in times of unrest. In the more peaceful period of the 1850s and 1860s, the trade union movement spread, mainly in the skilled and relatively well paid trades. These often developed their own insurance schemes for members, inde-pendently of the older friendly societies.

The first housing society was founded in Birmingham in 1781 for the purpose of 'raising by small periodical subscriptions a fund to assist the members thereof in obtaining a small leasehold or freehold property'. By 1874, there were some 2,000. There is an interesting example of a society in Swansea which operated a tontine: members subscribed for five years to buy five houses to let. When only ten members remained alive, they were to have the option of selling or keeping the houses. If they opted to keep them, the tontine would continue until only five were left alive, when they were to be allotted one house each.[17]

Housing societies developed into two rather different kinds of organizations: housing associations, which had a philanthropic element, and built for the working classes; and building societies, which were mainly a means of investment for the middle classes. Many subscribers made quarterly payments – they were not weekly wage earners, who were usually 'spent up' by pay-day. Building societies were not friendly societies, and their legal position was obscure until the passing of the Building Societies Act of 1836.

By the 1820s, few building societies were actually concerned with building houses. Their main activity was in lending money to others at interest. As the Royal Commission of 1872 reported 'Building societies do not build, they simply make advances on building'.[18] Cole and Postgate argue that building societies were not a mutual aid movement: they exacted high rates of interest, and if housing prices fell, the house-buyers had to stand the loss. Further, they were a force against social change, because people with a mortgage were afraid of social and economic instability.[19]

People's Banks grew naturally out of the collecting societies. As wages improved for some classes of skilled workers, they needed a safe place to keep their limited reserves. The working man was to become 'his own capitalist'.[20] By the second half of the nineteenth century, there were village banks and municipal banks among many other forms of savings institutions. The Post Office Savings Bank dates from 1861 – an innovation by Sir Rowland Hill, who introduced the penny post.

The co-operative movement had its origins in short-lived workers' co-operatives set up in the eighteenth century, and in the pioneer work of Robert Owen, who bought the New Lanark cotton mills in 1800, and set out to prove that capitalism need not mean exploitation. Owen was a model employer who failed to convince other factory owners of his day that it would pay them to look after their workers. When his attempts to secure factory reform failed, he moved steadily towards Socialism with a scheme to set up 'Villages of Co-operation' where the unemployed would be set to work. Jeremy Bentham was one of many influential people interested in his plans. But Owen parted company with many of his supporters when, long before Marx, he developed a system whereby the currency was based on the human labour employed in production, not on demand and supply. The Owenite villages including New Harmony, his North American settlement, had a relatively short life.

But the idea of linking labour directly to the sale of goods without the intervention of the capitalist class survived. In 1844, a group of flannel weavers in Rochdale set up a shop in a warehouse in Toad Lane to sell their own produce. They were 'followers of Mr. Owen', but they dealt in money. The new factor was that they sold at market prices, but gave members of their society a dividend on their purchases which could be reinvested. This encouraged 'moral buying as well as moral selling'.[21] Though the local shopkeepers tried to put them out of business by undercutting their prices, the 'divi' proved a powerful incentive.

In the event, Co-operative production did not last for more than a few decades, but Co-operative retailing flourished. In the long term, the Co-operative movement did not overturn capitalism, but it became a wide-spread working-class movement with political influence and many services to offer to its members, including adult education and investment.

From 1854, when the Prudential was set up as a joint stock company, mutual aid insurance schemes began to be overtaken by the commercial insurance companies. By 1872, the 'Pru' had more than a million policy-holders. But there were some social dangers in this new movement. A Royal Commission in 1871–1874 recommended that limits should be placed on the insurance of children's lives by their parents in a period when child life was cheap; and 'everyone who wanted to have a flutter was being urged to have sixpence on grandmother'.[22] Acts of 1875, 1896 and 1909 led to successive restriction of the right to insure the lives of others.

All these developments showed a sturdy independence among the more prosperous and regularly employed working classes, who wanted to distance themselves from the hopelessness and helplessness of poverty. Only the trade unions and the co-operative movement kept their original radical stance. The other mutual aid movements tended to draw the working man into small-scale capitalism.

Self-Help

In *Voluntary Action*, Beveridge avoids the term 'self-help', preferring 'personal thrift'. It is possible that he wanted to keep the subject of individual saving clear of the views of Samuel Smiles, whose book *Self-Help* enjoyed a remarkable success in the late Victorian period. Smiles' views were looking very dated by the time *Voluntary Action* was published in 1948.

'Heaven helps those who help themselves'. Smiles announced at the beginning of *Self-Help*, published in 1859. An example of his own philosophy, he was apprenticed to a group of medical practitioners at the age of fourteen (his father died of cholera) and he studied in his spare time, gaining a medical diploma at the University of Edinburgh. He abandoned medicine, first for journalism and then for the exciting new world of the developing railway system. After some years of being secretary to the Board of Management for Leeds Central Station, he moved to London to manage the South-Eastern Railway in 1854; and throughout his career, he wrote and lectured on his main theme, which was the importance of encouraging providence and industry. 'The spirit of self-help is the root of all genuine growth in the individual', he told his public, '. . . help from without is often enfeebling, but help from within invariably invigorates'.[23]

Bad luck or lack of opportunity was no excuse. 'There is . . . a Russian proverb which says that Misfortune is next door to Stupidity'. Men who lamented their luck were merely 'reaping the consequences of their own neglect, mismanagement, improvidence or want of application'.[24] There were splendid examples in the developing industrial economy of men who had started from humble beginnings, and achieved wealth and fame: Isaac Newton, James Watt, inventor of the Spinning Jenny, Robert Stephenson, inventor of the steam engine, Isambard Kingdom Brunel, the great engineer – the list was long; and Smiles dealt sharply with the argument that the achievement of such pioneers was chiefly due to talent, quoting Voltaire and Beccaria to the effect that talent was much less important than industry, diligence and continuous application. Given continuous application, almost anyone could become a great musician or a great artist. Michelangelo, for example, completed the ceiling of the Sistine Chapel through continuous application. Shakespeare is dealt with in a chapter on 'Great Men of Business'. Smiles praises his industry in managing the Globe Theatre; ignores the literary value of the plays entirely, and then compliments the playwright on having 'prospered in his business and realised sufficient to enable him to retire upon a competency to his native town of Stratford-upon-Avon'.

This remarkable work was rejected by one publisher, but taken on rather doubtfully by another, who found that he had a best-seller on his hands. Books did not sell in millions in Victorian times, but *Self-Help* had unprecedented sales which ran into tens of thousands. It was translated into French, Dutch, German, Danish, Swedish, Spanish, Italian, Turkish, Arabic, Japanese and 'the native tongues of India', and widely circulated in the United States.[25] Queen Victoria recorded that she wept when she read it, because it was so beautiful.

Smiles (that was his real name) preached a gospel of social optimism. *Self-Help* was followed by a series of other books with similarly promising titles: there was *Character* (1871), *Thrift* (1875) and *Duty* (1880). These never achieved the overwhelming success of *Self-Help*, and over the years the message became somewhat repetitive; but it had made its mark.

Thrift was a particularly sharp attack on those who asked for help:

> We often hear the cry raised, 'Will nobody help us?' It is a spiritless, hopeless cry. It is sometimes a cry of revolting meanness, especially when it issues from those who, with a little self-denial, sobriety and thrift, might easily help themselves.[26]

Thrift and industry enabled 'the poorest man to achieve honour, if not distinction. The greatest names in the history of art, literature and science are those of labouring men'. Thrift and industry were the essence of civilization: for 'the savage is the greatest of spendthrifts . . . he has no forethought, no tomorrow'. Anyone – anyone at all – could rise from the depths. 'The Parthenon began with a mud-hut'.

Smiles writes much about the qualities of a True Gentleman: he was after his fashion, an egalitarian, for these were qualities of character, not of birth and social advantage. He is the apostle of social mobility. 'Truthfulness, integrity and goodness . . . form the essence of the manly character'. Little is said about the female half of the population, though any women readers could take hope from the improving story of the Helpful Wife. When this woman was married, she stipulated to her husband-to-be that she must have threepence, the price of a pint of ale, every day. Though puzzled, he agreed. The time came a year later when (having indulged heavily in drink himself) he was short of money. His wife then triumphantly brought out of her stocking three hundred and sixty-five threepences, for she had saved the money instead of drinking it away. 'The wife's little capital was the nucleus of frugal investments that ultimately swelled out into a shop, a factory, a warehouse, a country-seat, and perhaps a Liverpool mayor.'[27] In a rapidly-expanding economy, all things seemed possible.

Despite his strictures on Shakespeare and Michelangelo, Smiles did not wish to be thought a Philistine. He wanted to better the conditions of working-class life, and advocated free public libraries, free education, and museums. The poor could appreciate the beauties of nature, and bring flowers into their homes. Pictures, prints or engravings that represented 'a noble thought . . . a heroic act' might be bought for pennies.

Nobody reads Smiles any more. Nevertheless, he articulated an important strand in Victorian experience, and there were some grains of truth in his insistence that the age of the common man had arrived, and that those who were born poor need not despair. He did provide some sense of worth and dignity for the industrious working man. His work is also of some value because of the biographical studies he undertook on the new men of the industrial age: he wrote a life of George Stephenson, and his three-volume work on *The Lives of the Engineers* (1861–1862) became a classic.

But his frequently-repeated theme about the value of self-help and the undesirable effects of philanthropy provided the well-to-do with a defence against compassion. When social misery was so apparent, and social despair so prevalent, it was profoundly comforting for his huge public to be told that individuals were responsible for their own condition, and that any attempt to help the unfortunate was 'enfeebling'. The poor need trouble their consciences and their purses no longer.

Contrasting philosophies

In the Victorian context, philanthropy, mutual aid and self-help were contrasting and often competing philosophies. Philanthropy was tender-minded, stressing the extent of social misery. At worst, it was patronizing and snobbish, but at best, it had the merit of reaching the poorest and most disadvantaged classes in a divided society, and developing a public conscience about conditions which no civilized society could tolerate.

Mutual aid was an intensely practical movement for the better-off and more regularly employed members of the working classes. It was not a way out of poverty, but it was a means for supporting and protecting members of societies against sudden financial disaster.

Self-help was tough-minded, of greatest use to the individualistic and hardworking who were prepared to overcome obstacles of any kind in order to further their own ambitions. For such people, the developing capitalist system, the opening up of roads, railways and international trade, offered many opportunities of advancement. But however crass its expression, the self-help movement did mirror the breakdown of the traditional class barriers, and offer self-respect and hopes of a better future to those who were prepared to work for them.

Over a century later, it is not necessary to argue the merits of any one of these movements to the detriment of the others. The three voluntary movements were in many respects complementary to one another, providing different pieces of the jigsaw of future social service provision.

FIVE

Darkest England and the Poverty Surveys

The need for information about changing social conditions was well recognized before the end of the eighteenth century, but much of the early work was anecdotal and impressionistic. Investigators who attempted to convey factual information could only list what they had found, relying on the accumulation of material to prove their case, because they lacked the techniques for processing and analysing data.

The introduction of the National Census in 1801 and the Registration of Births, Deaths and Marriages Act of 1836 led to a new framework of investigation in which it was possible to obtain statistical information about the whole population for the first time, and statistical techniques began to be developed and refined. The Statistical Society of London was paralleled in other major cities, and the study of patterns of sickness and mortality developed comparatively rapidly. These were a matter of hard data: people were born, got married, had children, and died from carefully classified causes; but despite the pioneer work of Chadwick and his colleagues, the development of social statistics, involving softer data about living standards and the meaning of poverty took longer. The Social Science Association, founded in 1857, created a new focus for social analysis, but much of the early work was localized, and the techniques comparatively shaky.

The 'African Parallel'

The popularity of Henry Mayhew's *London Labour and the London Poor* (1851) indicates how much the field of social investigation was lagging behind that of medical investigation at the mid-century. Mayhew was a journalist, and he conducted his own colourful investigations of low life, concentrating on street traders and the criminal classes. His stereotyped sketches of such categories as 'Bawds', 'Procuresses, Pimps and Panders', 'Fancymen', 'Sneaks or Common Thieves', 'Magsmen or Sharpers', 'Beggars and Cheats' provided lively reading for his public, but scarcely added to the sum of knowledge about poverty. The general impression was that the poor were artful and amusing, and their way of life foreign to his respectable readers.

British imperialism had entered its expansionist phase, and many remote areas of Asia and Africa were being explored. As information filtered back about the lives and customs of 'primitive' tribes (some of which were later found to have very complex social systems) it was inevitable that comparisons would be drawn between their condition and that of the poorer classes in Britain. Mayhew used such reflections to support the somewhat startling theory that the London poor were *not English*: 'Each civilised or settled tribe has generally some wandering horde intermingled with, and in a measure preying upon it'. The Fingoes (literally beggars or outcasts) preyed upon the Kaffirs of southern Africa, the Lapps preyed upon the Finns, the Bedouins on the Fellahin of North Africa and Egypt. His conclusion was that 'there are two distinct races of men':

> We, like the Kafirs [sic], Fellahs and Finns, are surrounded by wandering hordes – paupers, beggars and outcasts, possessing nothing but what they acquire by depredation from the industrious, provident and civilised portion of the community.[1]

The identity of this nomad race could be ascertained by the shape of their heads (low-browed and small-skulled), by their unintelligible language – 'greatly advantageous in the concealment of their designs' – and by their deplorable personal habits:

> The nomad, then is distinguished from the civilized man by his repugnance to regular and continuous labour – by his want of providence in laying up a store for the future – by his inability to perceive consequences ... by his passion ... for intoxicating fermented liquors ... by his comparative insensibility to pain –

by his immoderate love of gaming . . . by an immoderate love of libidinous dances – by the pleasure he experiences in witnessing the sufferings of sentient creatures . . . by the looseness of his notions as to property – by the absence of chastity among his women.[2]

Many of these strictures might equally well have applied to wealthy young men about town; but the theory that the poor were not only embarrassing and a nuisance, but foreigners as well, evidently appealed to his readers.

General William Booth of the Salvation Army also saw the 'African Parallel', but came to very different conclusions. *In Darkest England, or The Way Out* (1890) is a passionate plea for social reform. Booth drew on the exploration of Henry Stanley in the Congo. Stanley's dramatic rescue of David Livingstone in 1871 in an expedition funded by the *New York Herald* had excited much public interest, and his subsequent accounts of the life of the forest pygmies were eagerly received. As General Booth said, they presented 'a terrible picture':

But while brooding over the awful presentation of life as it exists in the vast African forest, it seemed to me only too vivid a picture of many parts of our own land. As there is a darkest Africa, is there not also a darkest England? Civilisation, which can breed its own barbarians, does it not also breed its own pygmies? May we not find a parallel at our own doors, and discover within a stone's throw of our cathedrals and palaces similar horrors to those . . . existing in the great Equatorial forest?[3]

He wrote 'not in despondency, but in hope'. In England at least, the problems were soluble. For 'Darkest England' was only a fraction of 'Greater England', and there was wealth enough to rescue the 'submerged tenth' of the population.

This last phrase caught the public imagination in a way Booth cannot have expected. In the ensuing years, efforts were made to breed out the 'submerged tenth'. The science of Eugenics was in its infancy and its principal exponent was Francis Galton, a cousin of Charles Darwin. Galton's *Hereditary Genius* (1869) argued that mental ability, aptitudes and qualities of character, like such physical characteristics as hair colour and eye colour, were directly transmissible from one generation to the next on the principle of Mendel's Law: mathematicians tended to have mathematical children, musicians begat musicians. Conversely, criminal tendencies, mental illness, mental handicap and fecklessness ran in families. Mayhew regarded the poor as alien and predatory, William Booth saw them as lost and helpless, the eugenicists argued that their condition was hereditary; but none of these lines of approach added what would now be regarded as scientific data to the debates about poverty.

Charles Booth and the development of quantitative techniques

Charles Booth, a Liverpool businessman and not related to the Salvation Army leader, first decided to carry out a survey because he thought that the extent of poverty was grossly exaggerated, and he distrusted figures put out by a Marxist group, the Social Democratic Federation. The secretary of the S.D.F. was F. D. Hyndman, who had been Karl Marx's pupil, and Marx's daughter Eleanor ('Tussie') was a member. Hyndman is vague about dates and methods, but some time before 1883, the S.D.F. carried out a survey in working-class areas of London, and came to the conclusion that some 25 per cent of the working population was living in poverty. The publication is not listed among Hyndman's works, and it appears to have drawn a good deal of criticism, as Hyndman writes 'Of course we Socialists were denounced as deliberate falsifiers of facts and exaggerators of the poverty of the mass of the people'.[4]

Charles Booth was a staunch Conservative. He was convinced that the S.D.F. conclusion was a substantial over-estimate, but when he looked for accurate data to disprove the figure of 25 per cent, he found none. In 1883, he read a paper to the Royal Statistical Society in which he complained that many of the official figures were meaningless: the basic work of enumeration was poorly performed, and the categories in which information was collected varied from decade to decade.[5] He called on Hyndman, and informed him that he intended to investigate the matter himself. Hyndman later wrote, 'Mr. Booth even [went] so far as to denounce me in a quiet way for putting such erroneous, and as he termed them, "incendiary" statements, before the people'.[6]

Booth used the new organizational and statistical techniques of the business world to which he belonged in what was to be the first major social survey. He financed all his own work. One of his voluntary assistants in this enterprise was his cousin Beatrice Potter (later Mrs Sidney Webb), who wrote a vivid description of 'Cousin Charlie' in her autobiography: tall, abnormally thin, ascetic, looking like a university professor or a priest, or 'with another change of attire . . . an artist in the Quartier Latin'.[7] He was not at all like a great captain of industry.

The framework of investigation resembled a major military operation. Booth's headquarters were at Toynbee Hall, the first of the great university settlements in London. There was a Poverty Map, with flags indicating the areas under investigation. He organized a two-tier exercise: most of the information was collected from School Board Officers, appointed under Lowe's Education Act of 1870 to investigate the reason for children's non-attendance at school. The central team received and cross-checked the information.

Booth's major findings were published in 1889. What he had discovered was that Hyndman's 25 per cent was not an overestimate but an underestimate. His own classification of the London population[8] showed 30.7 per cent of the population in poverty.

Category			
	A.	Loafers, drunkards and semi-criminals	0.9 per cent
	B.	Casual hand-to-mouth earnings	7.5 per cent
	C. D.	Seasonal or small regular wages	22.3 per cent
	E. F.	Regularly and fairly well-paid	51.5 per cent
	G.	Lower middle class	
	H.	Upper middle class	17.8 per cent

Table 5.1. *Charles Booth's classification of the distribution of poverty*

Most of those in categories A to D were people who had a precarious existence through no fault of their own. Low wages and the precarious nature of seasonal and casual work were the major causes of poverty.

Booth's first volume was published at top speed – written in his spare time. Since he continued to run his shipping business in Liverpool, made frequent trips to the New York office to oversee the work of his brother, and lived the life of a country gentleman at Gracedieu Manor in Leicestershire, most of it must have been written on trains and ships. The demand was pressing – papers to London societies had aroused interest, and the first printing was quickly sold out. Most reviewers were adulatory – though the writer for the *Athenaeum* sniffed 'The book is entirely without literary merit, but contains information useful for philanthropists'.

Booth had discovered his life-work. In all, he was to publish seventeen volumes, piling fact on fact. The Poverty Enquiry ran to four volumes, and was followed by the Trades (Industry) Enquiry, volumes on Religious Influences and a final volume on Social Influences, published in 1903; and nearly all of it is unreadable.

Booth was aware of this himself. He wrote with difficulty, running to many drafts. He lived with working-class families, slept in doss-houses, and experienced the life of poor people at first hand. He 'walked in faith' that somehow the piling up of information would 'make the path more clear', but further enquiries only 'enlarged the wilderness of figures'. In the Trades Enquiry, he retained his belief in the efficacy of the capitalist system, but hoped to find some way of relating employment conditions to social conditions. He was disappointed, and his wife related that the study 'fell flat' on publication. His study of Religious Influences took him round the churches and chapels, the Gospel Halls and the Salvation Army Citadels in a ceaseless search for information. He developed a map with symbols – 'scarlet for places of worship, black for houses licensed to sell intoxicating drinks, and a lovely blue for the schools of the Board'; but though Professor Alfred Marshall from Cambridge found his report 'An angelic book, holy and beautiful outside and in', there was bitter criticism from the churches.

Booth's final volume was short. He was sure that the enquiries he had carried out were worthwhile (they had cost him some £33,000 of his own money) and that his methods of investigation were sound; but he could not see where they led. He was acutely aware of the limitations of his own work. 'The dry bones [of the argument] lie scattered over the long valley,' he wrote. 'May some great soul, master of a subtler and nobler alchemy than mine, disentangle the confused issues ... and make these dry bones live, so that the streets of our Jerusalem may sing with joy'.[9]

From a modern viewpoint, Booth's work has marked limitations. The scope of his surveys was not clearly delineated: the first volume related only to East London, and though he subsequently extended the work to other districts of the metropolis, he certainly did not cover the whole of London. He talked about a 'Poverty Line', and suggested that this might be drawn at an income of twenty-one shillings a week for a 'moderate family', noting that it would vary with circumstances; but he did not investigate either the size or the age of the family members. His biographer, Professor T. S. Simey, explores his definitions of poverty, and finds them 'imprecise'.[10]

Despite the concern which led Booth to devote much of his life and much of his fortune to the study of poverty, he could be judgemental – he wrote that drunkards, criminals and prostitutes ought to suffer 'all the natural consequences, short of actually perishing from cold and hunger'; but he was overwhelmingly convinced by the evidence that poverty was not a personal failing, but a failure of social organization. He modified his adherence to capitalism sufficiently to advocate a doctrine of 'limited socialism' for the poor: services should be provided for the underprivileged, to bring them up to the level where they could hold their own in a capitalist society.

Booth lacked the capacity to develop conceptual frameworks; but his contribution to the development of social policy and methods of social investigation was greater than he knew. He was the first person to ask 'Who are the poor?' and to replace stereotypes and prejudice with factual answers. He used quantitative methods of investigation. He pioneered the technique of the large-scale social survey in Britain. He made an early contribution to the categorization of social class. He made out a case for minimum standards of social provision – even if he did not wholly believe it himself. If he provided only the 'dry bones' of the argument, there were others who could bring them to life.

Seebohm Rowntree and the York Studies

One of the many people impressed by Charles Booth's work was Seebohm Rowntree, a young industrialist working in the family firm at York. At the end of the nineteenth century, Rowntree's was rapidly developing chocolate production, and employed some two thousand workers. The Rowntree family were Quakers, with a strong tradition of social concern. Seebohm Rowntree had visited slums in Newcastle, and studied food chemistry at Owen's College, Manchester (now the centre of the University of Manchester, and at that time surounded by slum property). He had corresponded with Charles Booth, and determined to carry out a similar survey in his own city of York, to establish whether Booth's findings were particular to the London area, or whether the problems were equally to be found in provincial cities.

Seebohm Rowntree was somewhat disingenuous in claiming that York was a 'representative' provincial city. It was his own city, and he was determined to work there. Though York had a mixed industrial pattern, and a fair spread of wage levels it was already a well-known tourist centre. York Minster and the Roman and Danish heritage were major attractions. But if the tourist trade lessened the city's claim to be typical, it also ensured that the findings of the survey would receive attention from people who were attracted to the city.

Work on the survey began in 1899. Seebohm Rowntree was 28 years old, and had been relieved from his more pressing duties in the Rowntree Works by the appointment of a second industrial chemist. Like Charles Booth, he was determined that the most up-to-date quantitative methods would be employed. Unlike Booth, he had a discrete area to work in. York was a reasonable size – some 15,000 houses, a population of 75,812. Rowntree excluded the 'upper class', including Booth's Class H, who kept at least one servant, and reduced his population to 46,754.

He was not happy with Booth's two-tier survey method – the information provided by School Board Officers and other informants had proved to be of variable quality. He had only two paid investigators, but he determined on a first-hand investigation, with a questionnaire of his own design. Since sampling had not yet been invented, that meant knocking on every door. The investigators knocked on every door; and when Rowntree discovered that one of them was producing unreliable results, he had the visits repeated. The work was meticulous. It also had the advantage that Rowntree had studied Booth's work in detail, and so could be more precise about his objectives, The survey, *Poverty – a Study of*

Town Life, was completed within two years, and published in 1901.

Rowntree took Booth's description of the poverty line and elaborated it. He developed two concepts of poverty – *Primary Poverty* and *Secondary Poverty*. These were carefully defined. Families were in primary poverty when their income was insufficient to provide the basic necessities for biological efficiency: food, fuel, shelter and clothing, even if every penny were spent on these four items. People were in secondary poverty when their income would have been sufficient to cover the four basic necessities, but where some of the money was diverted to other purposes. It is important to note that this second category did not imply a moral judgement that the money was misspent. Rowntree recognized that in some cases, the cause might be drinking or gambling; but he was at pains to point out that the money might be spent on other essentials – necessary household replacements, trade union dues, fares to work, or helping some less fortunate member of the family. He also made the point that living effectively on a minimum income required almost superhuman powers of energy and intelligence, which did not come easily to people living on the breadline.

Booth had noted that the poverty line would move, depending on the circumstances of the family. Rowntree worked it out in detail. As a nutritional chemist, he knew what people should eat to keep fit, and how much a minimum diet cost. In the end, to prove his point, he selected a diet given to him by the Local Government Board, which was less generous than that available at the time for able-bodied paupers. He checked his prices in the back streets of York. He checked local rents, and the cost of clothing in the cheaper shops, and the price of fuel. He took into account the size of the family and the age of the children.

His conclusion was that the wages paid for unskilled labour in York were insufficient to 'maintain a family of moderate size in a state of bare physical efficiency'. According to his calculations, 9.91 per cent of the working class population of York were living in primary poverty, and 17.93 per cent in secondary poverty. Though his figures were not directly comparable with Booth's, because both the base and the definitions differed, the total of 27.84 per cent was sufficiently close to Booth's figures to make a public impact.

Rowntree's second conceptual beakthrough was in the formulation of the *Poverty Cycle*. Working-class families went through predictable periods of relative poverty and prosperity. A couple would be living in or near poverty while their children were young; rise to comparative affluence as the children began to work and bring in wages to the household; sink back into poverty when the children left home to start their own families, and the man was no longer able to work in old age. Meanwhile, the children would have started on their own poverty cycle in their families of marriage, poverty, comparative affluence, and poverty again as they too became old. Here was the basic analysis which was to lead in time to contributory old-age pensions and family allowances.

Rowntree's findings on family incomes strongly supported Booth's. He estimated that a man, wife and three children of given ages needed 21s.8d. a week to keep them out of primary poverty. Booth's estimate had been 21s. The average weekly wage in York at that time was between 18s. and 21s.

Like Booth, he found that the major cause of poverty was not individual weakness of character, but 'the adverse conditions under which too many of the working class live'. He reinforced Booth's findings about the consequences of seasonal or casual labour, which made it impossible for a family to budget, since their earnings were so uncertain. These were the economic causes of poverty. The social causes were poor health services, poor housing, and a lack of education for living; and state intervention was needed. Though 'the dark shadow of Malthusian philosophy' had passed away, he insisted that 'No civilisation can be sound or stable which has as its base this mass of stunted human life'.[11] Rowntree's single volume, written with a dispassionate clarity, showed that the situation Booth had described was not only a metropolitan problem – it existed in York, and almost certainly in other cities throughout the country.

The Critics

Charles Booth was a Conservative, and a member of the new aristocracy of the industrial age. Many of his own social circle thought him a socialist, but criticism was relatively muted. Rowntree was a Liberal, a Quaker and a provincial, and his work had a sharper cutting edge. The criticism was consequently more vocal.

Much of the initial opposition to his ideas came from the Charity Organisation Society. The COS secretary, Charles Loch, was scathing about Rowntree's 'generalisations cloaked in numerical phraseology' and accused him of recommending the creation of 'a recognised servile class – paupers, old age pensioners and State-dependent wage-earners'. Rowntree pointed out in his sober way that the problems of poverty were often submerged – wives and children went without in order to keep the wage earner healthy enough to earn; and that poverty had long-term consequences – 'the high death rate among the poor, the terribly high infant mortality, the stunted stature and the dulled intelligence'.[12]

His findings were to have a considerable influence on the Liberal Government which took power in 1906, and formed the background to their social reforms. Rowntree would have been the first to admit that his work was dependent on Charles Booth's – but then, Booth's work was dependent on Hyndman's. Marxist, Conservative and Liberal formed an odd chain in the development of survey methods.

More recently, Rowntree's work has come under strong attack from members of the Child Poverty Action Group, a Fabian-inspired organization, on the grounds that poverty is relative (in relation to the standard of living of other people in the same society) rather than absolute (a measure of bare physical subsistence). Peter Townsend finds Rowntree's scales too arbitray and too harsh, pointing out that the diet he used was one designed for American convicts, and harsher than that used at the time by the Local Government Board for workhouses.[13] Rowntree's Human Needs Diet was certainly barely eatable. Miss Trudi Schultz of the Oxford University Institute of Statistics was still reworking it annually in the late 1960s. At that time, it cost just under £1 a week per head, and consisted largely of porridge, oatmeal, pulses and herrings – items which do not figure largely in working class diets.

Robert Holman echoes Townsend's criticisms and concludes that Rowntree 'ignored social, cultural and psychological needs';[14] but both Holman and Townsend miss the point. Rowntree was not arguing that the working classes should be able to live at this stringent level. Asa Briggs, Rowntree's biographer, emphasizes that Rowntree deliberately chose the starkest of theoretical measures in order to demonstrate to his fellow industrialists that workers could not possibly maintain their biological efficiency on current wage levels. In their own interests, if they wanted a fit workforce, they must provide a better standard of living for the workers. He quotes Rowntree's own statement to show how totally unacceptable this minimum standard would be in real life:

> A family living upon the scale allowed for in this estimate must never spend a penny on railway fare or omnibus. They must never go into the country unless they walk. They must never purchase a halfpenny newspaper... They must write no letters to absent children, for they cannot afford to pay the postage... They cannot save, nor can they join a sick club or Trade Union, because they cannot pay the necessary subscriptions. The children must have no pocket money for dolls, marbles or sweets. The father must smoke no tobacco, and must drink no beer. The mother must never buy any pretty clothes for herself or her children... Should a child fall ill, it must be attended by the parish doctor ... should it die, it must be buried by the parish. Finally, the wage-earner must never be absent from his work for a single day.[15]

Rowntree was not arguing that people should live at this level of deprivation. He was pointing out how impossible it would be to do so. He hoped (unsuccessfully, as it turned out) to pre-empt the inevitable criticism from the COS. He said 'I chose this criterion because I didn't want people to say that "Rowntree's crying for the moon"'.[16] It was a tough argument for an age in which large sections of the work-force never escaped from the debilitating effects of extreme poverty and near-starvation. Arguments about 'relative poverty' belong to the 1960s. In 1901, absolute poverty was still a stark reality.

SIX

Bypassing the Poor Law

By the 1860s, both the Poor Law and the Public Health services had moved away from controversy and into a phase of consolidation. After the horrors of the Andover scandal, the Poor Law Board became directly responsible to Parliament, since its President was a minister, and Parliament could question, debate and investigate. The administration became less centralized, less doctrinaire, and to some extent less harsh. Inspectors turned to advising on workhouse management rather than applying blindly deterrent policies. Boards of Guardians had more freedom to respond to local conditions, and outdoor relief, never entirely abolished, was given more frequently. Diets improved, and interest revived in constructive forms of classification – schools for the children, transition to work for young people, separate wards for the sick, and a non-deterrent regime for the old people.

But the problems were enormous, partly because of the size of the pauper population. In 1865, Florence Nightingale sent her 'best and dearest' pupil, Agnes Jones, to be Matron of the Brownlow Hill Institution in Liverpool. She took with her twelve Nightingale-trained nurses. Within a month, she had dismissed 35 of the untrained pauper nurses for drunkenness. The number of pauper patients varied from 1,350 to 1,500, and the conditions reminded Miss Nightingale of the military hospital at Scutari.[1]

When Louisa Twining, the pioneer of workhouse visiting, visited an old lady of her acquaintance who had moved into a workhouse, she discovered that the master and the matron were the only staff – responsible for 500 inmates. Here was a new field for voluntary action. Local groups, mainly of women, were formed to visit the workhouses, read to the old people, take flowers to the sick wards – and keep a sharp eye open for abuses. They believed in 'working quietly' rather than in conflict; but they soon discovered 'the power of red-tape' – the Guardians who refused them admission, the staff who took their requests for admission as criticism of their own work, the endless delays, the perennial excuses. In 1857, Louisa Twining read a paper on the subject to a meeting of the Social Science Association in Birmingham, and the Workhouse Visiting Society was formed, with a prestigious committee. They campaigned for special sick wards and trained nurses, supporting Agnes Jones, who was to die young of typhus probably contracted in her own hospital. They found avenues of employment for young people – usually manual work for the boys, domestic service for the girls. Their main aims were:

1. The classification of the inmates and separation of different classes, in order that each class might receive the management adapted to its wants.

2. The election of a superior class of guardians . . . who would be able to discharge their duties in an intelligent and unprejudiced manner.

3. The appointment of a higher class of superintendents, with education and administrative powers to fit them for their posts.[2]

In many ways, it was a typical Victorian voluntary reform movement, but it had three distinguishing features: first, its publicity was sharply professional: Louisa Twining recounts in her *Recollections of Workhouse Visiting and Management* (1880) how memoranda were drafted for the Poor Law Board and for Members of Parliament, how she wrote articles for newspapers and journals, including The *Guardian*, *The Economist* and *John Bull*, how facts were collated and pressure was maintained. Second, it involved statutory-voluntary co-operation: while most of the voluntary societies ran their own separate services, the Workhouse Visiting Society existed to improve the one basic state service. Third, it was a feminist movement. As Louisa Twining pointed out, there were over 100,000 workhouse inmates in Britain, and more than half of them were women and girls. Yet the overworked matrons (often single-handed) were the only women involved in management:

No-one who had any knowledge of the work of the society . . . could fail to have observed that the point of *women's work* had all along been urged as of the most vital importance . . . a great part of the evils which had grown up around the system were owing to the fact that it was carried out entirely by men . . . educated women as Guardians, as matrons, as nurses, as inspectors, had been over and over again urged as the one hope of reform and amelioration.[3]

The Society promoted the election of women Guardians, and worked on boarding-out schemes for children. A triumph was the appointment of Mrs Nassau John Senior, the daughter-in-law of the economist, as the first woman inspector of the Poor Law Board. Unfortunately she became terminally ill after some two years of work, and had to resign, but a barrier had been overturned.[4]

All this activity improved workhouse conditions and administration. It played a large part in humanizing the 'hell-concocted Poor Law' at a time when the workhouse system continued to grow in size under the impact of population growth and violent fluctuations in the labour market. If the workhouses were not exactly welcoming, they were at least clean and well run, and no longer places of positive and deliberate cruelty.

The Public Health movement

After the conflicts and crises of the General Board of Health, the public health movement was also settling down to a period of consolidation. The Sanitary Act of 1866 put the control of pollution and epidemic disease firmly in the hands of the local authorities, and in the towns, where the worst problems existed, a new breed of public health doctors went to work to eliminate the worst problems. At central government level, there was a Medical Department of the Privy Council. Its chief medical officer was John Simon, who had been Medical Officer of Health for London, and his assistant was William Farr from the General Register Office. Together, they developed medical statistics, producing a series of brilliantly diagnostic reports on mortality and morbidity – the nature, distribution and effects of epidemic diseases, and the success or failure of different methods of control.

By this time, the theory of specific contagion was generally accepted, and the serious study of bacteriology had begun; but it was also accepted that bacteria flourished most freely in conditions of filth. Chadwick and Sir Benjamin Hall had both been right, and a new generation of doctors devised a system for dealing with epidemics. The pattern which emerged was as follows:

1. Medical advance: research leading to greater precision in diagnosis, specific modes of treatment and techniques of immunization.
2. Notification of individual cases; medical statistics: identification of black spots.
3. Elimination of causes.
4. Isolation of individuals, cleansing of premises, tracing of contacts.
5. Public enlightenment – overcoming secrecy, inducing people to come forward for treatment, development of immunization.[5]

The evolution of this system is one of the great successes of medicine, and it involved quite complex patterns of central-local co-operation. Smallpox came under control after the Vaccination Act of 1853; typhus, typhoid and cholera soon followed. The figures fell annually, and with startling effect. By the end of the century, the public health doctors had moved on to deal with the next most serious causes of early death – scarlet fever, diphtheria, tuberculosis; and the elimination of the causes of disease moved from fetid pools and poisoned pumps to the wider issues of pollution, dangerous trades, slum housing and overcrowding.

Though scarlet fever, tuberculosis and diphtheria were not finally to be conquered until the discovery of antibiotics in the 1940s, the pattern of public health care helped to reduce the incidence, and the same principles are applied today in the treatment of venereal disease and AIDS. In the second half of the nineteenth century, every area had its great isolation hospital. In more recent years, these hospitals have stood empty, or have been devoted to other purposes, as improvements in treatment meant that the work could be handled by general practitioners or in hospital out-patient clinics.

An outstanding feature of Simon's work at the Medical Department of the Privy Council was the encouragement of a new generation of local authority public health doctors. Simon expressed the view that Edwin Chadwick – 'a man of very high mark' – had perhaps been in too much of a hurry, and that this had led him into centralizing policies when 'the people and their representative bodies should have made their way in a necessarily gradual process of education'.[6] In the second wave of reform, following the Sanitary Act of 1866 and a very thorough review of the situation by the Sanitary Commission of 1868, the public health service was built up from the local communities, not down from Whitehall, and with manifestly better results.

The Local Government Board, 1871

Public health work had started in the Poor Law Commission, with the work of Kay, Arnott and Southwood Smith, and the preparation of Chadwick's *Report on the Sanitary Condition of the Labouring Population*. Between 1848 and 1871, public health developed separately; but it was evident that the Poor Law Board and the Medical Department of the Privy Council had overlapping responsibilities and a need for liaison.

In 1871, the Local Government Act set up a new form of central administration – the Local Government Board. This combined the work of the Poor Law Board, the Medical Department of the Privy Council and a small Local Government section in the Home Office. But what might have been a useful merging of skills and responsibilities was frustrated by the structure of the new body. The Sanitary Commission of 1868 had recommended that Poor Law and Public Health should run in tandem, with separate secretariats; but there was one administrative structure – 'virtually a continuance of the old Poor Law Office' – and a single secretariat. 'It was as if the Act had ordered that the old Poor Law Board, subject only to such conditions of consultation and reference as itself might impose on itself, should be the Central Sanitary Authority for England' wrote Simon twenty years later. He added temperately enough that the situation was 'not of unclouded promise for sanitary administration'.[7] A highly-specialized department had been replaced by an all-purpose one in which public health interests were regarded as of comparatively minor importance:

Within the jurisdiction of the Local Government Board are many objects which are only sanitary in a remote instrumental sense, and some which are not sanitary at all; questions of local elections and finance, and boundaries and arbitrations, questions of mere common or commercial convenience in various local matters, questions as to highways and lighting, as to markets and their stalls and weighing machines, as to hackney-carriages and public bathing, as to local steam-whistles and public clocks.[8]

The Poor Law Board and its staff took all the senior positions in the new Board. Simon suffered personally in the reorganization, being reduced from the status of administrative head to that of technical adviser. He stayed on for another six years before retiring, but he thought the new administration was 'grievously wrong'.

The Poor Law was entering on a new period of rigidity and parsimony. Shortly before the dissolution of the Poor Law Board, in 1869, the Goschen Minute had outlined only a minimal and deterrent service, any rehabilitative work being left to the voluntary organizations. The new Local Government Board took an exceedingly narrow view of its own powers and duties, and the broader aims of preventive medicine and public health work were neither understood nor supported.

In the towns at least, the initiative in public health had passed decisively to the local authorities. The Public Health Act of 1875 was a great consolidating measure which laid down extended responsibilities for sewage, drainage, refuse collection, offensive trades, food inspection, infectious diseases, epidemics, hospitals (including isolation hospitals), street cleansing and housing. All areas were to have a Medical Officer of Health, full-time or part-time.

The development of local authorities

In 1888, the local government system was at last rationalized. The County Councils Act set up a comprehensive structure. London was a special case, administered by the London County Council. Other towns of medium or large size were designated county boroughs, with their own councils. County councils took the major responsibility for the rural areas, but because of the distances involved (and the relative slowness of communication at that time) some responsibilities were left with district and parish councils. The problems of disease and sanitation and overcrowding were essentially urban problems, and it was in the growing metropolitan areas that local government became a strong force for reform. Though the system led to many boundary disputes between county boroughs and their surrounding county councils, it endured for nearly a century, until the county boroughs were absorbed into the county councils in 1975.

Two points are worthy of note: first, a coherent network of locally elected authorities was set up, replacing a jumble of old municipal authorities and *ad hoc* bodies. It was clear to the general public who the members of the authority were, what powers they held, and how they exercised them. The system was democratic and accountable. Further, a single local authority in the towns could appoint its own officers and develop its own expertise in the light of local knowledge. A career service of local government officers was beginning to be built up. As local government developed and strengthened, it became possible for more responsibilities and services to be delegated from central government. In the next few years, other services were to be developed and co-ordinated at the local level.

A major responsibility delegated to the new local authorities in 1888 was that for main roads, and 'the new road era began'.[9] Turnpike Trusts, by which individuals or groups who had developed roads could charge a toll for their use, were virtually ended in 1895. The development of modern methods of transport radically changed the lives of people living in rural areas:

> In the 80s the only link between the village and the market town was often the carrier's cart which journeyed between them once or twice a week. Not only had the oldest inhabitant never seen the sea or even visited a town, but the children had to put up with the education which the village could provide.[10]

The railways developed first, then the motor car and the bicycle 'heralded the renaissance of the road, and the intermingling for good or ill of the country and the town'. The Daimler petrol engine, developed in the 1880s, solved the technical problem of the ratio of power to weight (an early 20 h.p. steam carriage weighed some four tons). In 1896, the Act of 1865 which required all cars to be preceded by a man carrying a red flag was repealed. The bicycle was also becoming a common means of transport –

pneumatic tyres were invented in 1889. After 1909, money was raised from petrol duty and motor vehicle licences to develop the roads, and local authorities became very active highway authorities. Housing responsibilities developed out of public health concerns. The Artisans' and Labourers' Dwellings Improvement Acts of 1875 and 1879 gave local authorities the power to purchase land in slum areas and redevelop it. In 1890, following a Royal Commission on Housing which made detailed recommendations, a consolidating Housing Act gave the new local authorities power to clear whole areas; to repair and improve houses, and to build new houses of better quality. 'The government which in the 1840s had begun to take responsibility for providing drains, became responsible . . . for the quality of the houses'.[11]

An Education Service developed slowly from the time of Althorp's first grant of £20,000 to the voluntary societies in 1833. For much of the nineteenth century, its growth was hampered by the competition between the Established Church and the Dissenters. The only matter on which the two parties agreed was that education was a religious matter, and that state intervention must be fought at all costs. Forster's Education Act of 1870, which is usually celebrated as the major initiative in state education, merely made it possible to fill in the gaps in a very uneven provision, and established the right of every child to education in theory; but it was not until 1880 that Mundella's Act specified that the right could be exercised between the ages of five and ten, and not until 1895 or even later that the last remnants of fee-paying (3d a week) were finally abolished. *Ad hoc* School Boards were responsible for the state schools until 1902, when Balfour's Education Act secured uniformity of administration by placing the funding for all schools, statutory and voluntary, in the hands of the local authority.

One of the effects of universal schooling was to present the problems of poverty in a new and acute form. School attendance officers reported that there were children who could not come to school because they had no clothes to wear, or no boots for their feet. Teachers reported that it was impossible to teach hungry children: they simply put their heads on the desks and went to sleep. So some local authorities, like the LCC Education Department, developed schemes in which soup and bread were available at a penny a day for those who could pay, and free for those who could not. The COS bitterly opposed these schemes. 'A PENNY GIVEN AND A CHILD RUINED' was the heading of one COS leaflet published in 1883. 'To feed their children is to debase the moral standard ... by practically inviting parents ... to spend in idleness or drink the time and money which should have been given to making provision for their family'.[12] But child poverty and child hunger were becoming visible, and local authorities were moving from a concern with the environment to a concern for individuals.

Maternity and Child Welfare

The reports of Charles Booth and Seebohm Rowntree were influential in creating informed opinion about the physical effects of poverty. Perhaps even more startling, and of greater immediate impact, was a single fact: when conscription was introduced in Britain for the first time in the Boer War, 40 per cent of the recruits were unfit for service. After the war, the Balfour Government set up an inter-departmental committee to consider the problems of what Seebohm Rowntree had called 'this stunted mass of human life'. An inter-departmental committee is a quieter and less publicized procedure than a Royal Commission, and generally works faster. Its members are senior civil servants. They meet as part of their working life, out of the glare of publicity, and as representatives of particular departments of state. They are usually concerned less with debating major issues of principle than with ways and means – how to get things done. The Inter-Departmental Committee on Physical Deterioration had an unmemorable title, but its subject was one of considerable importance, and the findings were wide-ranging and authoritative.

At that time, wars were still fought with men rather than with technology. The huge and highly disciplined German army was known to be preparing for war: could Britain only muster an army of weaklings to oppose it? This simple image – the well-fed arrogant German soldier in a spiked helmet and the weedy, under-nourished English youth – drove out the last remnants of Malthusian thinking. Children suddenly became important: they represented the future. And the needs were not only for defence in case of war in Europe. The British Empire had expanded at a remarkable rate in the late Victorian period. Fit young men were

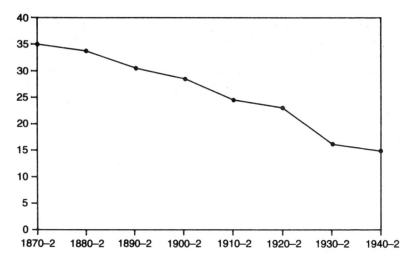

Figure II Live births per thousand population, United Kingdom 1870–1940
Source: Annual Abstract of Statistics, 1989, table 2.16.

needed for India, for Canada, for Australia, for all those areas coloured red on the maps of the world where British jurisdiction ruled.

It was beginning to be realized that this demand for 'fit young men' depended on the birth and rearing of fit children, and the statistics were alarming: the birth-rate was dropping, the infant mortality rate (ie the proportion of babies dying before their first birthday per thousand born) was not. In 1870–1872, the crude birth-rate was 35 per thousand population, and the infant mortality rate 150 per thousand births. In 1900–1902, the crude birth-rate had dropped to 28.6 per thousand population, and the infant mortality rate had dropped very little, standing at 142 per thousand births. The worst year was 1899, with an infant mortality rate of 163 per thousand: of every hundred children born, sixteen would die before their first birthday. Astonishing medical advances had been made in dealing with epidemic diseases, but the causes of infant mortality were more complex and more personal: they included insanitary home conditions, malnutrition, inhibited attitudes to pregnancy, attendance by ignorant and untrained midwives, poor baby-feeding practices, sheer lack of knowledge and lack of care. Epidemic diarrhoea was the main killer. And many of the children who did survive grew into sickly adults.

The recommendations of the Inter-Departmental Committee covered a variety of issues, and most of them involved extended activity in local authority Health and Housing Departments. The most progressive were already carrying out pioneering work in maternity and child welfare.

Health visiting had been initiated by the Ladies Sanitary Reform Association in Manchester and Salford in 1862, when it was proposed to have 'a lady superintendent for each district, and a health visitor who was a working woman'. Florence Nightingale, who totally lacked class consciousness where nursing was concerned, endorsed it as 'a new work and a new profession for women'. Milk depots (where mothers were encouraged in breast-feeding, and supplied with dried milk if this was not practicable) were the main weapon against epidemic diarrhoea. These were developed from the model of a clinic set up in Paris by Dr Pierre Budin, and soon developed into general maternity and child welfare clinics, where mothers were given advice on a variety of child-rearing problems, and the welfare of babies could be monitored.[13]

Obstetric practice was improving. Back in the 1840s Dr Semmelweiss had watched hospital doctors in Vienna go straight from dissecting corpses to delivering babies without washing their hands, and had associated the fact with puerperal fever. The practice of asepsis, or 'Listerism', as it was called, spread slowly. Sir Arthur Newsholme, later Chief Medical Officer of Health to the Local Government Board, could recall his own days as a fourth-year medical student in the late 1870s:

I saw a surgeon pick up a forceps from the floor, and use it again forthwith. The coats in which some surgeons operated were old frock coats, used repeatedly without adequate cleansing. . . And one saw threaded needles with silken threads hanging down attached to the well-worn coat of the house-surgeon, ready for the surgeon in the later stages of his operation.[14]

Though the hospitals were improving under the twin influences of asepsis and better nursing care, most babies were born at home, and without medical attention. Most villages and city areas had a woman, recognized by her neighbours, who assisted other women in childbirth, and usually laid out the dead as well. The trade was often passed down from mother to daughter. Some of these women were highly competent and some were drunken and sluttish. Gin, which was still very cheap, often provided an anaesthetic for the woman in labour, and a pick-me-up for her attendant. In the last two decades of the nineteenth century, there was a protracted battle over the status of midwives. The medical profession, by that time secure in their own professional status, objected to any formal recognition being accorded to these women. The midwives contended that assisting at a birth was a special skill, not simply a branch of medicine; that the presence of a doctor was usually not necessary and was often undesirable; and that many medical practitioners had no experience in obstetrics.

It was comparatively easy to prescribe training and registration for future midwives; but a particular problem for the parliamentary drafters was that of the 'bona fide midwives', the very mixed group of women already in practice. There were obvious objections to giving them all status; yet they could not be forbidden to practise, because there were as yet no trained women to take their place. The Midwives Bill came before a weary Parliament repeatedly for some twenty years. To medical obstructionism and drafting problems were added political problems which delayed and frustrated parliamentary procedure. These were difficult years, when the House of Lords was asserting its powers, and the Irish members, demanding Home Rule, were frustrating many kinds of legislative effort. It was not until 1902 that the Midwives Act reached the Statute Book. The untrained 'bona fide midwives' had finally been 'blanketed in' – that is, given a licence to practise because there was no alternative to their services. For the future, there would be a Central Midwives' Board responsible for proper training in midwifery, and the local authorities would supervise registers of midwives competent to practise.[15]

Maternity and child welfare measures were to have the same effect on infant mortality that the public health measures of the earlier period had had on epidemic diseases: the infant mortality rate fell steadily from the alarming figure of 163 per thousand births. Today it is a little over nine per thousand births, and still falling.

By the early years of the twentieth century, a broadly-based

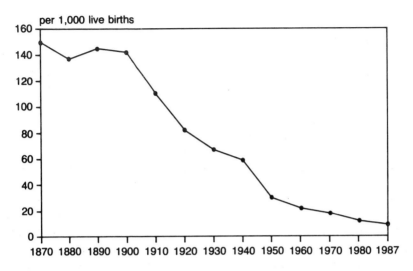

Figure III Infant mortality, England and Wales, 1881–1987
Source: Annual Abstract of Statistics, 1935, table 29, and 1989, table 2.21

system of central and local government agencies had been developed to provide for health and welfare needs: only the Poor Law – aloof, deterrent, unco-operative – remained outside the structure. So what was to be done about the Poor Law?

SEVEN

Victorian Values or Socialist Visions?

In 1905, in the last few months of the Conservative Balfour Government, a Royal Commission on the Poor Laws was appointed. It was to work for nearly five years, and to provide a classic statement of two opposing views of poverty.

The chairman was Lord George Hamilton, a former Under-Secretary of State for India and First Lord of the Admiralty. Lord George, though not a leading Conservative politician, was a respected one. As a free-trader, he had resigned from the Government in 1903 in protest against Austen Chamberlain's protectionist tariff policy. He was a very experienced chairman, and a man of integrity without strong views of his own on the subject of poverty. He must have seemed the ideal chairman for the Poor Law exercise; but the membership of his Commission was to be dominated by two groups who took up irreconcilable positions: the Charity Organisation Society and the Fabians.

The Charity Organisation Society

Three leading members of the COS were appointed to the Commission: Charles Loch, Helen Bosanquet and Octavia Hill.

Charles Loch was appointed Secretary of the COS in 1875, when he was only 26 years old. He said on appointment that the task required 'The heart of a Dickens and the will of a Bismarck',[1] and he never lost his iron grip, though the Dickensian heart was seldom in evidence. He was to remain the chief administrator of the COS for nearly forty years, organizing endless committees of

investigation into Housing, Unemployment, Vagrancy, the care of
blind, deaf and epileptic children, and many other subjects; giving
evidence to parliamentary committees, writing indefatigably,
founding the Charities Register, the Charities Digest, the Charity
Organisation Review. In all this useful and constructive work, he
remained strongly opposed to any intervention by the state in the
provision of social services, even to schemes for old-age pensions,
believing that the poor must save for their own old age, and that
state grants would pauperize them. He was still opposing old-age
pensions when he finally retired in 1914.

Under Loch's direction and control, the COS spread. The first
district offices were set up in areas in London where the rich and
the poor lived closely together – Marylebone, St George's Hanover
Square, Paddington, Kensington, Westminster. It proved harder
to organize charity in areas like Whitechapel, Shoreditch or
Bethnal Green; but by the end of the nineteenth century, the
movement had spread to many parts of London and to some of the
major provincial cities. These district offices investigated individual cases of poverty in depth, passing on those they considered
'deserving' to other agencies for action. They might ask one
society for a donkey for a coster-monger, so that he could ply his
trade, and another for a sewing machine for a widow, so that she
could make clothes for her children. They were often criticized for
arrogance and self-righteousness; but they remained convinced
that the only constructive way to meet the problems of poverty was
to investigate every case – and that most, on investigation, would
be found to be unworthy of help. In his book *Charity Organisation*,
Loch wrote his own commentary on Charles Booth's findings,
pointing out that 'only' 13.5 per cent of the population of East
London were estimated to be in dire poverty, and suggesting that
careful and rigorous enquiry would reduce that number to a much
lower level.[2]

But the COS did develop a degree of expertise in dealing with
family problems, and this formed the basis for the development of
social casework. Early developments in training social workers, in
the University of Birmingham from 1908 and in the London
School of Economics from 1913, relied heavily on fieldwork
experience in COS agencies.

Helen Bosanquet was the wife of Bernard Bosanquet, the Oxford
philosopher. Both the Bosanquets shared Loch's perspective.

Helen Bosanquet had already made a reputation as a speaker and writer on COS subjects as Helen Dendy before her marriage. In 1893, in a book edited by her husband, she commented that applicants for charity might at first sight seem eminently deserving, but prove on closer examination to be drunkards, spendthrifts or 'quarrelsome and lazy'. She cited the case of a workman who had 'thrown away place after place':

> Of course, the more chances he was given, the more he wanted, and now it has come to this, that his wife and daughter go out to work while he sits home and minds the baby. A little wholesome starvation at the beginning of his career might have taught this man a lesson he would never have forgotten, and enabled him to preserve his manhood.[3]

Octavia Hill, the housing reformer, was also a keen supporter of the COS, but her approach seems to have been less abrasive than that of Loch or Helen Bosanquet. Her slogan was 'not alms, but a friend'. In her early work, she befriended families in tenements in what seems to have been a warm and personal relationship, but she believed that they had to be helped out of a financial muddle of debts and pawn-tickets into managing their resources. She interested John Ruskin in her plans for a contractual relationship between poor tenants and their landlords. The tenants would agree to pay their rent regularly, and not to vandalize the property. They were visited, and helped to budget. In return, the landlord agreed to keep the property clean, and in a good state of repair. Ruskin, who was a philanthropist as well as a writer and a poet, was impressed by these ideas, and bought houses for Octavia Hill to manage. She soon put the enterprise on a business footing, and provided a return on capital of 5 per cent to investors. The Church Commissioners offered her property to manage, and she took over the running of some of their worst properties in the slum areas of London, training her own workers. So began the profession of housing management.[4]

Octavia Hill's interests moved steadily outwards: from individual families paying their rent to blocks of flats, to play streets for children, to town planning and the idea of a Green Belt – the 'green lungs of London'. She was also a founder-member of the National Trust, set up in 1895; but her work with COS arose directly from her relationship with tenant families. She would investigate their budgets, and taught her workers to do the same. If there appeared to be a need for assistance, clients would be sent to the COS. At least three other members appointed to the Poor Law Commission had extensive COS and Poor Law experience. They formed a formidable and united group: but they faced a formidable opponent.

Beatrice Webb and the Fabians

Since the Commission was appointed by a Conservative Government, and the Liberals were in opposition, no Liberals were appointed to it. Beatrice Webb, formerly Beatrice Potter and Charles Booth's assistant on the great poverty surveys, was the only Fabian Socialist, and her appointment seems to have been a miscalculation: the Prime Minister knew Mrs Webb socially, and understood that she was interested in poverty. His advisers appear not to have realized that a lady who dined with the Prime Minister could possibly be a Socialist.[5]

The Fabian Society, founded in 1884, believed in evolutionary change rather than revolution – it was named after Quintus Fabius Maximus, the Roman general who 'hastened slowly'. They had become the research arm of the Labour movement. Beatrice's marriage to Sidney Webb was the commencement of an outstanding joint career in scholarship and politics.

The Webbs were to be involved in many left-wing enterprises, including the publication of the *New Statesman and Nation* and the foundation of the London School of Economics, where they both taught for many years. Sidney Webb became a professor, and eventually a cabinet minister in a Labour Government in the late 1920s. They became great admirers of Soviet Russia, and their *Soviet Communism* was a classic of the 1930s. The partnership between the Webbs was so close that it is often impossible to distinguish the work of Sidney from that of Beatrice.

In *My Apprenticeship*, Beatrice Webb describes the COS as 'one of the most typical of Victorian offspring', and speaks of its activities with open contempt. She notes 'We fought each other's views to the death'.[6] Beatrice describes herself as temperamentally averse to the rough and tumble of argument (which was a very proper attitude for an Edwardian lady to take, though one

suspects that she had a combative streak), but she became the
channel through which Fabian ideas, many of them put into draft
by her husband, were brought to confront a bewildered and
exasperated Commission. The Fabians believed implicitly in the power of facts. One of
their earliest publications, dating from 1888 and regularly updated,
was *Facts for Socialists*. As Margaret Cole puts it, they believed
that:

> no reasonable person who *knows the facts* can fail to become a
> Socialist, or at the very least, to be converted to the Socialist
> policy – that out of their own mouths, or rather out of their
> published material, the defenders of capitalism can be made to
> prove that it is inefficient, brutal and idiotic.[7]

This belief is the key to Beatrice's behaviour on the Commission,
and also to the curious story of the Hutchinson Bequest, which was
commandeered by Sidney Webb to assist in founding the London
School of Economics. He was able to argue with perfect integrity
to the Hutchinson Trustees that the money would be devoted to
strengthening the cause of Socialism in accordance with the terms
of the bequest, and to the London Chamber of Commerce that
'the school would not deal with political matters, and nothing of a
socialistic tendency would be introduced'.[8] In his view, people
who honestly looked at the facts would inevitably come to Socialist
conclusions.

In *Our Partnership* (1948) Beatrice Webb gives extracts from
her diaries which contain a blow-by-blow account of the proceedings, and her changing view of the other participants as the debate
went on. She started with great hopes of the chairman, at first
describing him as 'this experienced politician and attractive grand
seigneur', but later judging him to be 'weak' and 'frightened'
under attack by the COS. She seems to have underestimated
George Lansbury, the Christian Socialist Member of Parliament
from the East End, referred to rather patronizingly in the early
days as 'our workingman' [sic]. Later, she learned to respect him
for his firsthand knowledge of poverty and his strong Socialist and
pacifist convictions. She thought Prebendary Russell Wakefield,
another Christian Socialist, a very dubious ally, but eventually
found that he would support her point of view. She was less

fortunate with her cousin Charles Booth, who was 'as delightful as ever', but 'losing his intellectual grip and persistency of purpose. Happily, he is unaware of it'.[9] But her view of the COS members did not change: she regarded them as merely uninformed and prejudiced, and nearly five years of weekly debate did not bend their convictions nor mitigate her scorn.

The Commission's work

There were two acknowledged experts on the Commission – Charles Booth, and a Poor Law historian, Professor William Smart. There were four senior civil servants – the Permanent Heads of the Local Government Boards of England, Scotland and Wales, and their Chief Medical Officer, whom Beatrice Webb called 'the big officials'. By the second meeting, she had found the procedure a shambles, and was demanding a much more organized way of working. From then on, she and Sidney worked together, drafting memorandum after memorandum, and submitting lists of proposals. 'My little tea-cup of a Royal Commission', she called it; but every meeting was exhausting. She recorded 'the clash of tongues', reproof from the chairman after a particularly bitter comment, and her own resolve to keep to good manners; but Charles Loch, normally the most controlled of men, repeatedly lost his temper and became 'white with rage' when she opposed his views, till Beatrice concluded that he must be seriously ill.[10] Reading between the lines, it seems that she tried to build bridges with most members of the Commission in the hope of converting them to Socialism; but her approach to Loch was a complete failure, and she was equally unable to come to terms with Helen Bosanquet, whom she consistently referred to formally as 'Mrs Bosanquet', describing her contributions to the Commission's debates as 'wonderful' and 'brilliant' in terms which leave no doubt about the sarcasm intended.[11] They were clearly not on each other's visiting lists.

Facts, facts, facts. The Commission's work was extensive, partly because Beatrice drove it on past the collection of opinions to the collection of empirical data. In all, its members visited 400 institutions, attended 160 meetings and interviewed Guardians from 200 Unions. They called for a mass of memoranda and statistical returns from central and local government. They enquired into systems of relief in other countries, including New Zealand and Canada. They collated data on trade depressions, on immigration and emigration, on the growth of trade unions, on the use of female labour. A report on the operation of Boards of Guardians seems to carry the mark of the COS. They were concerned about the system of election, and the poor quality of those elected. This was partly due to public apathy. Only 28.1 per cent of the population voted in the Guardians' elections in 1906, as against a 78.3 per cent vote for parliamentary elections. People became Guardians for the wrong reasons – often because they had political ambitions. The comment that 'Many men become Guardians as a stepping stone to the Town Council' may have been aimed at George Lansbury, who had begun his own political career as a member of the Board of Guardians for Poplar. In one instance 'A lady was beaten at the elections by a publican who brought twenty-five electors drunk to the poll'. Guardians were 'often totally ignorant of the procedure of a public meeting . . . ignorant and assertive'. Frequently they had no knowledge of the principles of public relief, or of the facts of individual cases. The conclusion was:

> It is not a question of the social status of the Guardians, still less of wealth or poverty; but it is a question of choosing, from whatever class of the community, experienced, thoughtful, and above all disinterested men and women, to perform a most important public service. We believe that there are many such men and women quite prepared to give the service, who will not face a popular election carried on under present conditions . . . and will not make the promises of liberal relief which are so potent in an election, and so fatal to good administration.[12]

An exhaustive Statistical Survey, published as Part II of the Report, was directed by Professor William Smart. It gave a breakdown of the pauper population as at 1 July 1907. There were 868,276 paupers – equivalent to the population of Liverpool. Of these, 27.6 per cent were men, 43.0 per cent were women, and 29.4 per cent were children. These figures alone should have been enough to end the persistent myth of the pauper as an able-bodied male. The age breakdown was even more telling: the number of paupers was only 3.3 per thousand in the 15–24 age-group and 6.6

in the 25–34 age-group; but it rose steadily to 163.0 per thousand aged 65–74, 275.9 per thousand aged 75–84, and 353.1 per thousand – more than one in three – of those aged 85 and over. The case for old-age pensions could not have been more clearly put; but these figures had no effect in modifying the COS view. Beatrice Webb set up investigations of her own, which were financed by Fabian sympathizers. At a meeting of the Fabian Executive in July 1907, it was decided to ask 'the richer members of the Society' to contribute to the cost, and Beatrice acquired her own research workers and secretariat.[13] An investigation on the effect of outdoor relief on wages elicited the information that there was no effect on wages – since hardly any able-bodied men received outdoor relief. This hardly matched the conviction that Guardians were handing out liberal relief to undeserving applicants.

Another enquiry was concerned with the effect of a refusal of outdoor relief on families. The report stated that in no case had this led to sustained assistance from relatives; and that no charity had provided more than spasmodic gifts. Unemployed men appeared to be disheartened by a refusal, and did not seem to make greater efforts to obtain work. There was often marked physical deterioration. 'If eventually they are forced to enter the workhouse,' reported the investigator, 'they do so with health gone, home gone, and spirit and courage shattered'.[14]

A report on the 150,000 children on poor relief painted a vivid picture of their condition. They were 'under-nourished, many of them poorly dressed and bare-footed ... the under-nourished child is easily tired, and usually slow, dull and listless, but he is often not to his knowledge hungry, and will refuse good food.' The problems of single mothers were described in this report:

> They have to take up the position of both parents, be bread-winner and housewife, keep house, often on an impossibly small sum, cook, clean, mend and bake, often when others are asleep. Little wonder that they break down in health and courage, and become ineffective, colourless and whining.[15]

In May 1906, Beatrice Webb could see neither shape nor purpose to the Commission's deliberations. It became clear that she could not hope to convert her fellow members by argument: they had to be confronted head-on. In December of the following year, she submitted to the Commission a closely written document on 'the break-up of the Poor Law' which was 'received in stony silence'. 'The COS were chuckling at the defeat of my scheme ... by persistent discourtesy, they have absolved me from the obligations of good fellowship'.

This document was to develop into the Minority Report. 'There was coldness towards me', Beatrice notes in October 1908, 'and Lansbury says they are very angry at the length of my report'; and in November:

> The poor old Commission – and it is getting more old and weary, if not actually senile, with every week's sitting. It is floundering about in its morass of a report ... our document stares at them in a fine blue cover ... there it is, 300 pages of reasoned stuff, with a scheme of reform at the end.[16]

According to Beatrice, when the last meeting came, the final version of the Majority Report was not ready, so the Commissioners who supported the COS view had to sign blank pieces of paper. She implies that some of them may not have been quite clear what they were putting their names to. Only three other members joined her in signing the Minority Report – Russell Wakefield, George Lansbury and a trade union member, Francis Chandler. It should be said that this picture of the Commission's final stages is markedly different from that presented by Helen Bosanquet, who totally ignores the Minority Report, and treats the Majority Report as an uncontested triumph for rationality and common sense.[17]

The fact that there are two reports is not apparent fom the contents list of the official published version. It is presented as 'The Report of the Royal Commission on the Poor Laws' – with a dissenting minority view listed in small letters near the end. All the investigations (including those set up by Beatrice and paid for by the Fabians) are listed as part of the main report. In fact, the two sets of recommendations are of roughly equal length.

The Majority Report

Both the Majority and the Minority recognized that the existing Poor Law was obsolete, and wanted to hand its functions over to the county and county borough councils. Beyond that, they diverged. The views of the Majority commissioners were that the Poor Law needed reform, but that the principle of the Goschen Minute should be maintained – the public authority should provide only a basic minimum, and voluntary agencies should provide better standards for the 'more deserving'.

The 'leading defects of the Poor Law system' were that the Union areas were too small to meet the growing needs of administration; that the Poor Law system was isolated from other forms of local government, which were developing rapidly; that the Boards of Guardians were unsuitable administrators; and that there was too little central control. They recommended that:

1. The central authority (then the Local Government Board) should have a higher status, with a Secretary of State as its head.

2. Local administration should be undertaken by a committee of the county or county borough council.

3. The name of the service should be changed from 'Poor Law' to 'Public Assistance'.

4. Workhouses should be classified institutions, and their operation should be 'as far as possible curative and restorative'.

5. Outdoor relief (renamed 'Home Assistance') should be handled primarily by voluntary agencies, and conditional on recipients 'living respectable lives in decent houses'.

This last recommendation was an attempt to give a controlling role to the COS, with the state system as the last resort, in the spirit of the Goschen Minute of forty years earlier.

The Minority Report

The Minority Report analysis was of a completely different order. It was argued that poverty was not due to personal failing: it was an artificial problem, created by capitalist organization. All the apparatus of voluntary organizations, special administrative machinery and institutions were merely serving capitalist purposes. What was necessary was the total abolition of the concept of 'the poor' as a class and pauperism as a problem, and the total breakup of the Poor Law system.

In its place the Webbs proposed the principle of 'Administrative Functionalism'. This meant that people who were poor would be assisted by organizations framed to meet the different causes of poverty rather than its common effects. The main recommendations were as follows:

1. The problems of the able-bodied poor and the non-able-bodied poor (this rather clumsy phrase had replaced the 'impotent poor') should be separated.

2. *The non-able-bodied poor* should be the responsibility of the local authority, but of different committees with specialist staff: children would be the responsibility of the Education Committee, sick and disabled people the responsibility of the Health Committee, mentally ill and mentally handicapped people the responsibility of the Asylums Committee. These bodies already existed for other purposes. What was new was the proposed allocation to them of responsibility for individuals in need who had previously been classified as 'poor'. The local authority would be empowered to provide institutional or domiciliary care as required, and grants in aid would be provided from Government funds.

Each of these local committees would have a clear line of responsibility to a central government department: the Education Committee to the Board of Education; the Health Committee to a Ministry or Board of Health (not the Local Government Board, which was still dominated by the Poor Law ethos); the Asylums Committee to the Lunacy Commissioners. These central government departments would be responsible for administering the grants in aid, and setting down guidelines. Each would have its own inspectorate to ensure the maintenance of standards.

3. *The able-bodied poor* would be treated by totally different methods which emphasized the responsibility of the state to provide work rather than the responsibility of the individual to find it. A Ministry of Labour would be set up, with six sections: Labour Exchanges, Trade, Maintenance and Training, Industrial Regulation, Emigration and Immigration, Statistics. A government economic programme would be set up to meet the trade cycle on a ten-year basis: there would be high taxation during the boom years, and lower taxation and encouragement of investment during the years of slump. Labour Exchanges would be set up in every area. Casual labourers would be woven into two or more trades which might complement each other. There would be a reduction of hours for young workers, so that they had an opportunity for further education, to provide a way out of blind alley jobs.

4. *The wilfully idle* would be sent to a reformatory colony run by the Home Office. It is notable that the Webbs never denied the existence of a small group of people who would not work, and their view was the orthodox Marxist one: labour and self-maintenance were duties which the citizen owed the state, and those who did not accept those duties had to be taught to do so; but the proper management of the economy and the labour market would ensure that the stigma of idleness was not applied to people who were willing to work.

A bare recital of the main points of the two reports indicates that there was never any real possibility of unanimity, much as Beatrice Webb claims that she hoped for it. Unanimity would only have been possible on her terms. The majority and the minority proceeded from different views of Man, different views of society, different experience, different knowledge-bases.

The Webbs were so incensed by the way in which the reports were officially presented that they published the Minority Report separately at their own expense through the Fabian Society as *Break up the Poor Law and Abolish the Workhouse*. The Treasury intervened, claiming copyright, as it was technically a Government publication. Sidney Webb pointed out that the copyright was properly his, since the document was in his handwriting – final proof of the degree of his involvement in the Commission's work; and the Treasury withdrew its opposition.[18] No-one seems to have commented on the fact that Sidney was not actually a member of the Commission.

'If we had not taken steps' Beatrice wrote in February 1909, 'we should have been submerged completely'. The Webbs took steps. They embarked on two years of 'raging, tearing propaganda', lecturing or speaking five or six times a week. The National Committee for the Break-up of the Poor Law, soon re-titled the National Committee for the Prevention of Destitution, attracted 16,000 members. The campaign was enough to defeat the Majority proposals, but not enough to carry the country; for while the Commission debated, the Liberals (excluded from its membership) had been in power for three years, and had already embarked on their own programme of social reform. The great Conservative–Socialist debate was on the sidelines of current policy.

The long view

The recommendations of both majority and minority went on the shelf, and gathered dust for decades. So much heat and anger, so much work, so little result; but they were not forgotten. Over twenty years later, the Poor Law Act of 1930 implemented much of the Majority Report, creating Public Assistance Committees of local authorities and a reformed and more specialized Public Assistance Service. By that time, the COS had lost much of its influence, and the recommendations for a distinction between 'deserving' and 'undeserving' and for the enhanced position of voluntary agencies had been dropped. The Society never had the resources nor the organization to undertake such a role, and this fact was recognized in 1930 by a noted jurist, Sir Ivor Jennings:

> Unfortunately, the recommendations of the majority were coloured by the views of certain of the commissioners in favour of organised charity, and are now recognised to be hopelessly impracticable and undesirable.[19]

The Minority Report had a longer time to wait. The Webbs' campaign attracted considerable support, not least among the local authorities, in the few years before 1914. Like many other social movements, it was lost in the stress and muddle of the First World War. It then became part of a Socialist charter, to be implemented when a Socialist government had the power. Nearly forty years after its first publication, the first Labour Govenment with a clear majority in the House of Commons was to make it the basis for the 'Welfare State' legislation of the late 1940s.

'Hateful friction' wrote Beatrice Webb; but the research and the thinking and even the friction were to be valuable in the long term. Meanwhile in 1909, the Liberals were in office, and already devising their own solutions.

EIGHT

The Liberal Answer

The Liberals took power in 1906 with a parliamentary majority of 356. The pressure for social reform was gathering, and the Government was in a position to enact any measures it considered advisable. Fraser[1] takes the view that reform came slowly, and was mainly due to the small group of Labour MPs who now had a place in the House of Commons. He argues that the Liberals were much more concerned at the time with issues such as free trade, Chinese labour in South Africa, and the battle over denominational schools following Balfour's Act of 1902. Many Liberal MPs were Nonconformists, and religious issues were hotly debated.

A reading of the parliamentary debates for the period does suggest that a great deal of debating time was spent on these issues, and there is no doubt that the Labour members acted as a pressure group; but there is much evidence that the Liberal Government was strongly committed to social reform even during the two years 1906–1908 when the cautious and ailing Campbell-Bannerman was Prime Minister. After Asquith became Prime Minister in 1908, with Lloyd George as Chancellor of the Exchequer, the lines of a distinctively Liberal policy were much more clearly delineated, owing little to either Conservative or Socialist thinking. But the record even in the first two years is stronger than Fraser suggests.

The first two measures were admittedly apparently minor ones which seemed to lack the weight of positive Government sponsorship. The Education (Provision of Meals) Act of 1906 empowered all local authorities to provide school meals in elementary (primary)

schools, and to raise a halfpenny rate to provide free meals for
children who were 'unable by reason of lack of food to take full
advantage of the education provided for them'. This was a private
member's Bill, and not a government measure. The Education
(Administrative Provisions) Act of 1907 contained among many
other clauses an apparently unimportant proposal for medical
inspection of schoolchildren. In fact, this measure had very
wide implications: it gave wide powers of delegation to the
central Board of Education to organize measures for 'the health
and physical condition of children educated in public elementary schools'. In time, this led to the setting up of a Medical
Department at the Board of Education, close liaison between
health services and education services, and a system of school
clinics in every area. Since this was the first provision outside
the Poor Law for the health of a whole sector of the population,
it was in some sense the beginning of the National Health
Service.

By the end of 1908, at least six other measures which had
reached the statute-book testify to the Liberal Government's
strong concern for social reform: the Workmen's Compensation
Act of 1907, and five Acts passed in 1908: the Children Act, the
Incest Act, the Probation of Offenders Act, the Labour Exchanges
Act and the first Old Age Pensions Act.

The Children Act was primarily a consolidating measure, bringing together provisions spread over 39 different statutes for infant
life protection and the prevention of cruelty to children. It also
made the first separate provision for juvenile delinquency, setting
up special courts with a separate panel of magistrates. The
Children Act and the Incest Act had two major policy implications:
the recognition that children had rights, and were not simply the
property of their parents – a considerable incursion into the closed
circle of the Victorian family; and the understanding that there
was no sharp line to be drawn between neglected children and
delinquent children, since a poor home background might be a
contributory cause to either condition.

The Probation of Offenders Act provided the basis for the
system whereby some offenders might be allowed to continue to
live in the community, with a Probation Officer (usually a worker
from a temperance organization in the eary days) to 'advise, assist
and befriend' them. This was a first step in the development of

alternatives to prison, and a major contribution to the development of social work.

The Workmen's Compensation Act of 1907 provided compensation for industrial injuries in dangerous trades, and made it necessary for the employers to insure their workforce. Again, this was a first step in what was to become a national scheme.

The Labour Exchanges measure of 1908 provided a national network of labour exchanges, where those who were seeking work might find out what work was available. The state took over some 61 local labour exchanges already in existence, and run by municipalities. By 1913, there were 430 major labour exchanges, and over a thousand small rural offices. This measure owed much to the work of William Beveridge, who was recommended to Lloyd George by the Webbs.

The major pressure for reform in the period 1906–1908 came from Asquith at the Exchequer, and Lloyd George at the Board of Trade. They were already thinking about the possibilities of national insurance as a way of lifting the working population out of poverty, and the Workmen's Compensation Act and the Labour Exchanges Act were designed as preliminary steps in the fulfilment of this aim. A further step was the development of the first old-age pension.

The campaign for pensions for old people had by this time a long history of public support. The poverty surveys of Booth and Rowntree had made it clear beyond all doubt that old age was a major cause of poverty. The issues had been long-debated, and there was agreement in principle; but legislation had been held up by disagreement about the means: should the pension be contributory or non-contributory? How should it be financed? Could the country afford it?

The arguments in favour of a contributory pension were that it would be largely self-financing, and would not immediately affect the budget; and recipients would feel that they had earned their benefits by contributions. The arguments against were that a contributory pension scheme would take years to build up, and that most of the people who needed old-age pensions were women, who were unlikely to have paid contributions, since most women did not then have regular outside employment.

The terms of the Old Age Pensions Act of 1908 may seem timid by later standards, but represented a considerable advance at the time. The Act provided for a non-contributory pension of five shillings a week at the age of seventy for both sexes subject to a means test and a 'moral' test. The means test involved a full pension for those with up to £21 a year in income, and a sliding scale to £31.10s. a year, where the pension dropped to a shilling a week.

The 'moral' test meant that it was not to be given to people who were habitually drunken, had served a prison sentence in the previous ten years, were on poor relief or had habitually failed to support themselves. These provisions were to fall into disuse within a few years.

The positive elements were that the pension was non-contributory, and therefore not dependent on proving entitlement. It was paid through the Post Office, without stigma. Married women received the same pension as men and unmarried women – a proposal that a married couple should receive only 7s.6d. joint pension was defeated. The pension had nothing whatever to do with the Poor Law. Five shillings a week was not enough to live on; but for many old people, it was enough, with a little put by, to remove the ever-present fear of the workhouse. Flora Thompson tells in *Lark Rise* how the 'aged cottagers' of her village went to the Post Office with tears of gratitude running down their cheeks, because the pension would allow them to keep their independence; and how they said 'God bless that Lord George', because they thought only a lord could be so powerful and so kind; and how some brought flowers from their gardens and apples from their trees as presents for the girl behind the Post Office counter who handed them the money.[2] Few government measures can have produced so much simple happiness.

Meanwhile, the main debate about poverty went on. The Royal Commission on the Poor Laws continued to meet weekly. It is revealing to discover that, when the Webbs' Minority Report was in draft and circulating round the Commission, Lloyd George, by that time Chancellor of the Exchequer, asked for a copy, and the chairman refused to let him have one.[3] But before the Commission finally reported in 1909, Campbell-Bannerman had retired, Asquith had become Prime Minister, Lloyd George was Chancellor of the Exchequer, and Winston Churchill took over the Board of Trade.

The many biographers of Winston Churchill do not make much of this period in his life, when he was 'a Radical of Radicals',[4] and he and Lloyd George formed a partnership with common aims and ideals. The Welshman born in a cobbler's cottage in North Wales and the young Churchill shared one quality: a vision of a better Britain. Churchill told an audience at Blackpool that when he read Rowntree's *Poverty, A Study of Town Life*, his hair stood on end.[5] Lady Violet Bonham Carter, who first met him in 1906, when he was 32, wrote:

> The Liberal Government was determined to lay the ugly spectre of poverty, and to spread a net over the abyss. It is to Winston Churchill's signal credit that he embraced these aims, and fought with all his heart and might to realise them.[6]

As the Old Age Pensions Act reached the statute-book, Lloyd George went to Germany to study the scheme of health and unemployment insurance introduced under Bismarck.

The tour in August 1908, was an intensive one. Lloyd George and his official entourage visited a number of German cities, including Berlin, where they called at the Imperial Old Age and Invalid Insurance Offices, and dined with the Imperial Vice-Chancellor. They visited the docks and shipyards at Hamburg, holding discussions with trade union leaders and radical politicians. Though relations between Britain and Germany were deteriorating, Lloyd George seems to have been treated with much courtesy, and to have learned a good deal. On the train on the way back from Southampton to London, he gave a Press interview, and said that he was 'tremendously impressed with the finished character and perfection of the whole machine'.[7] The next step was to devise a broader contributory scheme for England and Wales which could be grafted on to the Old Age Pensions provisions.

The time was hardly propitious. There was a trade recession, a government committed to free trade could not raise money from tariffs, and before Asquith left the Exchequer, he had reduced the duty on imported sugar, which was a popular measure, but left very little provision for social insurance. The cost was estimated at £6 million. The money set aside was only £1.2 million. This disparity was to lead to the controversial 'People's Budget' of 1909, the first openly redistributive budget which proposed a super-tax of 6d in the pound and a tax on land values, and so to bitter conflict with the House of Lords in 1911, when the powers of the Lords in relation to Finance Bills were severely curtailed.

In 1909, the Royal Commission on the Poor Laws finally reported. Though the Majority and Minority Reports were fundamentally different in aims and scope, the two sets of Commissioners agreed in refusing to consider national insurance. The Conservative majority were opposed to it on the grounds that it involved state intervention. The Fabian minority were opposed to it on the grounds that workers on low incomes would not be able to afford contributions. According to John Burns, then President of the Local Government Board, Lloyd George was gleeful that he had 'dished the Webbs' and found a non-Socialist solution to the problems of poverty.[8] (Winston Churchill's alleged comment that he would not wish to be locked up in a soup kitchen with Mrs Sidney Webb seems to date from the same period. No doubt Beatrice Webb used all her considerable powers of persuasion.)

Once the Liberal Government had determined on an insurance scheme, there were four main decisions to be made:

1. Should it be contributory or non-contributory? If it was to be seen as an extension of the principles of mutual aid to the classes at greatest risk, it was necessary that it should be contributory: workers would pay contributions, and draw benefits in time of need.

2. Should it be financially watertight, like a commercial insurance scheme, or involve an Exchequer contribution? If contributions were to be fixed at a level which workers on low wages could afford to pay, an Exchequer contribution would be necessary. But what proportion should the Exchequer be prepared to meet?

3. Should it be a flat-rate scheme, in which everyone paid the same contributions and was entitled to the same benefits, or should it be wage-related? It was decided, on grounds of social equity and adherence to insurance practice, that it should be flat-rate.

4. Should the scheme work through existing agencies, or should special administrative agencies be set up? Setting up a national network of Government agencies would have been very costly, so it was decided to use the Friendly Societies to administer the scheme. (There was no special machinery for the non-contributory old-age pensions scheme of 1908. That was administered for some reason by the Customs and Excise Department.)

In the budget debate of 30 June 1910, Lloyd George had an answer for those who accused the Liberal Government of making 'reckless promises' to the people:

'What were these reckless promises?' he asked. They had made a 'reckless promise' about old age pensions, and there were already between 800,000 and 900,000 people receiving them. They had made another 'reckless promise' that the pensions would be extended to paupers, and on January 1 there would be about 240,000 aged paupers walking to the Post Office for their five shillings a week. They had made another 'reckless promise' about labour exchanges, and these were now in operation, and had provided work for 100,000 people. They had made another 'reckless promise' for next year that they would bring in unemployment insurance.[9]

The National Insurance Act of 1911

In its final form, the Act represented the settlement achieved after long and tortuous negotiations with powerful pressure groups: the friendly societies, the trade unions and the doctors. It had two distinct parts: unemployment insurance and health insurance. The unemployment insurance scheme originally covered only two and a quarter million workers, 90 per cent of them men. The contribution rate was 2½d a week for employees, 2½d a week for employers, with an Exchequer subsidy equal to one-third of the combined amount. It applied only to workers in fluctuating trades, such as building, shipbuilding and iron founding. Benefit was payable at a basic rate of 7s. a week for an adult male (slightly less for women and juveniles), subject to contribution conditions. There were no benefits for dependents, and proposals for widows' and orphans' benefits were dropped. Benefit was payable through the new labour exchanges, which could test the genuineness of claims by making them subject to the availability of suitable employment.

The health scheme had a different and wider basis. It applied to all manual workers between the ages of 16 and 70 earning less than £250 a year (£5 a week was then a good wage) and to non-manual workers earning less than £160 a year. Contributors registered with a friendly society of their choice, and there was a residual scheme, organized through the Post Office, for those refused by the voluntary societies on the grounds that they were poor risks. Contributions were 4d from the employee, 3d from the employer and 2d from the Exchequer – hence the popular election cry of 'Ninepence for fourpence'. The scheme originally provided for sickness benefit (10s. a week), disablement benefit (5s. a week) and a maternity grant of 30s. on the birth of a child, doubled if both husband and wife were insured. If the worker needed medical attention, there was a 'panel system' by which he could choose a doctor from a list kept by the local insurance committee.

'I do not pretend' said Lloyd George, 'that this is a complete remedy. Before you get a complete remedy for these social evils, you will have to cut deeper'.[10] But it was a notable beginning.

The National Insurance Scheme in Practice

National insurance was introduced in 1912. Insured people had a card for unemployment insurance, usually kept by their employers, to which stamps were affixed weekly, thus emphasizing the contributory aspects of the scheme. (Some ladies in Mayfair and Belgravia, appalled at the prospect of having to keep cards for their staff, founded a society which campaigned against 'licking stamps for Lloyd George',[11] but in fact domestic servants were not included in the classes of employees covered). The health insurance scheme, run through the friendly societies, meant a continuation of the existing practice by which agents went from door to door, collecting dues weekly.

For central government, the schemes involved major calculations of risk: the study of economic and demographic trends, estimates of the likely risks of sickness and unemployment. There was no experience of this kind of actuarial work in Whitehall, and it was anticipated that the unemployment scheme would run smoothly, while the health scheme might run into difficulty, because the incidence of sickness was unpredictable.

In the event, the health scheme presented little difficulty. The days of the major epidemic diseases were over, and the scheme was actuarially sound. The big friendly societies made large profits, and ploughed some of them back into additional benefits for their subscribers. The employment scheme started well enough in the two years before the First World War. By 1914, the Fund had a balance of over £3 million, and only £700,000 had been paid out in benefits. During the war, coverage was extended to munitions workers, who were likely to be thrown out of employment when hostilities ended. At the end of 1918, there was a healthy surplus of £15 million. The Government made 'Out of Work Donations' to former munition workers and ex-servicemen, and it seemed that the adjustment to peace-time conditions was proceeding without major problems. Government optimism ran so high in 1920 that the scheme was extended to all manual and non-manual workers earning less than £250 a year apart from agricultural workers and people in permanent employment, such as railway workers and local authority employees, and plans were made to introduce benefits for dependents – 5s. for a wife, and 1s. per child. At that time, an adult man's contribution was 4d a week, and the basic benefit 20s. But in 1921, unemployment began to rise sharply, and the problems began.

NINE
The Hungry Thirties

Up to the time of the First World War, the great powers ran their own budgets, and paid relatively little attention to the state of each other's economies. The world after 1918 was to be very different: communications improved, international trade increased, and booms or slumps became impossible for individual countries to control. There were theories about 'the trade cycle', which was thought by some economists to occur at regular intervals on an international scale; but the sudden growth of unemployment in 1921 in the aftermath of war seems to have taken the Liberal Government by surprise.

By the end of 1921, 14 per cent of the insured workforce were unemployed, and the reserves of the Fund had shrunk to £1 million. Two separate Acts had been passed raising contributions and cutting benefit. That was the beginning of years of frantic juggling with the figures: raising contributions, cutting benefits, setting increasingly stringent conditions before workers were entitled to claim, increasing the waiting period before benefit could be taken up. Table 9.1. indicates the major changes which took place up to 1931.

This table tells its own story of the efforts to keep contributions within what a working man could afford to pay, to pass more of the burden on to the employer, to reduce the Exchequer contribution (but then to accept that it must be increased) and the decline of benefits to a level on which a family could barely live.

The 'Geddes Axe' of 1922, the General Strike of 1926, when organized Labour brought the country to a near standstill, and a

Contributions for an adult male worker			
	Worker	*Employer*	*Exchequer*	*Benefits*
Nov. 1920	4d	4d	2d	15s
July 1921	7d	8d	3d	15s
Nov. 1921	9d	10d	6d	15s
Jan. 1926	7d	8d	6d	18s
Apr. 1926	7d	8d	6d	17s
Apr. 1929	7d	8d	7½d	17s
Oct. 1931	10d	10d	10d	15s.3d

Table 9. 1: *Unemployment Insurance: contributions and benefits 1920–31.*
Source: Royal Commission on Unemployment Insurance, chairman Judge
Holman Gregory, *Final Report*, HMSO Cmd. 4185, 1932, pp. 19–20.

worsening international economic situation, culminating in the
Wall Street crash of 1931 are all reflected in the figures.

The 'Geddes Axe', named after Sir Eric Geddes, Secretary to
the Treasury, was a policy by which Government cut public sector
employment and state subsidies. It was the beginning of a period
of retrenchment based on the economic understanding of the
day: that costs had to be cut in order to balance the budget.
People in work should accept salary cuts (and the salaries of civil
servants and teachers were cut, in some instances by 10 per cent
or more). The number of jobs was regarded as fixed, so that
people who did not 'need' a job were dismissed, or expected to
retire from the job market. Married women were expected to
retire from paid employment, and to be dependent on their
husbands. (It was quite common in the 1930s for young women
teachers or civil servants who wanted to continue working to
conceal the fact that they were married, keep their single names,
and wear their wedding rings on chains round their necks.)
Older workers entitled to a minimal retirement pension were
expected to give up work 'to make a job for a younger man'.
Wages were cut in many trades, and the combined effect of low
wages and rapidly rising unemployment inevitably led to industrial
conflict.

At that time, coal mining was by far the largest industry in
Britain, with over a million workers, and the miners were the
pacemakers in terms of industrial relations. By 1925, British mines
were running at a loss, due to the import of cheap coal from
Germany and Poland. The mine owners cut wages, lengthened

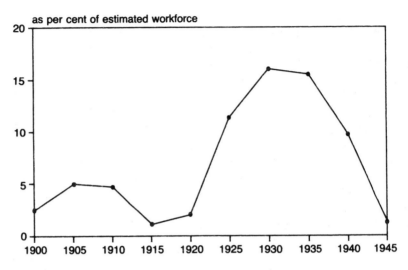

Figure IV Unemployment, United Kingdom, 1900–1945
Source: Annual Abstract of Statistics

hours of work, and often ignored safety regulations in an attempt to reduce production costs. Miners had a particular solidarity, born out of the hazardous and gruelling nature of their work, and their resistance to these measures soon developed into acute class conflict. The mine owners threatened a lock-out. The Trades Union Congress backed the miners, and other unions joined the strike.

The General Strike of 1926 lasted only eleven days, but it virtually brought the country to a standstill. The Government tried not to become involved, arguing that this was a private dispute between employers and employees, but was soon sufficiently alarmed to make plans for dealing with civil war. Britain was divided into ten autonomous regions, each with a civil commisioner who could act independently of Whitehall. When the workers on the printing presses came out on strike, and there were no newspapers, Winston Churchill ran an official Government paper which demanded 'unconditional surrender' from the strikers. Churchill's political stance had changed. As A. J. P. Taylor comments, the call to 'unconditional surrender' was to be used to better effect in the Second World War.[1]

There was an appeal for conciliation from King George V, and another from the Archbishop of Canterbury, backed by the leaders of other churches; but the risk of civil war was never a real one. Organized labour had tried its strength, and it was not strong enough. The trade unions were beaten, their funds depleted. The miners stayed out of the pits for six months before they were 'driven back to work by starvation'. A. J. Cronin's *The Stars Look Down* tells the story of the miners' strike in a powerful novel of the period.

Wal Hannington's *Unemployed Struggles 1919–1936* records the hunger marches organized by the National Unemployed Workers' Movement through those long and desperate years. Hannington was an engineer who became the leader of the NUWM, and took part himself in the marches, which were to become a repeated feature of English life for sixteen years. On the first march: 'Many men took to the road even without overcoats, much less blankets and other necessary kit. There were no food kitchens for the contingents. There were no assurances of food or guarantees of places to sleep. It was an adventure which only men with deep-seated grievances would be prepared to undertake'.[2] The men came from Glasgow, Lancashire, South Wales, Tyneside and the Midlands, often ragged and half starved. They came in their thousands and tens of thousands, walking for weeks, sustained at first only by a sense of common purpose and a sense of injustice. Public sympathy was roused in time: church halls and other buildings were made available to them, local committees arranged food and shelter. The Lord Mayor of London raised a relief fund of over £1 million for the unemployed.

In London, year after year and time after time, the marchers filled Trafalgar Square, and marched through the City and the West End. In Edinburgh on one occasion, 20,000 converged on St Giles' Cathedral, and some 2,000 ended by sleeping in the gutters in Prince's Street. When two miners died on one London march: 'Their bodies were returned to their native soil. In the funeral procession which marched through London, the coffins were covered with the red flag of the workers, and on each stood an unlighted miner's lamp. The silent march to Paddington station was most impressive; thousands on that great station stood hushed in silence as the marchers bore the bodies of their dead comrades to the van of the train'.[3]

Probably few of the marchers were Communists, as Hannington

was, and even Communist sympathies were with the British workers rather than with Moscow; but successive governments, both Conservative and Labour, saw them as a political danger rather than as citizens asking for help. There were scuffles, and baton charges by the police, and threats of military action. Wal Hannington and his colleagues told the troops that if they were ordered to fire on the unemployed, they should remember their working class origin, and not shoot their brothers. For this, they were convicted on charges of 'preaching sedition', 'uttering seditious libels' and 'incitement to mutiny amongst H.M. Forces' and sent to prison.

It was a good way to make martyrs. Crowds formed outside, singing 'The Red Flag' and 'The Internationale' in support. Hannington says that there were untrue allegations that the National Unemployed Workers' Movement was supported by 'Bolshevik gold'. The ranks of the marchers were infiltrated by 'spies and agents provocateurs', who tried to turn the movement to a violence which would have justified a violent response.[4] But the men (and some women) who marched were not demanding the overthrow of government. They wanted work. Photographs of the period show them as gaunt and hopeless, many of them prematurely old.

George Orwell, in *The Road to Wigan Pier*, gives an unforgettable picture of life in a decaying Lancashire town. He is appalled by the dirt, the squalor, the revolting food, 'the sense of stagnant, meaningless decay ... the monstrous scenery of slag-heaps, chimneys, piled scrap-iron, foul canals, paths of cindery mud' in a place where people 'go creeping round just like blackbeetles, in an endless muddle of slovened jobs and mean grievances':

> For this in part is what industrialisation has done for us. Columbus sailed the Atlantic, the first steam engines tottered into action, the British Squares stood firm under the French guns at Waterloo, the one-eyed scoundrels of the nineteenth century praised God and filled their pockets – and this is where it all led.[5]

Orwell sees all this with great clarity – perhaps the more so because he was not born to it. (He was the son of an Indian High Court judge, and an Old Etonian). But like Charles Booth, he knew the smell and the taste of poverty at first hand. He knew the impossibility of living a decent life on unemployment benefit in 'any hole or corner slum, any misery of bugs and rotting floors and cracking walls, any extortion of skinflint landlords and blackmailing agents'.

He estimated the extent of misery: if two million people were registered unemployed, that did not mean that the rest of the population was comparatively well-off. When the destitute, the people who failed to register, the dependent families of unemployed men, the families on starvation wages, the old people unable to earn a little or to get help from their children and 'other nondescripts' were added, he calculated the total at near ten million people.[6]

Two factors mitigated the harshness of the reduced benefits: the introduction of dependents' allowances – at first intended to be only a temporary measure, but incorporated as a permanent part of the scheme; and the introduction of 'uncovenanted benefit', later called 'transitional benefit' for workers who had exhausted their benefit rights. This gave them an extra period of benefit at a lower rate.

Blanesburgh and Holman Gregory

In 1925, when the situation seemed to be improving slightly, the Minister of Labour appointed a Committee to review the unemployment insurance scheme under the chairmanship of Lord Blanesburgh. It sat through the General Strike and the panic measures of 1926, and concluded gloomily 'even actuaries are not prophets'.[7] No-one had foreseen the extent of unemployment, and the financial drains on the scheme. Witnesses who gave evidence to the Blanesburgh Committee advocated their own remedies. Some thought that the scheme should become non-contributory (since the needs were so much greater than the workers' capacity to pay contributions). Others thought that it should be abolished altogether (since it had degenerated into 'public charity'). The Committee's conclusion was that the scheme was sound, but that benefit should be paid indefinitely to those out of work without regard to contribution conditions. The main cause of the problem was thought to be the trade cycle, but the Committee took the view that major booms and slumps were predictable enough to be taken into account in actuarial calculations.

'The rather stupid Blanesburgh Committee' wrote Beveridge to Churchill,[8] were recommending the prediction of the unpredictable, and the abolition of the insurance principle which he had fought so hard to establish. In 1930, the Labour Government appointed a higher level investigation, a Royal Commission under the chairmanship of Judge Holman Gregory. But before that Commission could complete its task, a Treasury Committee, the May Committee, reported that the budget must be balanced at all costs, and that Britain must continue to pay off the national debt. Cuts in unemployment benefit were therefore inevitable. The Labour Government fell on the issue. The King asked Ramsay MacDonald to head a National Coalition Government, and the Labour movement never forgave him for doing so. MacDonald went to the country. An election was fought largely on the issue of whether the unemployed should receive 17s. or 15s. 3d. a week, and whether they could live on the latter amount. Ramsay MacDonald, returned to power, presided over the cut in unemployment benefit to 15s. 3d., and Britain abandoned the gold standard, which was a considerable blow to national morale and to the country's economic standing.

Two years later, the Holman Gregory Commission produced its final report. They had a much clearer policy to offer than Blanesburgh. Insurance was defined as:

> a contract whereby an individual or a group of individuals pays a premium in return for a guaranteed indemnity against a specific loss . . . premiums should be so adjusted as to cover the payment out, together with administrative expenses.[9]

At that time, the unemployment insurance scheme covered 12.5 million workers out of a total workforce of 18 million. In October 1931, 2,726,000 were drawing unemployment benefit, and a further 526,000 were drawing transitional benefit, which could run for up to 100 weeks. If the insurance principle was to be maintained, the scheme should be limited to those whose contributions entitled them to benefit. Those who had exhausted benefit should be funded by a separate mechanism; but the Commission was emphatic that this should not be administered by the Public Assistance Committee:

The ordinary Poor Law services of the Local Authorities must remain to meet the needs of all who are in distress from causes other than unemployment . . . but we desire as far as possible to distinguish for separate treatment those whose distress is due simply to unemployment, *and whose distress is due to no personal or moral defect*. (author's italics).[10]

This showed a remarkable shift in opinion from the heyday of the Charity Organization Society. If it was illogical to leave other categories of people in need to the Poor Law, that was not the Commission's concern; but members were quite clear that the Poor Law was not a suitable mechanism for the relief of the unemployed. Some other body was necessary 'to take the dole out of politics'.

The result of these considerations was the Unemployment Act of 1934, which set up the Unemployment Assistance Board. This was seen at the time as a considerable step forward, safeguarding the position of the long-term unemployed and making special provision for them. The UAB developed its own scales of benefit, and its own means test. But the popularity of the new Board soon diminished when it was found that its scales of benefit were actually lower than those given on Public Assistance, and the means test was considerably harsher. This was the Household Means Test, which involved calculations based on the income of the total household, including working children, aged parents and lodgers.

Orwell pointed out that the Household Means Test broke up families. Adult sons or daughters tended to move out rather than have most of their wages deducted as a household contribution. Old-age pensioners were no longer welcome in their children's homes if most of the pension was counted against unemployment assistance. When people are living on the breadline, they cannot always afford family feeling. The authorities were constantly on the look-out for 'scroungers', and neighbours would inform on each other:

The favourite joke in Wigan was about a man who was refused relief on the grounds that he 'had a job carting firewood'. He had to explain that he was not carting firewood, he was doing a moonlight flit. The 'firewood' was his furniture.[11]

The Holman Gregory Commission had noted that unemployment was not a single phenomenon: it took many forms – short-term and long-term, intermittent or continuous, due to a variety of international, national and local factors. Measures to deal with the situation were outside their terms of reference; but though the Commission insisted that the unemployed were 'not a standing army', there were areas of Britain where they were precisely that. In Jarrow, the unemployment rate reached 67 per cent. In Glasgow, the cranes stood idle on the Clyde. In South Wales, the iron foundries stood smokeless. In the coalfields where the pits had been closed, in the mill towns of Lancashire, there was simply no hope of work, and whole communities were near starvation. These were widely known as 'Distressed Areas' or 'Depressed Areas'. The Government response was no more than a token one. The Special Areas Act of 1934 provided a more acceptable description, and set up a fund of £2 million to stimulate economic development. As Wal Hannington, was to point out, this was less than half the beet sugar subsidy for the previous year, and less than the beef subsidy for six months.[12]

Liberal and Labour Members of Parliament condemned the scheme as merely palliative. Lloyd George, who had not lost his gift of words, told the House of Commons, 'The age of miracles is past. You cannot feed the multitude with two Commissioners and five sub-Commissioners. The new Commissioners are being sent on their apostolic mission, not without purse and script, but pretty nearly that – just with a little bit of cash, to deal with a problem costing £100,000,000 a year'.[13] The Commissioners were not even given the task of creating jobs. They were to improve the economic development of the area; but they were not allowed to use their meagre funds to supplement any scheme for which a central government grant was payable to a local authority. As Wal Hannington commented, 'if the Ministry of Transport [offered] a local authority a 60 per cent grant towards making a new road, and that authority could not afford to find the remaining 40 per cent, the Commissioners were not permitted to bear any of the local authority's portion, even though the road would lead in their opinion to the economic development of the area'.[14]

The Commissioners had the greatest difficulty in discovering what they might and might not do, and the results of their efforts

The scales at the left-hand side indicate respectively the actual Bank Rate of discount per cent, the percentage of trade union members not returned as unemployed, the number of marriages in England and Wales per 1,000 of the population, the number of indoor paupers in England and Wales per 10,000 of the population, the gallons of beer consumed, and the nominal capital of new companies registered, in pounds, per head of the population. No scale is given for the Foreign Trade curve. Unless the contrary is stated, all figures apply to United Kingdom generally.

Figure V. Beveridge's economic and social indices, 1930.
Source: William Beveridge, *Unemployment: a problem of industry*, Longmans Green, revised edition, 1930, p.44.
Note: Beveridge's intention was to illustrate the correspondence between fluctuations in the unemployment rate and those of other, possibly related, indices.

were not impressive; but by the time they were in full operation, the shadow of long-term unemployment had begun to lift. The mines, the shipyards, the mills and the foundries were busy again, preparing for the war which was only too clearly coming.

Maynard Keynes published his *General Theory of Unemployment, Interest and Money* in 1936, though the ideas were current in left-wing circles some time before that, and had been partially anticipated in the Webbs' Minority Report of 1909. Keynes pointed out that unemployment had a multiplier effect. The unemployed became a charge on the budget, paid no taxes or insurance contributions, bought few consumer goods, and so depressed demand still further. The downward spiral could be reversed by public investment in times of depression, and higher taxation in times of prosperity would provide the resources. This view of economics was unacceptable to the Conservative government of the mid-1930s; but as Fraser points out, the Baldwin

Government 'unconsciously proved Keynes right'.[15] By the second half of the 1930s, rearmament provided the public investment. The downward spiral was reversed, but the lessons of the Great Depression were not forgotten.

Better or worse?

If the 1930s were years of great deprivation and misery for some, there were also signs of development. The very depth of misery in the 'Special Areas' stimulated efforts to improve the health and social services. It is notable, for instance, that in Merthyr Tydfil and some of the towns of south Lancashire, the infant mortality rate actually went down in the 1930s, as doctors and nurses strove to counteract the effects of poverty and malnutrition.

The Poor Law was dying at last. National insurance had lifted whole classes of the population out of its reach. Despite the difficulties of operating the basic sickness and unemployment scheme introduced in 1911, the Widows Orphans and Old Age Pensions Act of 1925 had introduced new contributory schemes to cover the risks of bereavement and old age. Though there were gaps and anomalies in state pension schemes, they guaranteed a minimum income to most working class people. Improvements in health services, housing and education were all contributing to a better society.

The Local Government Act of 1929 finally transferred the remaining Poor Law functions to committees of the county and county borough councils, ending the rule of the Guardians. They were permitted to have up to one-third co-opted members, allowing for the recruitment of local expertise, and some of the co-opted members were to be women. There were to be sub-committees for various purposes – Finance and General Purposes, Institutions, District Assistance (out-relief) and so on. Institutions were to be regularly inspected.

The complementary Poor Law Act of 1930 at last renamed the service as 'Public Assistance'. Paupers became 'rate-aided persons', and workhouses became 'Public Assistance Institutions'. A Public Assistance Service was set up, with examinations and regular opportunities for promotion, on the lines proposed by the Majority Report of 1909. There was, however, no provision for the voluntary services to take on the 'deserving' cases: the Goschen Minute had

had its day, and Public Assistance no longer attempted to distinguish between the 'deserving' and the 'undeserving'.

But though a Public Assistance service was still necessary to deal with residual poverty, successive governments were concerned to decrease its scope. The Unemployment Assistance Act of 1934 made separate provision for the long-term unemployed. The Blind Persons Act of 1938, which made special provision for blind people mandatory, revealingly specified that it should be 'not by way of the Poor Law'. Bernard Wickwar, who published a textbook on the Social Services in 1936, wrote about 'The Rump Poor Law', and looked forward to the demise of the 'two-headed monstrosity' which did not meet the needs either of those fit for work or of those who could not work.[16]

Seebohm Rowntree, by this time over 60, decided to undertake a second study of York:

> In 1935, I determined to repeat the investigation made in 1899, and to find out what changes had occurred in the living conditions of the workers during the thirty-six years which had elapsed since my previous investigation was made ... in every well-conducted business, a balance-sheet based on a physical stock-taking is prepared periodically: if this were not done, it would be impossible accurately to assess the measure of success which had been obtained.[17]

Again he carried out a house-to-house investigation, covering 16,362 families 'comprising practically every working-class family in York'. He had been told about the technique of random sampling, but was not certain that it would produce accurate results, so he had every family investigated, and then drew samples of one in ten, one in twenty, one in thirty, one in forty and one in fifty from his data to see if the results tallied. His conclusions were that sampling was reasonably accurate if applied to large populations, but that it produced substantial inaccuracies when applied to smaller sub-samples.[18] He employed seven investigators 'on whose work full reliance could be placed', questioned them closely on their returns each week, and instituted check visits to verify their data.

It was extremely difficult to make comparisons over nearly four decades – so much had changed. This time, Rowntree fixed the

Poverty Line at 43s. 6d. a week for a man, wife and three children. He found that 31.1 per cent of his defined 'working class population' lived below this level, and that 14.2 per cent had less than 33s. 6d. a week. For this latter group, more than half the total income was made up of state benefits – health insurance, unemployment insurance, pensions, Public Assistance. Unemployment accounted for nearly half of the most extreme poverty in the city. The chief causes of poverty were inadequate wages, the unemployment of the chief wage earner, and old age; but there was a paradox in that the increased numbers of old people in poverty actually represented social advance: old people lived longer, and more were able to live alone:

> Today ... such people can manage to live, though in primary poverty, on their state pensions, often supplemented by a grant from the Public Assistance Committee, and by some additional source of private income. A few, for instance, keep a lodger, others earn a few pence or are paid in kind for rendering small services. To 'mind the baby' for a neighbour while the mother is out, or to wheel a pram on washday and do any necessary errand, will probably mean a square meal or a 'mash of tea' and some coppers, as well as discarded garments, if the neighbour's husband is in good work.[19]

Another and less encouraging reason for the increased numbers of old people in poverty was that, in time of mass unemployment, employers would use the excuse of the pension to dismiss a worker of pensionable age. In 1899, there had been a high demand for workers, and because there was no state pension then, employers had usually allowed those who wanted to continue working to do so.

People were drinking less than in 1899, Rowntree observed, because there were other leisure attractions. 'Cinema, wireless, bicycles ... excellent roads, free libraries ... cheap books, parks and public gardens, swimming baths, cheap railway facilities, 5,000 houses with gardens, a first-rate repertory theatre and a music hall, both with seats at low prices, adult educational classes and an educational settlement. It is an amazing list!'[20] He noted, but did not understand, the 'craze for gambling', particularly the football pools. On the whole, he thought that the standard of living was about 30 per cent higher than in 1899, but his rather convoluted statistical exercises do not really provide a firm basis for this estimate. The only figure he was prepared to stand by was his figure for primary poverty. In 1899, this had been 15.46 per cent of his sample. In 1936, it was 6.8 per cent. In York, the main causes of improvement were a reduction in the size of the average family, an increase in real wages, and the growth of social services; but Rowntree still found 'social ills to be diagnosed'. He might have found more if he had conducted his study in one of the 'Special Areas'.

In 1937, PEP (Political and Economic Planning, one of the leading social research organizations of the day) produced its own national reports on the state of the Social Services and the Health Services. The Social Services report described Public Assistance as 'the last resort', accounting for only 12 per cent of total expenditure on public social services. The main recipients were as follows:

age	number of persons	per cent of age-group
0 – 15	460,030	4.6
16 – 64	640,289	2.3
65 plus	287,401	8.7

Table 9.2. *Persons in receipt of Public Assistance, 1 January 1936*
Source: PEP Report on the Social Services, 1937, p. 144.

Of the 16–64 age-group receiving public assistance, slightly over one-third were physically or mentally unfit; but in the 65 plus age-group, nearly 90 per cent were unfit. There was still a substantial amount of need among old people – and it could hardly be argued that they should stay within the scope of the Poor Law when steps had been taken to provide a less stigmatized service for long-term unemployed and blind people.

PEP concluded that much had been done, but in a pragmatic and incremental way which meant that the principles had not really been examined. There were many anomalies, particularly in the operation of the Unemployment Assistance Board and the local authority Public Assistance Committees. UAB and PAC served the same need, but the UAB's service was available only to an arbitrarily defined sector of the population – able-bodied unemployed who earned less than £250 a year when in employment, and who had been in insurable occupations. The result was that, if a man earning £6 a week became unemployed, he would have to go to the PAC, while his office boy would come within the scope of the UAB. When families were considered, the anomalies increased; for the UAB was only concerned with workers, not with their wives and children. If a man covered by the insurance scheme was unemployed and ran out of benefit, he could claim from the UAB; but if his wife became ill, the PAC would have to provide for her and the children. What purpose was served by having two poverty services with different scales and different discretionary rules?

The administration was little short of chaotic; for the Public Assistance Service was responsible through the local authorities to the Ministry of Health (set up in 1919 to replace the old Local Government Board: it had taken nearly fifty years for health interests to defeat Poor Law interests at central government level); but unemployment assistance was administered by a central organization, the UAB, with its own local offices; contributory old age pensions were administered by the Ministry of Health through the Post Office, but the non-contributory pension started in 1908 was still administered by the Department of Customs and Excise.

So there was a mass of provision, but there were too many ill-defined agencies, and many people were not provided for. The next step was rationalization:

> We attach great importance to the emergence of a mature philosophy and a broad strategy of the social services which can take the place of piecemeal political and administrative improvisations.[21]

The Report on the Health Services pointed out that the health insurance scheme created 'wide and irrational divergencies' consequent on the different benefits offered by different friendly societies. Since the scheme did not extend to dependents, it covered 'barely half of the ill-health risk of those contributing to it'; and since only employed people were eligible, the self-employed, such as small shopkeepers and traders, had no cover.

PEP was concerned to study the economics of ill-health:

Many of the costs of ill-health cannot be measured in money. The subjective element in the endurance of pain and sickness cannot be estimated . . . but the cost of treatment and maintenance of sick persons is susceptible to measurement in money; it would also be possible, if data were available, to put a money value on the work lost through sickness absence from regular employment.[22]

The money value of work lost was estimated, after tentative calculations, at £285 million a year. Expenditure on preventive services came to no more than £117 million a year, and the expenditure on medical research was 'possibly one-fifth of one per cent of the natural expenditure and wastage through ill-health'.[23] What was needed was a health service, which would maintain people fit for work, rather than a sickness service, which dealt with ill-health after it had occurred:

Millions of pounds are spent in looking after and trying to cure the victims of accidents and illnesses which need never have occurred if a fraction of this amount of intelligence and money had been devoted to tracing the social and economic causes of the trouble.[24]

War was to be the rationalizer of a confused situation, and the philosophy came from that long-term student of social insurance and the labour market, Sir William Beveridge.

TEN

War, Peace and the Beveridge Plan

The Second World War changed the face of Britain. The Boer War had been comfortably distant. The war of 1914–1918 had involved rationing and shortages and price rises, and a few desultory air raids, but most of the action had been in the Flanders trenches; but after the 'phoney war' of 1939–1940, in which nothing very much seemed to change, the whole population was virtually on active service. There was conscription – from 1941, for women as well as men. Street signs and road signs disappeared, lest they should guide the invaders, and the country was plunged into darkness. London and other major cities were bombed nightly for long periods. The civilian population grew used to spending its nights in air raid shelters – the Anderson shelter, made of corrugated iron, had to be erected in a hole dug in the garden; the later Morrison shelter, about two feet high, fitted under the dining-room or kitchen table. In London, more old people died as a result of falling down in the black-out than were killed in air raids (one of the reasons for the formation of the National Old People's Welfare Association, now Age Concern). Children were evacuated from the cities, to live with strangers in unfamiliar environments. Some came back, in spite of the bombs, because family ties were stronger than fear. Hospital beds, particularly those for chronic patients, were hastily emptied, and the Emergency Medical Service took over about half the country's hospital accommodation for war casualties. Exhausted doctors and nurses often worked round the clock. Four million paper coffins were prepared for the victims of air attack – most of them, fortunately, remained unused.

The British troops came scrambling back from Dunkirk in 1940, and France fell. Air raid wardens, a new and sometimes authoritarian breed, enforced the black-out and spoke of the 'Red Alert' which would signal a massive German invasion. Much of the adult population was in uniform, and the uniforms of other nations (Free French, Canadians, Norwegians, Danes, the United States and many others) were to be seen on the streets. Life was frequently boring and intermittently frightening, and there were shortages of everything – food, even bread and potatoes, clothes, transport, accommodation; but the problems were not the problems of the 1930s. Unemployment disappeared by 1941, and the 'Special Areas' no longer existed.

War and social policy

The history of social policy in the Second World War, written in meticulous detail by Richard Titmuss, concentrates on three themes: the evacuation of nearly four million mothers and children, the care of the homeless, and the Emergency Medical Service. Titmuss concluded:

> By the end of the Second World War, Government had, through the agency of newly established or existing services, assumed and developed a measure of direct concern for the health and well-being of the population which, by contrast with the role of Government in the nineteen-thirties, was little short of remarkable. ... it was increasingly regarded as a proper function or even obligation of Government to ward off distress and strain among not only the poor, but almost all classes of society.[1]

This had not happened in any planned or ordered sequence, and was not always the result of deliberate intent; but social values changed, particularly after Dunkirk. 'If dangers were to be shared, then resources should also be shared'. War had unexpectedly turned out to be 'a great engine of social advance'. There was a new altruism, and a new passion for social justice.

It is certainly the case that the common experience of privation and danger did much to heal the gap between the social classes; and that from this new sense of 'community' came the demand for a more open and egalitarian society. In the Forces, men and women of very different social backgrounds were brought together, and often shared devastating experiences. Evacuation took children out of the slums – the 'unkempt, ill-clothed, under-nourished and often incontinent children of bombed cities',[2] and prodded the conscience of the well-to-do in the more peaceful rural areas. People accepted an unprecedented degree of government intervention in their lives – conscription, direction of labour, having troops and children billeted in their homes, the compulsory takeover of land and property, Excess Profits Tax – for the sake of winning the war; but it is doubtful whether the wartime experience alone is sufficient to explain the Khaki Election of 1945, when Winston Churchill was summarily swept from power, and a Labour Government with a large majority set about creating a 'Welfare State'.

The demand for a reconstruction policy started early in the war. A Post-War Problems Committee of the Conservative Party, chaired by R. A. Butler, was meeting as early as the summer of 1941, and a minister of state with responsibility for reconstruction was appointed in the same year. The demand and the response came less out of wartime experience, which was then of under two years' duration, than out of the still recent memories of the 1930s. One generation of men had fought a war, and had been promised 'Homes for Heroes'. Those promises had not been kept. There was a grim determination that this should not happen again. Politicians who wanted to mobilize effort for victory could only call on the people to make sacrifices if they demonstrated clearly that new promises would be made, and that this time they would be fulfilled.

The Labour Party, though not officially in power, was in a position to campaign for new and more egalitarian social provision. From May 1940, Churchill headed a Coalition Government in which Labour politicians, including Clement Attlee, Ernest Bevin and Herbert Morrison held office. Attlee was deputy Prime Minister. Though membership of the Coalition had the effect of somewhat stifling criticism of the conduct of the war, it gave the Labour politicians a position from which to begin planning for peace. They had the support of William Temple, Archbishop of York until 1941 and then Archbishop of Canterbury, whose paperback, *Christianity and the Social Order*, was a best-seller.

Temple presided over the Malvern Conference of 1941, which remains a basic statement of the Christian view of social justice. He argued that the private ownership of major resources was a stumbling-block to the development of a truly Christian society. Professor Arthur Marwick, who has specialized in the impact of two world wars on British life and thought, describes how the centre movements of the 1930s 'sand-blasted by war, began to take on a much harder political edge, eventually going into service on behalf of the Labour Party';[3] but the primary motive which powered the move to Labour was not a love of collectivism. By 1945, most people had had enough of barracks, barbed wire and taking orders, and there was an overwhelming desire for individual freedom and small-scale family life. It was not even a desire for Socialism as such. It was the spirit of 'never again'. Pauline Gregg notes, 'the German war was over. Domestic issues were uppermost in people's minds – the events of 1918–39 rather than of 1939–45. The Election was a challenge to all the Governments of the past unhappy twenty years'.[4] Fraser comes to a similar conclusion: 'The nation was expressing an opinion not on the previous five years, but on the decade before that'.[5]

Two services which had dominated the social provision of the 1930s had undergone fundamental changes due to war conditions. The Poor Law had disappeared at last. In 1940, the Unemployment Assistance Board, which was no longer needed, gave way to the Assistance Board, which catered for a very different type of client. Among the categories of people who needed emergency help in wartime were such previously unthought-of categories as seaside landladies (put out of business when defence regulations put the coastal areas facing Europe out of bounds to civilians), people who were bombed out, and arrived with no possessions of any kind; and refugees from Europe. When Norway was about to fall to the German advance, the entire fishing fleet from Bergen sailed for England – and arrived unannounced in Blackpool. Wartime needs were sudden and urgent. They had nothing to do with the pre-war debate about the nature of poverty.

In 1940, the Household Means Test, which had aroused so much opposition, was replaced by a personal Means Test. The immediate reason for this was that families were broken up by conscription and the direction of labour, and many people were living in 'scrambled' households. To amalgamate the income of the householder with that of billetees and lodgers would have resulted in obvious injustice. Similarly the patchy provision of hospital and health services could never be the same again. Private, voluntary and local authority hospitals had been arbitrarily merged in the Emergency Medical Service. Many mental hospitals had been taken over – their most disturbed patients confined to a few wards while the rest of the accommodation was used for military or civilian war casualties. The process of amalgamation swept aside many existing barriers. Former Harley Street specialists were working side by side with colleagues from the Public Assistance Service, psychiatrists with colleagues in general medicine, consultants with general practitioners. If the needs were acute, and the services stretched to the limit, the destruction of the organizational frontiers between different kinds of medical care held promise for the future.

Wartime shortages led to many extensions in social services. School meals and milk were universally provided – no longer a relief measure for low-income families, but a basic social service for all children. There were special services for expectant mothers – orange juice, vitamins, cod liver oil, which led to an unusually healthy crop of babies, but in wartime, babies were scarce, and they and the schoolchildren represented the future of the race. There was a massive expansion in nursery provision, so that mothers could work in factories or on the land – a policy which was fairly rapidly put into reverse when the war was over and the men came home.

But if the war accelerated social change, it also distorted it. Wartime social values tend to be primitive: the fighting services come first, the back-up services, such as coal mining, heavy engineering and armaments manufacture second, children (the next generation of the fighting and back-up services) and by extension their mothers third, and the rest of the population nowhere. This set of priorities was exactly reflected in food rationing. The Forces got comparatively large allocations. Miners got an extra cheese ration (for protein); children got the occasional egg, and the first bananas and oranges when the war was over; expectant mothers were given their special supplies. Old people got only an extra tea ration.

War meant a return to tribal priorities, because all aspects of social life were necessarily subordinated to the war effort. The comforting picture of an England united in community spirit, class barriers swept aside, preparing for the brave new world, may owe more to the efforts of the Ministry of Information than to reality. Certainly the chronic sick, the disabled and the infirm elderly came very low down on the list of priorities. But there was a desire to plan for a better society when the war was over, and the wartime Coalition Government was aware of it. If great sacrifices were called for, it was necessary to demonstrate that this time they would be rewarded.

The Beveridge Report

When Arthur Greenwood, a Labour member of the Cabinet, took over responsibility for 'social reconstruction', the Trades Union Congress pressed him for a review of policies for national insurance, and an inter-departmental committee of civil servants was set up. Sir William Beveridge, Master of University College, Oxford, and former Director of the London School of Economics, who had spent much of his earlier life in the Civil Service working on insurance problems, was appointed as chairman, charged with the apparently innocuous task of rationalizing social insurance provisions. Beveridge saw his opportunity, and took it.

The final Beveridge Report is printed as 'by Sir William Beveridge'. Though much of the background work was done by other individuals, he explained in the Report why he alone took responsibility for it:

All the members of the Committee other than the Chairman are civil servants. Many of the matters deal with in the Report raise questions of policy, on which it would be inappropriate for any civil servant to express an opinion except on behalf of the Minister to whom he is responsible; some of these matters are so important as to call for decision by the Government as a whole.[6]

Beveridge was determined to set out a far-reaching plan for postwar social security which went far beyond his terms of reference. Greenwood took the decision to allow Beveridge to put his plan in full – and thereby set the framework for a 'Welfare State'.

The plan was an astonishing mixture of social vision and practical realism. Beveridge started from three guiding principles:

1. Any proposals made were to take account of the experience of the past, but to ignore sectional interests. Beveridge could remember the negotiations over the National Insurance Act of 1911, which was very much an affair of pressure groups, and the uneasy compromises with the approved societies and the doctors. 'Now, when war is abolishing landmarks of every kind, is the opportunity for using experience in a clear field'.

2. There were five 'giants on the road to reconstruction': Want, Disease, Ignorance, Squalor and Idleness. The plan which followed was designed to attack Want and provide income security; but this was to be seen as 'one part only of a comprehensive policy of social progress'.

3. Social security should be achieved by co-operation between the state and the individual. The state would provide 'security for service and contribution'; but this would be a national minimum, on which individuals might secure extra protection for themselves and their families through voluntary contributions. The state plan would provide benefits 'as of right and without means test' so that 'individuals may build freely upon it'.

In this third section, Beveridge was doing three things: he was trying to mark the end of the Victorian view of charity; he was assuring the commercial insurance companies that they would not be put out of business by an extension of state schemes; and he was stating a Liberal principle of freedom of individual choice.

The scheme for the abolition of Want was carefully set out in a form which would make it easy for the public to retain and recall. Numbers helped with the mnemonics. There were six fundamental principles of social security, six classes of the population to be covered, and eight primary causes of need to be remedied.

The six fundamental principles[7] were adequacy of benefit; flat rate of benefit; flat rate of contribution; unification of administrative responsibility; comprehensiveness; and classification. The rate of benefit would be adequate for the ordinary needs of living, and it would be the same for all causes of the interruption of earnings – unemployment, sickness, disability, maternity, widowhood, retirement. The contributions would be on a flat rate, irrespective of income, and not income-related: this preserved the insurance element, and prevented the scheme from becoming 'an income tax assigned to a particular service'. There would be one Social

Insurance Fund, with local offices. Individuals would pay a single contribution weekly.

'Comprehensiveness' meant that the scheme should provide for all the basic and predictable needs of the population. 'It should not leave either to National Assistance or to voluntary insurance any risk so general and so uniform that social insurance can be justified'.

'Classification'[8] meant that the scheme should provide for the needs of all sections of the population – employed and self-employed, housewives without paid employment, others of working age, those too young or too old to earn. These made up the six classes of the population. The ways in which they were to be given insurance coverage, and the needs covered, were carefully tabulated. The needs of the different classes would vary – for example, a self-employed person would not be eligible for unemployment benefit, but would need coverage against disability; a full-time housewife would not be covered for disability, but would have cover for 'special needs arising out of marriage', such as childbirth and widowhood.

The eight Primary Causes of Need and the provision for each [9] are listed in Table 10.1. They were a direct extension from the work of Booth and Rowntree on the causes of poverty. (Seebohm Rowntree was one of Beveridge's advisers).

Need	Provision
Unemployment	unemployment benefit
Disability	disability benefit or industrial pension
Loss of livelihood	training benefit
Retirement	retirement pension
Marriage needs of a woman	marriage grant maternity grant maternity allowance maternity benefit widow's benefit guardian benefit
Funeral expenses	funeral grant
Childhood	children's allowances
Illness, disability	medical treatment and rehabilitation

Table 10.1. *Beveridge's proposals for meeting the Eight Primary Causes of Need*

The retirement pension would be payable at the age of 60 for women, 65 for men; but the cost of retirement pensions was estimated to be heavy, and those nearing retirement at the time of the introduction of the scheme would not have paid enough in contributions to qualify for the new increased benefits. Beveridge therefore proposed that there should be a twenty-year period over which benefits would be scaled up to full value. He also introduced an incentive for people of pensionable age to continue in work after their official retirement date. Those who were fit to do so and wanted to go on working would continue to pay contributions, and would receive a higher rate of benefit when they finally retired.

The 'marriage needs of a woman' were carefully thought out. At this time, there were estimated to be 9.3 million 'housewives', and only 1.4 million women of working age in paid employment. There was to be a grant on marriage (presumably for setting up house); a grant for the birth of a child; a maternity allowance for women confined at home; [10] and thirteen weeks of maternity benefit at the full benefit rate for women in paid employment, who could claim in their own right.

Beveridge recognized that widowhood was a severe financial blow to many women, but he wanted to avoid what was widely regarded as a mistaken policy introduced by the Widows, Orphans and Old Age Pensions Act of 1925. That Act introduced a pension of ten shillings a week, payable on the husband's contributions, for any woman who was widowed before she reached her own retirement age. Though the pension could be lost if she remarried or cohabited with another man, there was no lower age limit. Some 'ten-shilling widows', widowed in their twenties or even their teens, were entitled to claim for the rest of their lives. Beveridge's conclusion was that this was inappropriate – the amount was too small, and the period too long. If a woman was young enough and fit enough to work, it would be better for her to re-train and find employment after a period of adjustment. He recommended that widows should receive the full benefit rate for thirteen weeks. After that, there would be guardian benefit for a widow with dependent children at home. Other widows under the age of 55 would be expected to seek employment in their own interest, and if necessary to take a training course (with re-training benefit at the standard rate). Those of 55 and over would be treated as though they had reached the pensionable age of 60.

From his involvement with the approved societies and commercial insurance, Beveridge knew of the importance which many working-class people still attached to a 'proper' funeral, and how many took out a small policy and paid contributions all their lives to avoid being buried 'on the parish'. He thought that this was a predictable need, and one of deep emotional content. Accordingly, he proposed scales which would provide for a decent, plain funeral. This was only to apply to people under the age of 60 at the time the scheme was implemented, to keep the cost down.

The last two categories of need – childhood and illness – brought the subject into the contentious area of Beveridge's three basic assumptions.[11] These were:

A. Children's allowances.
B. A comprehensive Health Service.
C. Full Employment.

It is easy to appreciate why Beveridge argued that these provisions were essential to the success of his social insurance scheme. The campaign for family allowances, which arose out of the findings of Booth and Rowntree, had a long history, and is chiefly associated with the name of Eleanor Rathbone.[12] An allowance scheme would ensure some relationship between family size and family income. The Health Service would be both preventive and curative: 'it is a logical corollary to the payment of high benefits in disability that determined efforts should be made by the state to reduce the number of cases for which benefit is needed'. The argument for full employment took a similar line: 'unemployment, both through increasing expenditure on benefit and through reducing the income to bear those costs, is the worst form of waste'. Mass unemployment was demoralizing to the fit; it prevented those with partial disabilities from having 'a happy and useful career'; it gave the sick no encouragement to get well; it wasted national resources in labour; and it placed an impossible strain on any insurance scheme.

Unemployment could not be entirely avoided: there would always be some 'irregularities of work' resulting from trade conditions – what is now called 'frictional unemployment'; but Beveridge estimated that this should not affect more than 8.5 per cent of the insured workforce at any one time, and that it should be temporary in nature. 'It should be possible to make unemployment of any individual for more than 26 weeks continuously a rare thing'.

The Beveridge Report was published in December 1942 – just before Christmas, and only weeks after the Battle of El Alamein, which was the turning point in the Desert War in North Africa. Winston Churchill, with his flair for a popular and dramatic act, ordered that all the church bells should be rung to celebrate victory. The significance of this was that church bells all over Britain had been silenced since September 1939 – they were only to be rung to sound the alarm in the event of a German invasion; but now the threat of invasion was past, the bells could be used for their proper purpose, and there was a new mood: victory was possible, the war could be ended, and planning for peace could begin in earnest. Beveridge's report came out at exactly the right time.

The popular Press, coining a phrase, spoke of Social Security 'from the cradle to the grave'. There was immediate recognition that the report was a blueprint for a new and more egalitarian Britain, which could heal the scars of war and the older but enduring scars of the thirties. Beveridge (who can still sometimes be seen in a televised film clip, small and spare, explaining in precise terms the logic and common sense of his plans) became a national hero. From that time on, Beveridge's plans, and Beveridge's assumptions, were firmly written into the political agenda.

The Conservative Party tended to regard the report as unrealistic. Winston Churchill thought that no energy could be spared from the task of winning the war, and was wary of 'false hopes and airy visions of Utopia and El Dorado'.

I have so far refrained from making promises about the future. We shall all do our best, and we shall do it much better if we are not hampered by a cloud of pledges and promises which arise out of the hopeful and genial side of man's nature, and are not brought into relation with the hard facts of reality.[13]

Though this reaction has been much quoted, it should be said in fairness that Churchill was heavily preoccupied at the time – he was about to leave for Casablanca, and a crucial conference with Roosevelt and Stalin about the conduct of the war. But later, having read the scheme in detail, he concluded that it constituted 'an essential part of any post-war scheme of betterment'.[14] Could Churchill – could the Conservatives – be trusted? Some alarm was created in the Forces, when the Army Bureau of Current Affairs issued Beveridge's own summary of the Report, and then withdrew it two days later on orders from the War Office.[15] It was three months before the Report was debated by the House of Commons, and then Members of Parliament were invited only to receive and 'welcome' the document. There were no proposals for action, though Labour members moved (and lost) an amendment calling for implementation. The Coalition Government held together for the purpose of winning the war, but was deeply divided on party lines about plans for peace.

Beveridge was to entitle his autobiography *Power and Influence*. His influence was far-reaching, but the power soon passed into other hands. Despite his popularity in the country, and his growing international reputation, he writes that 'While the British people and the free world outside Britain were applauding the Beveridge Report, the Government of Britain, other than the Minister of Information, showed to the report an attitude of marked reserve, and to its author an attitude which developed from ignoring him into boycott'.[16] The one person in Government who supported Beveridge was Brendan Bracken, the Minister of Information, who saw the immense potential of the Report as a weapon in the battle for morale; but when Beveridge asked to see Churchill, the Prime Minister was 'too busy' to see him (again, there were reasons: he was suffering from pneumonia at the time). When a woman Member of Parliament asked Churchill in the House whether Beveridge was being consulted on the implementation of his plans, the reply was brief – 'No, sir'. The question was repeated in an unmistakably feminine voice, and the reply came again – 'No, sir'.[17]

Beveridge went on to write a book on Keynesian lines – *Full Employment in a Free Society* (1944); but the Government refused him official co-operation even from officials he had previously worked with, and succeeded in reducing the impact of this second report by publishing its own version first. Beveridge felt 'like a small boy racing a railway train.[18] Power had escaped him, though his influence was to endure for many decades and to reach many countries.

Public Debate

The Minister for Reconstruction was now Lord Woolton, a Conservative peer. In the aftermath of the Beveridge Report, government departments began to produce their own plans for reconstruction; but if the original intention had been to take the steam out of the Beveridge proposals, it was soon modified. The plans, in response to public opinion and the logic of the situation, became steadily more progressive. The so-called 'White Paper Chase' of 1943–1945[19] included White Papers on the plans for a National Health Service, education, social insurance and assistance, the location of industry, planning for the countryside, land tenure, and other policy issues. These will be discussed later in relation to subsequent legislation.

This was open government: the White Papers and explanatory pamphlets were sold on every bookstall, and discussed by groups all over the country, and wherever in the world the Armed Forces were based. In the days before television, and at a time when the radio was used mainly for urgent news broadcasts, a main method of dissemination was through adult education groups. The Army Bureau of Current Affairs, undismayed by its experience over the Beveridge Report, published over fifty pamphlets of its own which were used by Forces education and discussion groups. The Workers' Educational Association had a national network of classes attended by a wide cross-section of people – teachers, doctors, local authority administrators, railway workers, miners, housewives, factory workers and many others. Each group had its 'book box'. 'Current Affairs' or 'Social Reconstruction' was easily the most popular subject in the last years of the war, and the book boxes contained the Beveridge Report and the White Papers straight from the Stationery Office. University Extra-Mural Departments ran longer and more academic classes on similar subjects.

Never before or since has there been so much committed public debate in Britain about the shape of social policy. Perhaps there was not much else in the way of popular entertainment; but week by week, groups of up to fifty or sixty people met all over Britain in pubs and chapels and school halls, braving the blackout and sometimes the bombs to discuss subjects such as 'Are the Social Insurance proposals fair to widows – to retired people – to the disabled?' 'Flats or Houses?' 'Will the doctors join a Health

Service?' 'Do we want a tripartite Education Service?' 'Can unemployment really be cured?' The Beveridge Report had been the first stage in an irresistible process.

It is important to note that three major social measures – the Education Act of 1944, the Disabled Persons Employment Act of 1944 and the Family Allowances Act of 1945 – were sponsored by the Coalition Government, and passed when there was a Conservative majority in the House of Commons. Some 'Welfare State' legislation was backed by all three major political parties (Beveridge was a Liberal); but the return of a Labour Government in the 'Khaki Election' of 1945, it was believed largely on an overwhelming anti-Conservative Forces vote, ensured that the policies would be whole-heartedly implemented.

This was the first General Election for ten years – the last had put the Baldwin Government into power in 1935. It was a new world.

ELEVEN
Setting up the 'Welfare State'

In the years 1944–1949, Beveridge's 'Five Giants' were systematically tackled by legislation. The Labour Government was convinced, in Hugh Dalton's words, that it was 'walking with Destiny',[1] and despite all the problems of moving from a wartime economy to a peacetime economy, it put the creation of a new and more egalitarian social order at the top of the political agenda.

Many city centres were in ruins. The factories had to turn from heavy engineering to the production of consumer goods. The troops had to be brought home from Europe and the Far East, and demobilized. The task of rebuilding took place at every level, from the international and national levels to the rebuilding of the lives of individual families, as men and women separated by war were reunited, sought jobs and homes, set up house, and had their postponed families. The birth-rate soared – and so did the divorce rate, as some hasty wartime marriages failed to survive the transition. Everything was in short supply; but gradually, the basis for post-war England was established on the lines which Beveridge had planned.

Whether those plans would have been carried through with the same vigour if Winston Churchill had remained Prime Minister must be a matter for conjecture. The young Churchill had worked with Lloyd George on health and unemployment insurance, and set William Beveridge to work on labour exchanges in the early years of the century. The older Churchill had seen the need for post-war planning, and had suggested the compiling of a 'book of

Figure VI Live births per thousand population, United Kingdom 1939–1951
Source: *Annual Abstract of Statistics*, 1952, table 15.

the transition' for the move to peacetime conditions; but he had insisted that the war must be won first, and he was deeply distrusted by a radical electorate which had bitter memories of the Conservative governments of the 1930s.

His successor, Clement Attlee, was almost tailor-made for the task of bringing a 'welfare state' into being. As a young lawyer, he had given free legal advice to clients at Toynbee Hall. He was secretary to Sidney and Beatrice Webb's National Committee for the Prevention of Destitution, set up in 1909 to campaign for the Minority Report. He had been a Lecturer in Social Science and Administration at the London School of Economics when Beveridge was the Director. This 'sensitive, sincere, shy ... self-effacing, somewhat chilly little man' according to one American commentator[2] had very clear ideas on the policy which a Labour Government ought to follow:

> Our policy was not a reformed capitalism, but progress towards a democratic socialism ... the war had shown how much could be accomplished when public advantage was put before private vested interest. If that was right in war-time, it was right in peace-time.[3]

So, in the period of Attlee's premiership, Beveridge's plan and Beveridge's assumptions were translated into a statutory framework for defeating the 'Five Giants'.

Want

In 1944, the Ministry of Reconstruction had issued two White Papers on Social Insurance.[4] Both were summarized in a pamphlet, price 3d, which was probably one of the most successful exercises in communication between a government and its people. Graphics and scaled diagrams were used to illustrate a complex scheme in which all would take part, and which all would be able to understand.

The Family Allowances Act, 1945, introduced an allowance of 5s. a week for every child under the age of 16 except the first. This limitation was a way of restricting the cost at a time when a great many first babies were being born. It was assumed that a young couple could maintain the first baby, and that the state contribution need not begin until they produced the second. Many organizations were swift to point out that the first child was the expensive one: most working women gave up work before the first baby was born, so the family was dependent on one income rather than two. The pram, the cot and the baby clothes had to be purchased for this baby – they could always be passed on for subsequent children. Family allowances for the first child were not introduced until April 1977.

The National Insurance Act 1946, introduced 'an extended scheme of national insurance providing pecuniary payments by way of unemployment benefit, sickness benefit, maternity benefit, retirement pension, widow's benefit, guardian's allowance and death grant'. All Beveridge's principles were accepted. The only modifications were that the marriage grant was omitted (at a time when the marriage rate was high, this must have seemed an unnecessary inducement to matrimony); the retirement pension was to be paid in full from the beginning of the scheme, instead of being scaled up over a period of twenty years; and the central authority was the Ministry of Pensions and National Insurance (MPNI), not a Ministry of Social Security. In 1946 and the following years, war pensions to the disabled were of great importance. It was decided that the Assistance scheme should be

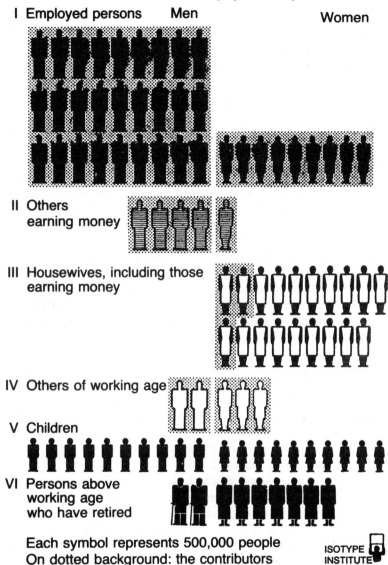

Each symbol represents 500,000 people
On dotted background: the contributors

ISOTYPE
INSTITUTE

Figure VII The Six Classes of the Population in the Social Insurance Proposals of 1944.
Source:Social Insurance: Brief Guide to the Government's Plan, issued by the Minister of Reconstruction, HMSO, 1944.
Note: This popular version of the Plan cost 3d. Note the Isotype technique for the presentation of statistics.

separately administered, like the Unemployment Assistance Board of the 1930s, to keep the topic out of politics.

Unlike commercial insurance, the insurance scheme was not financially watertight: money was to be paid in from the Exchequer and the Reserve Fund, and part of the individual's contribution was to be paid into the fund for the new National Health Service; but the principle of contributions from the employee, the employer and the state was preserved, and a new principle was that the amount of benefit was to be enough 'to maintain health and working capacity'.

Schedules set down the amount of contribution and benefit in great detail: for an adult man in full employment, the initial rates of contribution were employee: 4s. 9d.; employer: 4s. 0d.; Exchequer: 1s. 1d. The balance of payment had therefore shifted from the state, which now provided only 1 per cent of the total, to the employee and employer. Every employee had an insurance card – self-employed people kept and stamped their own cards – and the benefits payable were clearly set out. The standard rate of benefit for all contingencies was 26s. a week for both sexes. For an adult dependent, there was a payment of 16s., and for a child dependent, 7s. 6d. It was relatively easy for people to calculate what their entitlement was, and what they would receive in return for contributions.

The National Assistance Act 1948 introduced complementary provisions for people who, for one reason or another, were not adequately covered by the insurance scheme. It was subtitled 'An Act to terminate the existing Poor Law' and section 1 began, 'The existing Poor Law shall cease to have effect'. The change of terminology to 'Public Assistance' in 1930 was ignored in the Labour Government's determination to sweep away a system it regarded as repugnant. Some Labour MPs, from working class families, had personal experience of its operation.

The wartime Assistance Board was replaced by a new body, the National Assistance Board. It was to 'promote the welfare' of 'persons in Great Britain who are without the resources to meet their requirements, or whose resources. . . must be supplemented to meet their requirements'. The NAB was not merely to keep recipients at a minimal subsistence level, but positively to promote their welfare; and the provisions applied irrespective of any kind of qualification except that the recipient be human, and on British soil. 'Requirements' were to be defined by the NAB, and there was provision for an appeals procedure. The grants were to be made in money. In the United States and some other countries, experiments were being made with vouchers for particular purposes, such as clothing or food; but it was decided that families were the best judge of their own needs, and that payments should be made in cash, not in kind. If some misspent the money, that was a small price to pay for the preservation of individual choice and the minimization of bureaucracy.

Under Part III of the Act, every local authority was to provide two classes of accommodation: 'residential accommodation for persons who by reason of age, infirmity or any other circumstances are in need of care and attention which is not otherwise available to them'; and 'temporary accommodation for persons who are in urgent need' (section 29). 'Part III accommodation' as it became known, was to be of a new and better standard. Aneurin Bevan introduced these clauses in the House of Commons with the words, 'The workhouse is to go'.

Part III of the Act also made provision for non-residential services: local authorities were to have 'power to make arrangements for promoting the welfare' of disabled people, including those who are blind, deaf, dumb, or otherwise handicapped. Provision could include workshops, work at home, helping in the sale of the products of such work, and the provision of recreational facilities. Local authorities might give financial support to voluntary organizations for some of these purposes.

An interesting contrast between the National Insurance Act and the National Assistance Act is in the degree of delegated legislation. The insurance scheme was set down in terms of actual sums of money, because of the heavy expenditure involved. This is still the case, and as adjustments are made in contributions and benefits, for inflation or other reasons, new legislation is necessary. Generally there is at least one National Insurance Act a year. The National Assistance scheme was intended to have much smaller financial implications (since most of the population would be eligible for insurance benefits) and the main purpose was the enabling of local authorities to develop residential and community services as required. It therefore set down principles, and left the details to be worked out.

Disease

The National Health Service Act 1946, laid down a commitment to the health of the nation in the following terms:

> It shall be the duty of the Minister of Health . . . to promote the establishment . . . of a comprehensive Health Service designed to secure improvement in the physical and mental health of the people . . . and the prevention, diagnosis and treatment of illness. . . . the services so provided shall be free of charge, except where any provision of this Act expressly provides for the making and recovery of charges (section 1).

Plans for a National Health Service had been long discussed, and involved complex issues. The main problems were the status of the large and prestigious voluntary hospitals, which were engaged in teaching and research, and were unwilling to be downgraded, as they saw it, to the status of the former Poor Law infirmaries; the interests of the local authorities, which had done much to improve these same infirmaries, and did not wish to lose jurisdiction over them; and the resistance of medical specialists and general practitioners, who wanted to preserve a degree of professional autonomy, and were unwilling to become employees in a salaried service.

Discussions and negotiations with these and other professional groups, such as opticians, dentists and nurses, began early in 1943. The Brown Plan of 1943 reputedly provided for the continued independence of the large voluntary hospitals, which would take patients from the Health Service on contract, but this plan was never published. The Willink Plan of 1944, produced by a Conservative Minister of Health and published as a White Paper,[5] set down the principle that good medical facilities should be available to all without regard for the patient's ability to pay. It was acknowledged that the existing services were fragmented and limited in scope. A national service would be set up, but both patients and doctors would be free to use it or not – there would be no compulsion. The question of whether the general practitioner service should be salaried or paid on a per capita basis was left open.

Intense public debate was in progress when the war in Europe ended, the Labour Government took office, Aneurin Bevan became Minister of Health, and the negotiations got tougher. Bevan, formerly a miner from South Wales, had his own very strong views about both the abolition of the Poor Law and the need for a National Health Service. His father, also a miner, had died from pneumoconiosis – and without compensation from the mine owners, because the condition was not then scheduled as an industrial disease.[6] The medical establishment initially regarded him as an enemy: he was to prove a highly intelligent and skilled negotiator with a thorough grasp of principle. He held long and protracted negotiations with all the interest-groups involved, chaired many committees and conferences himself, and drove a more radical scheme through with the minimum of concessions. The National Health Service Act became law in 1946, but the date when it was to come into operation was put forward to 5 July 1948. This was because new machinery had to be set up, there were major staffing implications, and it was necessary to co-ordinate the legislation with the National Insurance Act and the National Assistance Act, which had the same appointed day.

In the final plan, all types of hospitals were brought under the control of the Ministry of Health, but with two kinds of status. Most hospitals, whether previously voluntary, municipal or private, were placed under the management of Regional Hospital Boards. There were 13 RHBs, the areas being based on the 13 Civil Defence Areas set up in wartime. At a lower administrative level, hospitals were administered by Hospital Management Committees, each being responsible for a small group of hospitals in a particular area.

In an ingenious compromise, the major voluntary hospitals, which carried on most of the medical training and research, were exempted from this structure and designated 'teaching hospitals'. The basic plan was for each RHB to have one such hospital as its centre, working with a university medical school. Teaching hospitals were to work in partnership with the RHBs, but to be administered separately by Boards of Governors responsible directly to the Minister of Health. All hospitals in England and Wales were brought into the NHS apart from a few small private or charitable hospitals which were 'disclaimed' by the Minister, usually at their own request.

Consultants were to be employed by the RHB or the Board of Governors, but were allowed to work on a sessional basis which left them time for private patients. Hospital care was to be without basic charges, though there was provision for amenity beds (section 4) and private beds (section 5); but any bed set aside for private patients was to be made available if necessary for 'any patient who urgently requires accommodation on medical grounds, and for whom suitable accommodation is not otherwise available'.

Local authorities, which lost their hospitals when the Act came into force, became responsible for a consolidated range of public health services – district nursing, health visiting, midwifery, maternity and child welfare, home helps, ambulance services, vaccination and immunization. They were to organize health centres (a development strongly opposed by most general practitioners) and they acquired sweeping, if somewhat obscure powers, under section 28 of the Act, which ran:

> A local health authority may with the approval of the Minister, and to such extent as the Minister may direct shall, make arrangements for the purpose of the prevention of illness, the care of persons suffering from illness or mental defectiveness, or the after-care of such persons.

The NHS Act provided a broad framework, but allowed for a considerable degree of delegation. It left scope for the local authorities to innovate, scope for the Minister to require them to provide certain services, and scope for these services to cover any kind of care or treatment not provided by the hospital service. The section was designated to run parallel with section 29 of the National Assistance Act, described above, which gave the local authority similar powers in relation to people suffering from long-term disability or infirmity. Though the services were as yet undeveloped, these two sets of provisions provided a basis for the growth of community care.

General practice was to be administered by Executive Councils, one for each local authority area. There were separate committees for medical, dental, pharmaceutical and supplementary ophthalmic services. The national Medical Practices Committee was responsible for the provision of medical practices – designating new ones in under-doctored areas, and closing down practices in areas where in their judgement there was a surplus. General practitioners, who had previously bought and sold their practices, were compensated for the loss of right to do so. Aneurin Bevan commented on the NHS Act afterwards:

The field in which the claims of individual commercialism come into most immediate conflict with reputable notions of social values is that of health. ... Preventable pain is a blot on any society. Much sickness, and often permanent disability arise from failure to take early action, and this in its turn is due to high costs and the fear of the effects of heavy bills on the family. ... You can always 'pass by on the other side'. That may be sound economics. It could not be worse morals.[7]

Idleness

Contrary to many of the fears expressed during the war, the maintenance of full employment was not to prove a problem in post-war Britain. The Coalition Government had committed itself in the White Paper of 1944[8] to a basically Keynesian analysis. However, it was notable that, whereas Beveridge was insistent on a policy of 'full employment', the official document spoke only of 'high and stable employment'.

Government spending was high, particularly in the public sector, as the mines, the electricity and gas industries, the iron and steel industries and the railways were nationalized. There was no lack of work to be done in reconstruction, and a high employment rate was to continue through to the early 1970s. Though there were more than two million unemployed in 1947 – the main year of demobilization – they were quickly absorbed back into the workforce. Overall economic planning brought new industries to the former distressed areas. There was work for almost everyone who wanted it, and the trade cycle, which had dominated economic thinking in the 1930s, appeared to have disappeared for all time. There was considerable optimism that planning and regulation could create economic stability, and prevent the recurrence of widespread economic distress.

Ignorance

Like the NHS Act, the Education Act of 1944 was the result of long and careful consultation with professional and other interests, and similarly it steamrollered a variety of patchy provision into a national system. Free education was to be provided all the way from the nursery level, through primary school, to three kinds of secondary school and beyond, to further and higher education. The Act usually bears the name of R. A. Butler, the Conservative Minister who presided over its passage through Parliament. It was the result of protracted discussion and the work of two influential committes. The McNair Committee had formulated an ambitious plan for teacher training, including extended grants and maintenance awards for students in college, links between the training colleges and universities, and a longer and more liberal training, lasting for three years instead of two.[9] The Norwood Committee had laid down principles for secondary education for all children. Education was to be for three purposes: for work, for citizenship and for the individual – 'to help each individual to realise to the full the powers of his personality'.[10] It was recommended that the existing mix of grammar schools (fee-paying for most pupils), central schools, technical schools, commercial schools and senior elementary schools should be shaped into three kinds of secondary school available without fees: grammar schools for the more intellectually minded; technical schools for those who would benefit from a technological education, and 'secondary modern' for the rest. There was to be 'parity of esteem' between the three groups, and children would be tested and directed to an appropriate school at the age of 11.

Subsequent criticisms of the tripartite system in education and the 11+ examination have been so devastating that it is necessary to stress how advanced these proposals were at the time. Butler was a Conservative with marked Liberal leanings (perhaps that is why he narrowly failed to become Prime Minister). He believed that education was the key to a better society. In the 1930s, a few working class children had struggled through to university level by means of scholarships. Now the whole education system was to be open to all on the basis of merit. The nation would have the benefit of the best brains and talents. Individual children would be able to make the best of their ability.

The 11+ examination was to be a means of distinguishing what the planners were convinced were three basic types of ability: the academic, the technological and the practical. The Hadow Report of 1926, the Spens Report of 1938 and the Norwood Report of

1943 – all produced by committees with eminent educationalists among their numbers – had agreed that the age of 11 was the right point for a break in the educational process, and that children of different types of ability might be distinguished at that point. What was new in 1944 was the determination to give them all equality of opportunity, with parity of esteem between the different types of school.

The McNair and Norwood proposals formed the basis of a White Paper, *Educational Reconstruction*,[11], issued in 1943. The proposals had the support of all the main political parties, and formed the basis of the new law.

So the Butler Act reached the statute book even before the end of the Second World War. The three types of secondary school were specified, the Board of Education was up-graded to a Ministry, plans were laid to raise the school leaving age from 14 to 15 and eventually to 16,[12], grants were provided for further and higher education, and education became a right instead of a privilege. As Pauline Gregg comments:

> The right to organised education has been one of the most keenly fought and most cherished prizes of the working classes; every section of the British working class movement since the Industrial Revolution has claimed the right to education, and has ascribed to it a remedial quality that would help the worker to better his own material condition, raise his class socially, and introduce justice and humanity over the land ... The belief in education as a philosopher's stone was naïve, at times pathetic ... and yet it has proved a mighty warrior for the working classes, and as a social leveller, it is matched only by wealth.[13]

Squalor

The Town and Country Planning Act of 1947 was similarly the result of long deliberation and the process of political consultation with the professions. In this case, there were three key reports: Barlow, Scott and Uthwatt. The Barlow Report of 1940 on the Distribution of the Industrial Population[14] acquired a new significance as factories moved out into the rural areas, bombing destroyed the fabric of the inner cities, and major replanning became imperative. After the Beveridge Report, it was seen as the major key to the defeat of his fifth 'giant'.

Sir Montagu Barlow and his colleagues had argued that the 1930s had been a period of haphazard growth, and that a small country with limited land at its disposal could not afford to continue unrestricted and unplanned building. Urban sprawl, ribbon development along main 'arterial roads', ramshackle developments of which Peacehaven in Essex was named as the prototype, could all be held in check by proper planning. The Barlow Report listed the advantages of population concentration: the proximity of production to markets, low transport costs, the availability of labour. The disadvantages were high site values in city centres, traffic jams and the steady exiling of the working population to the outer suburban areas, with consequent costs and fatigue in the daily journey to work. London and the population drain to the south-east were already special problems.

The Barlow Report argued that it was possible to achieve a balanced distribution of population. The members commended attempts which had been made before the Second World War to disperse industry and provide living accommodation within reach of work – the 'garden cities' of Welwyn and Letchworth, the satellite towns of Wythenshawe, near Manchester, and Speke, near Liverpool, the trading estates; but there was a need for a national plan. Members of the Barlow Commission differed in the degree of control which they thought necessary – the majority settled for a National Board with powers over London, with a remit which could be extended to other areas by Orders in Council. The minority wanted a Ministry with national planning powers.

The Scott Report of 1942[15] was concerned with the preservation of the countryside. While some of its recommendations (like the proposal that rural telephone boxes should be painted green instead of red, so that they might better blend with farms and fields) suggested a somewhat romantic view of country life, the basic findings were practical enough. The rural population was often assumed to have no problems. In fact, much rural housing was of a very poor quality; many people in rural areas still lacked main drainage, gas and electricity. The Scott Committee recommended that the standards which had been achieved in the towns should be extended to the country, which was underprivileged by comparison. This implied the nationalization of the essential industries, since it was improbable that private companies would go to the expense of extending supplies to sparsely populated areas. The Scott Report was also concerned with questions of rights of way and access, Green Belts round the towns, and the development of national parks, for the benefit of town dwellers and country dwellers alike.

The Uthwatt Report of 1942[16] was concerned with Compensation and Betterment: a dry title for an important subject. The Committee found that the powers of local authorities to undertake redevelopment were inadequate in view of the extent of wartime damage and the replanning which was necessary. The Uthwatt Committee recommended that local authorities should have sweeping powers of compulsory purchase – not merely for slum areas, but wherever it was necessary to replan whole areas for shopping centres, housing estates, roads and other purposes. There would be compensation for those whose property depreciated in value due to new developments such as roads or the building of new housing estates, and betterment charges against those whose property increased in value. A subsequent White Paper on land use was much debated. Of all the measures of social reform in the post-war period, this one most directly affected private property and individual ownership.

The main conclusions of Barlow, Scott and Uthwatt went into the Town and Country Planning Act of 1947. A Ministry of Town and Country Planning had already been set up in 1943 to deal with wartime land problems, and this was put on a permanent basis. All local authorities were required to prepare plans for their own areas. The Board of Trade was to approve new industrial projects, and there were to be grants and loans to attract industries to what were scheduled as Development Areas, to secure 'a proper distribution of industry'. New Towns were to be built, with full provision for work, residential areas and community life, to relieve the congestion on the cities. A National Parks Commission was set up, and the Nature Conservancy Council, which developed research on river and air pollution, litter and noise, was also established.

A Welfare State?

The social legislation of 1944–1949 was evolutionary rather than revolutionary, in the sense that it built on the legislation of the pre-war period, but made it more comprehensive and more rational. A muddle of provision which had developed empirically was replaced by a coherent network of co-ordinated services. It was the result of an unprecedented process of public discussion of a kind which was both informed (since the outstanding experts were involved in each field) and democratic. In each policy area, the process was built on past experience. Nothing was done in haste, and nothing was done without due consultation with all the interested parties. If the planners got it wrong, as they did in some instances, it was not through lack of consideration or lack of advice.

The 1940s were a period of great social idealism, and this was not confined to any one political party. All parties were united in the intention of bringing about a more secure and egalitarian society. While the return to power of the Labour Party in 1945 gave the plans a more radical impact, they were not exclusively Socialist plans. The legislation did not, of course, produce a Welfare State overnight. Getting the legislation through Parliament was only the first step, and there were major problems ahead.

TWELVE
Problems of Expansion

In the early post-war period, there was much discussion of 'Social Reconstruction'. This was not simply a matter of moving from a wartime to a peacetime footing – the aim was to create fundamental changes in the organization of society, and to heal the divisions between the social classes. Once the legislation provided the framework and the powers, there was a massive amount of detailed work to be done at both national and local level to set up the new machinery of state.

But the financial cost was high, and in setting up this new structure of services, Britain was borrowing against the future. War had left the economy in massive deficit. Britain had been virtually a front-line battle station for the Allied nations, and exports had all but ceased during the war years, while the labour force had been organized for war purposes, and was disorganized and de-skilled for the new peacetime world. President Roosevelt had promised Prime Minister Churchill a continuation of Lend-Lease (by which the United States provided Britain with consumer goods it could not produce under wartime conditions) after the end of the war to ease the transition back to peacetime conditions; but Roosevelt died, and was succeeded by Truman. Churchill was voted out of power, and was succeeded by Clement Attlee. The relationship between the American and British Governments changed abruptly from wartime collaboration to peacetime commercial trading. Barbara Castle, then a newly elected Labour MP, and later a leading Labour minister, recalls this as a direct action by the Truman administration to create difficulties for a socialist

Government in Britain, insisting that 'even ships which were already crossing the Atlantic changed their nature' as they became conveyors of goods which had to be paid for on docking rather than of a contribution from one ally to another.[1] Britain lacked hard currency, and vital supplies were involved.

So Britain faced the transition to peace and a new social order in acute financial difficulties. Food rationing had to continue, and was not finally abolished until 1951. Even bread was rationed. There were shortages of many kinds of basic commodities, the price of consumer goods soared, and taxation increased. There were repeated coal and power cuts – particularly severe in the bitterly cold winter of 1947. The Chancellor of the Exchequer, Sir Stafford Cripps, was known as 'Austerity Cripps'. The first Labour Government with a clear majority in the House of Commons started with popular support for its social programme; but by 1951, its popularity had evaporated in the face of continuing economic difficulties, and Winston Churchill was back in Downing Street. However, both Conservative and Labour governments accepted the framework of welfare legislation – it was part of the 'consensus government' which was to characterize the next forty years. There were some differences of emphasis – characteristically, Conservatives looked at cost, while Labour looked at benefits; but the battle against Beveridge's Five Giants continued.

When the new legislation came into effect in the late 1940s, the administrative implications were staggering. Boards, Committees, Advisory Councils and other bodies were created. Tens of thousands of staff had to be recruited, or transferred from old organizations to new ones, to learn new jobs and new ways of working. What was a Regional Hospital Board, and how should it function? How did the work of the Welfare Department of a local authority differ from that of Public Assistance? How did a secondary modern school differ from the senior section of an elementary school? How could the enormous and pressing need for family housing be met, when whole areas were devastated and needed to be replanned? There was no experience of such large-scale organization to draw on, and much to be learned.

Government and local authorities looked to the universities and colleges for training and research. Economists, sociologists and other social scientists found a new focus of interest, and the study of Social Policy and Administration mushroomed.[2] The new specialists devoted themselves to the study of 'social engineering' – how to develop the new services, identify the problems, and improve the quality of care. The result of this concentration of academic effort was a new flood of publishing – some of it critical, much of it impatient with the slow pace of progress; but few of the new social engineers doubted that the machine they had to tune was basically well designed.

Because this was a period of sustained high employment, 'Idleness' and 'Want' were not major problems. There was work to be had, and the National Insurance scheme was not unduly strained. Though there was a growing concern that the National Assistance scheme was not the minor service of last resort which Beveridge had envisaged (too many people, particularly old people, were claiming because benefits were below subsistence level), the scheme was viable. The other three 'giants' were more immediately resistive: in the Health Service, Town and Country Planning, and in the field of Education, there were fresh problems to be faced.

The National Health Service

The NHS initially offered a service which was 'free at the point of delivery'. Aneurin Bevan made it clear that it was not a free service, because the public paid for it through taxation and insurance. The point was that individuals did not have to pay directly when they were sick, or in proportion to the services they needed. This principle was questioned as early as 1949, when Bevan fought his Labour colleagues to prevent a small charge of one shilling on medical prescriptions, and to prevent the imposition of a financial limit on Health Service expenditure. Other Ministers complained that the NHS was 'the sacred cow' of Labour policy, since the claims of other essential services such as housing and education and investment for industry were set aside as the health costs soared. Disputes with Hugh Gaitskell, Stafford Cripps's successor as Chancellor of the Exchequer, played a major part in Bevan's resignation in 1951.[3]

Bevan argued that the high costs of the NHS were only a temporary phenomenon. The hospital and specialist service accounted for more than two-thirds of the total cost in 1950–1951. When outdated hospital premises, such as the former mental hospitals and the Public Assistance hospitals, had been brought up to an acceptable standard, and the backlog of untreated sickness had been dealt with, Britain would be a healthier nation, and costs would fall. Both Beveridge and Bevan had concentrated on the problems of making and keeping the working population fit for work, with the assumption that this would reduce absenteeism and increase national productivity.

This view was supported by the Guillebaud Committee of 1956[4] which examined NHS expenditure, and found that it had risen by 70 per cent since the introduction of the service in 1948. The conclusion was that the five years under review had been a period of inflation, and of working through short-term problems, but that there were no grounds for charges of extravagance, and the basic administrative structure of the NHS was sound.

But the opposition was gathering. The medical profession, which had assented to the scheme in 1946 with the greatest reluctance, repeatedly pressed for higher salaries, and in 1951, the British Medical Association threatened to withdraw from the NHS altogether: an eventuality which was seemingly only averted by a very large salary award in that year. Pharmaceutical costs spiralled, as they did in all countries. This was a period of great advance in pharmacology, as the antibiotics and the neuroleptic drugs were developed and refined. In 1952, the Churchill Government introduced charges for dentures and spectacles, thus breaching the principle of a service free at the point of delivery to the patient.

Right-wing critics became active. In February 1952, *The Times* published two articles on 'Crisis in the Welfare State',[5] arguing that Britain could not afford the extensive services planned in the post-war period. Two leading Conservatives, Iain Macleod and Enoch Powell, published a pamphlet[6] soon afterwards arguing that health and social services should only be provided by the state on a test of need – a view which ran completely counter to the Beveridge principles, and raised left-wing hackles about means-testing.

In the Health Service field, the political debate was both protracted and bitter. The opening attack came from John Jewkes, Professor of Economic Organisation at Oxford, who thought the problems were by no means of a temporary nature. They indicated 'a steady and continuous struggle on the part of the British Government to restrain the demand for medical services'. The choices were to restrict capital construction (in effect spending money on current account which should have been put aside for improving the infrastructure); to impose charges for specific services; or to restrict the services to special groups.[7] Jewkes, later the author of *A Return to Free Market Economics*, was followed by other free marketeers from the Institute of Economic Affairs. An influential paper was *Health Through Choice*,[8] which complained of 'a strange neglect of economic principles' in the introduction of a scheme which was free at the point of delivery, and deprecated the intervention of a third party, the state, in the relationship between doctor and patient. 'Consumer sovereignty' could be ensured only by the application of the laws of supply and demand, which meant paying directly for service received.

To this, Richard Titmuss responded by arguing that the simple laws of supply and demand could not operate in the Health Service: the patient could not exercise a free choice, because medicine had become highly technical, and he had to be able to trust his doctor; but could he trust his doctor in a free market, where the doctor–patient relationship was dominated by financial considerations? The result would be 'fee-splitting, commission-taking, canvassing, the dispensation of "secret remedies" and the employment of unqualified assistants'.[9]

The conflict between Professor Titmuss and his supporters and the Institute of Economic Affairs was to develop with considerable personal bitterness;[10] but one basic fact gradually emerged. Quite independently of the philosophical and political positions taken up by the protagonists, it became clear that the high costs of the NHS were not a temporary phenomenon, for a reason which neither Beveridge nor Bevan seems to have understood: *health services are self-expanding.* That is, the better a country's health services, the more will be needed. The reason for this is that good health services keep alive people who would otherwise die: handicapped babies survive, people who would have succumbed to the acute diseases of middle age live on to experience the chronic diseases of old age, old people live longer. Good health services do not produce a fit and healthy population overall: they produce an ageing population with a higher proportion of handicapped and infirm people.

The cynical version of this unhappy truth is the old Health Service slogan 'The only good health service is in the Congo'. Countries with very little in the way of health care for the general population can run very good acute services, because the potential population of chronic sick simply dies off. A more balanced view is that good and freely available health services do increase the national well-being. The fact that patients live on who would otherwise die is not a 'problem' but a proof of success. It is true that this success has to be paid for, and some limits have to be set to health service expenditure. However, throughout this period, Canada, the United States and Sweden spent considerably in excess of 6 per cent on health services, while Britain's expenditure remained below 5 per cent.[11]

Much of the subsequent history of the health services has been influenced by the need to preserve the acute (mainly hospital-based) services in the face of the increasing cost of advanced medical technology, while making less expensive provision outside the hospital sector for the growing volume of chronic need for care: in the main for physical and mental handicap, mental illness, and the infirmities of old age. These services, frequently neglected by local authorities before 1948, were often known as the 'Cinderella Services'. Though they achieved theoretical parity of esteem with the acute services in 1948, this was not to last. By 1962, considerations of the problems of expense and administrative fragmentation brought about a reversal of policy in which, slowly and inexorably, the care of the chronic sick was largely returned to the local authorities.

In 1962, the publication *A Hospital Plan*,[12] sponsored by Enoch Powell as Minister of Health, proposed new measures for 'the effective use of hospital beds'. Small local hospitals – the former cottage hospitals and small Public Assistance hospitals – were to be closed. Hospital care was to be increasingly concentrated in large District General Hospitals, which would offer fewer beds, but improved medical technology and expanded out-patient services. To parallel this, there would be a sharp downward revision in geriatric, mental handicap and mental illness beds. Provision for these patient groups would be developed by the local authorities.

The Hospital Plan made a major change in the function of the hospital. Previously, hospitals had been centres to which patients went when they were sick, for medical treatment and nursing care. Now the hospital function was to be diagnosis, assessment and treatment, rather than long-term care.

The results of this change have been profound. There were

sufficient medical reasons for shortening patients' length of stay in some circumstances – antibiotics reduced the risk of infection after an operation or after childbirth, and new and powerful drugs controlling mood swings, such as tranquillizers and anti-depressants, made it possible for many mentally ill and elderly confused people to sustain life in the community once a routine of medication had been established; but there has been continuing concern about the care of the chronic sick in view of the slow expansion of the community services. Attempts to pass the 'Cinderella Services' back to the local authorities in a social rather than a medical context were to create many problems. Professor Titmuss had some stinging comments to make:

> If English social history is any guide, confusion has often been the mother of complacency. In the public mind, the aspirations of reformers are transmitted by the touch of a phrase into hard-won reality. What some hope will one day exist is suddenly thought by many to exist already. All kinds of wild and unlovely weeds are changed by statutory magic and comforting appella-tions, into the most attractive flowers that bloom, not only in the spring, but all the year round.

So 'that exotic hot-house climbing rose, "The Welfare State"' was to be followed by 'the everlasting cottage trailer, "Community Care"', which would in fact have the effect of transferring chronic patients 'from trained staff to untrained or ill-equipped staff, or no staff at all'.[13]

The official plans for community care were set out in 1963 in a companion document to the *Hospital Plan*. This was entitled: *Health and Welfare: the development of community care*.[14] It lacked the conviction and force of the *Hospital Plan*, consisting only of general statements on the desirability of community care for phys cally and mentally disabled people and the elderly, and detailed returns from local authorities on the services they hoped to provide. Though the statistics were revised annually for some years, little attempt was made to explore and account for anomalies in provision, and there was no direct funding: earmarked grants from central Government for particular local authority services, which enabled Government to set and maintain standards, were abolished. Local authorities were given a block grant, and could decide for themselves how they allocated it. The Ministry of Health could do little more than suggest guidelines.

By 1965, the National Health Service was well established, and immensely popular with the general public. It had a remarkable success in the fields of general practice and acute hospital treatment; but it was not the service envisaged twenty years earlier. Means were already being found to limit the costs of an ever-expanding service; and the debate had become highly politicized.

Housing

One of the most acute needs at the end of the Second World War was the need for housing. There were still serious slum clearance problems from the pre-war period. There had been virtually no building for six years. Nearly half a million houses had been destroyed or rendered totally uninhabitable, and many more were badly damaged by bombing. There had been two million marriages in the wartime period. Many young couples, separated by war, were setting up house for the first time and ready to start a family. The birth rate went up sharply – to a peak of 20.7 per thousand population in 1947. The phrase 'homes for heroes' remained in currency to haunt politicians – and particularly Aneurin Bevan, who, as Minister of Health, was responsible for Housing as well as for the NHS.

The Town and Country Planning Act of 1947 had set out a framework on the lines proposed by the Barlow and Uthwatt Reports. The immediate need was to meet the housing shortage.

Under the Labour Government, the emphasis was on local authority housing, and no longer just for 'the working classes'. The Housing Act of 1949 laid down the principle that housing need rather than social class was to be the main criterion, and local authority Housing Departments worked on complex points systems which included social as well as economic indicators. In the immediate post-war period, the emphasis was on temporary solutions: bomb damage was swiftly repaired to provide reconditioned houses, families were housed in Nissen huts in abandoned Army camps, and the first 'pre-fabs' were provided, with a predicted 12–15 years of life. Some were to last much longer. At the same time Rent Restriction Acts kept down rents in the private sector.

New housing began to be constructed as soon as the labour force was reorganized. Between 1950 and 1955, well over a million new council houses were built, the peak figure being 300,000 in 1953.[15] After that time, there was a change in policy from the immediate satisfaction of housing need to an improvement of housing stock. The Housing Rents and Repairs Act of 1954 assisted house-owners and private landlords by making larger improvement grants available, and so enabling older houses to be brought up to standard. At the same time, local authorities began to develop ambitious plans for high rise flats, and the New Towns began to take shape.

The reasoning of the Barlow Report led inevitably to plans for high-rise flats. It was necessary for the labour force to be near industrial centres to reduce fatigue and the cost of travel; land was expensive and in short supply in a crowded island. It therefore made sense to build upwards rather than outwards. In addition, local authorities were concerned to provide accommodation quickly and cheaply, and there were techniques of prefabrication available which were particularly suitable for this kind of construction. Half a dozen large construction firms virtually cornered the field, and obtained most of the contracts.[16]

It was some years before the problems became apparent: the isolation of mothers with young children who could not go out to play; the isolation of old people, who could not face the stairs or the lifts; the poor quality of construction, and the lack of imagination in design; the vandalization of walkways and stairways. Public dissatisfaction with high rise council flats reached its peak in 1968, when a gas explosion at Ronan Point caused one corner of a block to collapse like a pack of cards. Though the blocks created in the 1950s and 1960s are still occupied in many areas, housing authorities now tend to be more careful in allocating suitable tenants. Some blocks have already been demolished – and some stand derelict because the cost of demolition would be too high.

New Towns such as Stevenage, Corby and Milton Keynes were created under the New Towns Act 1946. They were a development from the 'satellite towns' and the 'garden cities' of the pre-war years. Some twenty were set up in all, eight of them round London, catering for a total population of about three million people. The initial problems of siting were severe: it was necessary to avoid first class agricultural land, places of historical interest and beauty spots, and there were environmental interests and transport links to be considered. On the whole, the New Town policy has worked well: industry and housing have been successfully combined, and genuine communities have developed. Though many people have doubts about living in a totally planned environment, preferring communities which grow naturally, the standard of provision has been good, and the combination of housing and employment opportunities has in many cases developed successfully.

Up to 1957, the emphasis in national housing policy was strongly on local authority provision. In the privately rented sector, maintenance costs had risen sharply, and there had been a long period of rent restriction. Public opinion was sharply against 'Rachmanism' – exploitation by landlords who harassed their tenants into leaving so that they could sell the property or raise rents. But many tenants had a protected status, so that the owners could neither sell their property nor afford to keep it in good repair. There was a gradual realization that many private landlords were not wealthy and exploitative. They were people of limited incomes whose capital was tied up in an asset they could not realize. The Rent Act of 1957 was based on the simple economic theory that the abolition of rent restrictions would increase private sector provision by bringing market forces into play; but this did not occur. The next few years were to see the virtual disappearance of rented accommodation except at the top and the bottom ends of the market, because of more general economic trends.

In the late 1950s, interest rates rose, inflation set in, and house prices rose sharply. In 1945, only some 26 per cent of dwelling-houses in England and Wales were owner-occupied; but this figure rose to 47 per cent by 1966. A house became the best hedge against inflation, and mortgage relief made home ownership profitable in periods of high taxation. After 1955, the number of local authority houses built annually was sharply reduced, while the private rented sector almost ceased to exist.[17]

Education

The Education Act of 1944 had provided a structure for a service which would give every child equality of opportunity all the way from nursery school to university. The main lesson to be learned in this field was that equality of opportunity was not enough. The 11+ examination soon came under fire. The Act had proposed that grammar schools, technical schools and secondary modern schools were to have parity of esteem, but reality denied the statement. Despite efforts to upgrade secondary modern schools, to provide them with equipment and sports facilities equal to those of the more prestigious grammar schools, the pecking order remained obstinately unchanged. And was it really possible to classify children – to make decisions about their education which would affect their whole lives – at the age of eleven? The pre-war pundits had thought this reasonable. During the 1950s, the evidence grew that some children developed later than others; that the 11+ tests were often unreliable; that the children of 'bookish' parents did better than those from homes where books were unknown; that it was easier to get into grammar schools in some areas than others. Some children were coached, and some parents moved house to get into one of the better endowed areas.

In 1945, the Labour Government had accepted the principles of the Butler Act; this may have been, as Morgan alleges[18] because many of their leaders were themselves 'public school products'; it may have been because they respected the quality of teaching in grammar schools, and did not want to damage the academic standing of these schools; it may have been because the Butler Act had laid down an acceptable basis for the Education Service, and there was too much other legislation in progress to plan major changes so soon. But while the National Union of Teachers and some Labour backbenchers argued for 'multilateralism' – more than one stream under the same roof – it was not until 1951 that the Labour Party manifesto included a demand for comprehensive schools, and Labour lost that election.

From that time on, policy on secondary schools showed a clear political split. Labour championed comprehensive schools on the grounds that the tripartite system was socially and educationally divisive. The Conservatives championed the grammar schools on the grounds that the divisions were real. But the edge was taken off the controversy by the gradual abandonment of the 11+ examination. Schools experimented with transfers at 13+, 14+, 16+. Some universities and colleges began to accept students with 'unorthodox' academic backgrounds. Educational opportunity diversified, rather than being channelled through the narrow gate of a single examination. But in the 1950s and early 1960s, there was still a sharp awareness of the problems of children in the secondary modern stream. This led to the publication of two reports from official committees – the Crowther Report of 1959 and the Newsom Report of 1963.

The Crowther Report was entitled *15 to 18* and subtitled *Education in a Changing Word.*[19] It was concerned with further education opportunities for young school-leavers (at this time, the minimum school leaving age was still 15). Britain was lagging behind other countries – particularly Germany, which had made a remarkable economic recovery in the years since the war – in further education and apprenticeship schemes. The Crowther Committee outlined a twenty-year plan for developments in intermediate technology covering building, plumbing, carpentry, basic engineering skills, the catering and grocery trades, and other trades. These involved day-release and block release schemes, with the aim that every young person should have the opportunity of acquiring relevant skills after taking up employment. These proposals, which were fully implemented, have achieved relatively little public recognition, but have had a far-reaching effect in changing the occupational structure. Previously, the bulk of the working population was unskilled. Since the implementation of the Crowther report, young people have had the opportunity to acquire a trade or craft after leaving school through a technical college or College of Commerce.

The Newsom Report was concerned with 'children aged 13 to 16 with average or less than average ability'.[20] Its title was *Half Our Future* because these children represented 'half the pupils in secondary schools – half the citizens, workers, mothers and fathers of the future'. The Newsom Committee stated that there was 'much unrealised talent ... among boys and girls whose potential is masked by inadequate powers of speech and the limitations of home background'. The second volume of the report is drawn from case-studies and survey data: the children were divided into three groups according to ability: the 'Browns' the 'Joneses' and the 'Robinsons.' The 'Robinsons', who represented the lowest quartile, were smaller, lighter in weight, came from larger families, were more likely to have unskilled fathers, lived in poorer neighbourhoods, were given less homework, were more likely to leave school early and wihout qualifications, and were much less likely to belong to school societies or youth clubs, or to become prefects. It was a compelling picture of educational rejects who became social rejects. The recommendations included raising the school leaving age to 16 (which took a further nine years), measures for making teaching more relevant and linking it to youth employment, the avoidance of excessive grading, and 'a working party on general social problems in slum areas' – the proposal which led to the setting up of the Plowden Committee, whose report will be considered in the next chapter.

A further notable development in this period was the Robbins Committee Report on Universities.[21] This opened up the other end of the educational spectrum, and marked the high point of optimism in the educational field. By 1963, the children born at the time of the post-war 'population bulge' were approaching university age, so pressure on universities and other centres for higher education was increasing. The Robbins Report started from the premise that 'a highly-educated population is essential to meet competitive pressures in the modern world' pointing out that university education was available to a much larger section of the population in both the United States and the USSR, and that other countries were planning a considerable expansion. Britain needed new universities, and quickly. There should be broader courses for first degrees, designed to develop student potential rather than to instil information. Postgraduate education and research should be developed. Grants for vacation study and other activities, such as field work, should be made available. Staff-student ratios 'should not be allowed to deteriorate'.

The result was immediate acceptance by the Government, and a national enthusiasm for new universities. Some of these, such as Aston, Strathclyde, and Salford, were former Colleges of Advanced Technology, which kept their technological emphasis. Others were new creations, variously dubbed 'Plateglass' or 'Newbridge' universities – East Anglia, Essex, Kent, Lancaster, Sussex, Warwick, York – which inclined to a more traditional model. But there were experiments in plenty – in new types of courses, in new combinations of subjects, in new modes of organization. At the same time, there was a parallel expansion in other forms of higher education: technical colleges became Polytechnics, and Colleges of Further and Higher Education were set up.

The period from 1945 to 1965 was a very exciting one in the field of education – a time when all things seemed possible, and many of them were already happening. Conservatives looked for the implementation of the Butler system. Labour looked for a healing of the divisions in society. The emphasis varied from education as a means of personal fulfilment to education to meet national manpower needs. There was much debate about C. P. Snow's 'Two Cultures' – the liberal and the scientific – and the means of bringing them together; about comprehensive schools and grammar schools, about ROSLA (which meant 'the raising of the school-leaving age') and the proper age of transferring children from one type of school to another. There were experiments with Sixth Form Colleges. But very few voices were raised to query whether the money was well spent, or whether education could fulfil all the hopes which were placed upon it.

The Sixth Arm of the 'Welfare State'

It was becoming apparent that there was some truth in the assertion that the welfare legislation primarily benefitted the middle classes rather than the poorer sections of society. As T. H. Marshall was to comment later, 'This is inevitable when services previously confined to the lower income groups are extended to the whole population'.[22] If the stigma of means-testing was to be removed, then some relatively affluent people would benefit: that was the inevitable consequence of services provided as of right rather than as of charity. But there was an uneasy recognition that articulate people who could understand how the services worked, knew where to go for assistance, and could talk to professionals such as teachers and doctors as social equals, fared better than inarticulate people who lacked these advantages. So developed the idea that the five major social services were not enough: there was a need for a sixth service which could act on behalf of those who lacked the knowledge, initiative and energy to act for themselves.[23]

This was the rationale behind the rapid development of social work in the late 1950s and 1960s. In the immediate post-war period, Eileen Younghusband of the London School of Economics had produced two reports which demonstrated that social work was useful, but that it was not yet a profession.[24] Medical social workers, psychiatric social workers, probation officers and child care officers were being trained on separate courses, and found it difficult to communicate with one another. Many people in social work posts were unqualified or underqualified. They were lowly paid and lacked support services, such as car allowances or secretarial assistance. As a result of this analysis, the first generic course for social workers, in which those intending to enter different specialisms trained together at a postgraduate level, was set up at the LSE in 1954.[25]

At the same time, the separate organizations for different kinds of social workers had set up a Standing Conference, and began to produce their own literature on ways and means of working together. One of the problems which had emerged as the social services developed was that a single client or family might be visited by several social workers with different trainings and of varying degrees of competence, all giving different, and possibly conflicting, advice. The solution to this was seen as the case conference, in which workers would meet together and pool their knowledge of a case, choosing one of their members as the key worker. The journal *Case Conference*, founded in 1953, spread the new philosophy.

Government was cautious. In 1955, a working party was set up on 'Social workers in the local authority health and welfare services' – its remit officially restricted to these two underdeveloped fields, where qualified social workers were a rarity. Eileen Younghusband, who had hoped for a much broader-based enquiry, was disappointed, but accepted the chairmanship in the hope that the working party's findings would be relevant to the whole of social work. The Younghusband Report,[26] published in 1959, made proposals for a massive expansion in social work employment in local authorities; the provision of adequate support services; a new qualification, the Certificate in Social Work, which could be taken in two years in Colleges of Further Education; a national training council, to guarantee standards, and a National Institute of Social Work Training (the word 'Training' was later dropped) as a central staff college. While the universities, which could take only limited numbers of social work students, continued to provide courses of a higher academic level, the proposals for a second level qualification met with instant public approval. There were two full columns on the Report in *The Times* on 5 May 1959, and the leader on the same day expressed the view that the report 'fittingly inaugurates the second decade of the Welfare State'. There were debates in the House of Commons and the House of Lords. One Conservative MP thought it the greatest social document since the Beveridge Report, and the Government spokesman in the Lords called it 'a great and absorbing human document'.

The main proposals were implemented in the Health Visitors' and Social Workers' Training Act of 1962. As Eileen Younghusband had forecast, the students taking the new shorter courses soon outnumbered the university-trained students, and went into all kinds of social work, not only to the local authority health and welfare departments. The National Institute was set up in London, and social work entered on a new phase of unification and professional development. The Sixth Arm of the 'Welfare State' was in place.

The end of ideology?

In 1965, Professor T. H. Marshall of the London School of Economics summed up sixty or seventy years of 'the story of social policy' with the judgement that social welfare, once confined to 'the helpless and hopeless of the population', had been steadily extended to all citizens. There had been 'a convergence of principles and an integration of practices' to which all political parties had made some contribution: 'there is a growing measure of agreement on fundamentals. It is realised that many of the old antitheses are largely imaginary ... There is little difference of opinion as to the services that must be provided, and it is generally agreed that, whoever provides them, the overall responsibility for the welfare of the citizen must remain with the state'.[27]

Marshall thought that Britain might be approaching 'the end of ideology'. There was a new understanding of community living, and a new wilingness to share. Britain had moved a long way from the 'naked "cash nexus" described by the Poor Law Commission in 1909' to a recognition of citizens' rights and duties. The public/ private welfare debate was no longer important, and the arguments put forward by MacLeod and Powell against the extension of public welfare services were simply irrelevant.

Events were swiftly to prove him wrong. 'Consensus politics' in domestic policy certainly held in theory until the Thatcher Government substituted 'conviction politics' in 1979;[28] but the practical limitation and contraction of the public health and social services began almost before Marshall's book had reached the bookstalls.

THIRTEEN
Problems of Contraction

Labour won the General Election of November 1964. As in 1945, the economic situation was highly unfavourable. According to R. H. S. Crossman, 'The incoming Prime Minister was presented with a Treasury memorandum showing an £800 million deficit on overseas payments ... and even after the "Paris Club" of central bankers agreed, early in November, to make another £142 million loan to Britain, with a prospect of a further £215 million from the International Monetary Fund, the pound continued to weaken'.[1]

Harold Wilson's administration of 1964–1970 was followed by the Conservative administration of Edward Heath from 1970–1974. Labour returned to power from 1974–1979. Labour was thus in office for ten years out of fourteen between 1964 and 1979. During this period, the pressures for social reform continued, but were increasingly countervailed by international pressures on the British economy and the growing strength of the views of the New Right. The promises of 1948 began visibly to fail.

Race, gender and equality

The influx of immigrants from the 'New Commonwealth' had begun soon after the Second World War. The workers came from India and Pakistan, from Ceylon (Sri Lanka), from the West Indies, from Africa and other countries in the hope of better living conditions, often taking the more poorly-paid jobs and moving into the worst housing. Britain needed their labour, but by the mid 1960s, the numbers swelled by wives and children who came to join the workers, were growing, and the problems multiplying. As early as 1958, there were riots in Notting Hill which were thought to have had a racial element,[2] and conflict grew as the immigrants competed for better jobs and for housing.

The Race Relations Acts of 1965 and 1968 set up the Race Relations Board (now the Commission for Racial Equality) and made it unlawful to discriminate on grounds of colour, race or ethnic origin in the provision of goods, facilities, housing accommodation or land. Machinery for conciliation was set up to resolve conflicts, but a breach of the provisions constituted a civil offence which could lead to a court action and the award of damages. Discriminatory advertisements were prohibited.

Though both Labour and Conservative leaders were in favour of measures to promote racial harmony, there was a considerable undercurrent of popular resentment against 'the blacks'; and Enoch Powell, then Conservative MP for Wolverhampton, touched a raw nerve in 1968 when he advocated mass repatriation. Powell's speech at Birmingham opposed the provisions of the Race Relations Bill then going through Parliament. He warned that its implementation would 'risk throwing a match into gunpowder'. Britons would become 'strangers in their own country'; and he added 'Like the Roman, I seem to see the Tiber foaming with much blood'.[3] This classical allusion (Powell had at one time been a Classics professor in the University of Sydney) was lost on the Press, and possibly on the public. What became known as the 'Rivers of Blood' speech greatly inflamed racial conflict.

Richard Crossman, then Secretary of State for the Social Services, wrote in his diary a few days later: 'There's no doubt how last week has got to be described. It was Powell week, and we are still absolutely dominated by the effect of his Birmingham speech. There he is with his 40–50,000 letters streaming in, the marches from the docks and from Smithfield, all part of a mass response to a very simple appeal: "No more bloody immigrants in this country!" I haven't spoken to anyone who has talked to Enoch since his sacking'.[4] Powell had been summarily dismissed from a post in the Shadow Cabinet. Though the shock value of the 'Rivers of Blood' speech was high at the time, the immigration issue never again excited so much popular opposition.[5] After the 1971 Immigration Act, which limited the numbers of immigrants, the problems of ethnic minorities merged into the more general problems of poverty, decaying urban areas, and the maintenance of public order.

The movement to secure equal opportunities for women took a different and less explosive course.[6] The Labour Party had long had a commitment to 'equal pay for equal work' and this was achieved (at least in theory) with the passing, after a long parliamentary campaign, of the Equal Pay Act 1970. The Equal Opportunities Commission, which is concerned with discrimination against women in employment, was set up in 1975. There was some discussion at the time on the proposal to set up a single board to deal with both racial and gender discrimination, on the American model; but the organizations representing the ethnic minorities were opposed to this. They argued that the situation was different from that in the United States. Ethnic minority groups were relatively small in Britain, and most of their members were immigrants. Most women in Britain were British born, and they totalled more than half the population. It was thought possible that complaints from women would swamp any joint machinery which was set up. (It was also the case that some of the ethnic mninority groups, coming from male-dominant cultures, were not always enthusiastic about equal opportunities for women).

With many frustrations, and in a relatively unspectacular way, the work of the two Commissions has achieved a framework for a greater measure of equality of opportunity in Britain, and neither has been seriously challenged to date, though discrimination still takes many forms, not all of them capable of legal prohibition.

The 'Rediscovery of Poverty'

In 1966, two Fabian academics from the London School of Economics, Peter Townsend and Brian Abel-Smith, published a study on poverty, *The Poor and the Poorest*,[7] which demonstrated that the growth of affluence had left whole classes of society in poverty – particularly large families on low incomes, and those on National Assistance. A powerful argument for increased family allowances and a minimum income level (or alternatively a state supplement to low incomes) was carried forward by the Child Poverty Action Group (CPAG).

Pressure-group tactics were not new. What was new was that British pressure groups, learning from their American counterparts in the Civil Rights movement and the War on Poverty of the Kennedy-Johnson era, now enlisted the help of the media, and acquired a new skill in presentation. CPAG and the Low Pay Unit produced a stream of pamphlets based on research in the Fabian tradition to hammer home the message that poverty had not been defeated, and that much more should be done for people in need. Television, radio and the daily newspapers brought the issues to the attention of the public. Conservative and Labour ministers were bombarded with research material, focussing on one type of benefit after another, in an attempt to raise allowances and humanize a benefit system which was already showing signs of rigidity. CPAG had marked successes in improving access to and take-up of benefits, in securing new forms of allowances and easier conditions for awards. Training courses were introduced for Social Security staff, in which they were required to undertake role-play exercises, and to find out what it was like to be on the other side of the counter. The Welfare Rights movement developed branches in most areas of the country, giving advice to those in need of benefits. The Law Centre movement provided advice on legal issues to people who could not afford the ordinary processes of law. The Low Pay Unit carried out research on families with small incomes.

But the CPAG campaigns, despite their immediate successes, produced two adverse long-term effects: first, the policy of 'disjointed incrementalism' – fighting the case for one specific benefit after another on a narrow front – meant that the benefit system grew more complicated, and benefits for one type of need got out of step with those for others. The simplicity and comprehensibility of the Beveridge system was lost. Second, in dealing a blow to complacency about the 'Welfare State', the campaigns provided ammunition for the opposition. It was very easy to turn 'There is still much to be done' into 'The Welfare State has failed'.

The failure of the Welfare State was a favourite theme of the Institute of Economic Affairs, founded in 1964, which became the academic branch of the New Right. A flood of papers and pamphlets on monetarist lines countered the literary flood from CPAG and its allied groups, arguing a very different case: freedom involved choice, not state monopoly; competition meant greater efficiency; Britain must shake off the shackles of the Socialist-inspired bureaucracy. State welfarism was restricting choice and stifling enterprise. The IEA Hobart Papers, with titles such as *Housing and the Whitehall Bulldozer*, *After the NHS* and *Growth Through Competition* were widely circulated. While the Fabians and the CPAG concentrated on the needs of the underprivileged sectors of society, the IEA argued that Britain was becoming affluent, so that extensive compulsory welfare systems were no longer necessary.

The move to selectivity

Though the academic debate took place on overtly political lines, the necessity of abandoning Beveridge-type universalism was reluctantly recognized by the Left as well as the Right. In November 1967, the financial situation worsened sharply. Sterling was devalued, and public expenditure cuts became necessary. Labour was in power at the time, and it was a Labour Secretary of State for the Social Services, Michael Stewart, who convened a conference of senior academics and civil servants only a fortnight after devaluation to discuss a new policy situation. Britain's international trade position was increasingly unfavourable, and for demographic reasons, the social services would be under increasing strain. The birth-rate had dropped, and the proportion of old people in the population was rising rapidly. That meant that a smaller economically active population would have to support a larger dependent population. In these circumstances, no government could continue to expand the social services in response to all the demands which were being made upon it. Expansionism – the

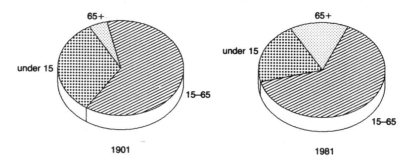

Figure VIII Age-structure of the population, 1901 and 1981
Source: *Annual Abstract of Statistics* 1989, table 2.3.

cry of 'More money, more staff, more training' would have to be replaced by a bleak attention to priorities.

The hard reality of democratic government was that no political party could hope to remain in power if it continued to raise taxes: the general public wanted a welfare system, but was not, in the last resort, prepared to pay for it. The only way to improve (or even maintain) the services in a situation of increasing demand and restricted resources was through the voluntary social services and charitable giving.

The message was unpopular, but the facts seemed incontrovertible. The result was a fierce debate in the Labour ranks on the subject of 'universality or selectivity'.[8] In *Social Services for All?*,[9] a Fabian symposium on the issues published in 1968, Peter Townsend argued that the debate was really about 'the kind and quality of society we wish to achieve in Britain', not about cash limits; but most writers were prepared to accept some degree of selectivity. Brian Abel-Smith described the 'slogans of the Beveridge era' as outmoded. There had never been 'social security from the cradle to the grave', and we had never abolished means-testing. Mike Reddin attempted to add up all the different forms of means-testing then in operation – for rate and rent rebates, home helps, day nurseries, children in care, educational maintenance, uniform grants, school meals, welfare foods for expectant mothers, contraceptives, residential care and other services. He estimated that there were at least 3,000 different tests, with different criteria and conditions. No one in authority appeared to be concerned about the cumulative effect on claimants, or the anomalies and illogicalities created.

Most of these Fabian writers were prepared by 1968 to accept some degree of selectivity. The broad outlines of 1948 had been replaced by an increasingly complicated welfare machine which seemed to be ill-adapted to meeting the needs of disadvantaged people. The way forward seemed to consist of two moves: a thorough reorganization of the services to make them more responsive and more efficient, and the development of new forms of special benefits for special needs.

Administrative reorganization in the 1970s

Social policy in the early 1970s was preoccupied with questions of reorganization. It was evident that the existing provisions in the health and welfare services were becoming cumbersome, and hampering development, but it was hoped that new administrative structures could cure the problems. The major reorganizations of the period 1970–1975 came in three areas: the local authority Personal Social Services, the National Health Service, and the structure of local authorities.

I   Reorganization in the local authority Personal Social Services

The Younghusband Report of 1959 had created a second tier of social workers, and done much to improve the supply of qualified staff; but it was clear that the services needed to be better organized. They were scattered between local Health Departments (dealing with sickness and maternity work), Welfare Departments (dealing with disability and the chronic infirmities of old age), Children's Departments (rapidly developing work with families where children were at risk), Education Departments (dealing with children in the school system) and Housing Departments (dealing with homeless families, rent arrears and evictions). An inter-departmental committee, composed of distinguished public figures, not civil servants, was set up in 1965 under the chairmanship of Sir Frederic (later Lord) Seebohm, and reported in 1968.[10] Its terms of reference were 'to review the organization and responsibilities of the local authority personal social services in England and Wales, and to consider what changes are desirable to secure an effective family service'.

The Committee's work was thorough, though the members were denied the opportunity to commission fresh research: they were told that this would be too expensive, and that it would take too long. The chief problem facing them was how to combine the scattered social work services of local authorities, and whether to place them under the aegis of any one of the 'parent' departments – Children, Health, Welfare, Education or Housing. Their conclusions were as follows:

1. There should be a new local authority department to provide 'a community based and family-oriented service available to all'.

2. This department should be free-standing, and not under the supervision of any other department.

3. It should combine the social work of Children's Departments

and Welfare Departments, both of which would disappear; Educational Welfare and Housing Welfare; and certain elements of the work of Health Departments: mental health care, home helps, day nurseries, residential Homes.

4. This new Department should be headed by a Director of Social Services, with chief officer status – i.e., equivalent to that of the Director of Housing or the Director of Education or the Medical Officer of Health.

5. The Social Services Department would have total responsibility for the social needs of the area: not only for those covered by statutory requirements, but for any needs which might arise.

6. The new framework was to be underscored by the concept of reciprocity: the Social Services Department would act as a powerhouse to ensure 'the greatest number of people ... giving and receiving service for the benefit of the community'. Individual volunteers would work with social workers, carrying out tasks and maintaining contact with clients under social work direction. Voluntary organizations would be funded and supported by the local authority, and would be free to criticize and stimulate the local authority into new forms of action.

These recommendations[11] became the basis of the Local Authority Social Services Act of 1970. The Bill had a stormy passage in two respects: first, there was immediate and powerful opposition from the medical organizations, which regarded social work as 'the handmaid of medicine', and wanted this new area of work to reinforce the dwindling empires of the Medical Officers of Health, soon to lose most of their public health work to restructured Hospital and Community Services. Second, though a Labour Government was in power at the time, it was clear that a general election was imminent, and that the Bill might fall. If the Conservatives were returned to power, it was thought that the Bill might not be reintroduced in the face of pressure from the medical profession.

The rapid and successful passage of the Bill owed much to the political energy of Lady Serota, a Labour peer and former Leader of the London County Council, who was instrumental in securing parliamentary support and parliamentary time for it. The Act received the Royal Assent on the day Parliament was dissolved.

When the new Directors of Social Services were subsequently appointed they found that much was expected of them. They had taken on very broad responsibilities involving an unknown volume of work. They had been told that there was no additional money available – the reorganized service was expected to be less costly, not more so; and they took over staff of very varying capacities and relatively narrow experience. There were new and heavy responsibilities. The Social Services Departments had to take over the management of the former approved schools for delinquent and neglected children under the terms of the Children and Young Persons Act 1969, and the development of services for disabled people under the terms of the Disabled Persons Act 1968. Both involved major changes with which the former Children's Departments and Welfare Departments had barely begun to cope.

In 1971, the year into which the Local Authority Social Services Act came into force, the unification of social work was finally achieved. The Act provided for the setting up of the Central Council for Education and Training in Social Work (CCETSW), which now supervises courses and qualifications for all social work students. CCETSW, which has its headquarters in London, is responsible for the validation of courses, the maintenance of professional standards, and the accreditation of qualified entrants to the profession. At the same time, the British Association of Social Workers (BASW) was formed from the amalgamation of the existing professional associations for psychiatric social workers, child care officers and almoners (now hospital social workers). Social workers in hospitals ceased to be employed by the National Health Service in 1974, and were transferred to the staff of the local authority, so that the local authority is responsible for hospital teams as well as area teams. In England, (though not in Scotland, where developments had started earlier and taken a different course) probation officers kept their own professional organization, and continued to be 'officers of the Courts'.

The demand for qualified social workers continued to rise. In 1971 CCETSW opted for a single qualification – the Certificate of Qualification in Social Work, which was awarded to all students on approved courses, from the two-year 'Younghusband' courses to Master's degrees in universities. In 1975, a new Certificate of Social Service, based on day-release for staff already in employment was introduced. The problem for CCETSW has been to secure as wide a base of training as possible, and the Council, constantly aware of the problems of expanding its work in a period of financial retrenchment, has opted for breadth rather than depth. The post-qualification courses recommended by the Seebohm Committee, which would have gone far to iron out the inequalities in basic social work education, have not materialized. The vast majority of social workers do not yet have the opportunities of advanced training available to nurses, prison officers or the police.

II Reorganization in the National Health Service

One of the first ominous signs of a changing economic climate was the introduction of charges for medical prescriptions by the Labour Government in January 1968. The argument proceeded on the now familiar lines of economic necessity versus social justice; but despite the strong opposition of the then Minister of Health, Kenneth Robinson (who had been Aneurin Bevan's parliamentary secretary in 1948) and of other Labour MPs, the selectivists won. There were exemptions from charges for patients over retirement age, and for those with chronic conditions; but prescriptions, like dentures and spectacles, were no longer 'free at the point of delivery'.

Reorganization would, it was hoped, bring about a more effective service. The NHS Act 1946 had set up a tripartite structure – hospital, local authority and general practitioner services – but there were few links betwen the sections. The three arms of the NHS grew steadily apart, and by the early 1960s, there was widespread unease about the basic structure. The Porritt Report of 1962[12] was the first to suggest thorough revision. The issues were debated for some years, while successive governments, both Conservative and Labour, issued two Green Papers, and a White Paper.[13] The final White Paper of 1972 put an end to protracted discussion, and led to the National Health Service Reorganization Act of 1974. The main features were as follows:

1. A new structure was set up, consisting of Regional Health Authorities, Area Health Authorities and District Management Teams.

2. The special status of teaching hospitals disappeared.

3. The former hospital services became 'Hospital and Community Services'. This meant that local authorities now lost all their health services apart from what had become minor environmental services

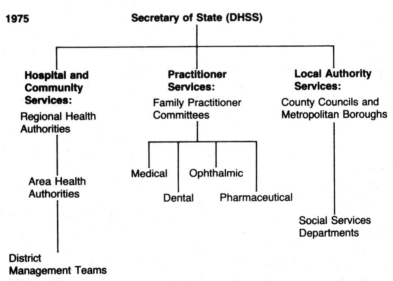

Figure IX. Structure of the National Health Service in 1948 and 1975
Note: Area Health Authorities were abolished in 1982, and District Health Authorities introduced.

– pollution, food and water inspection and so on. The position of Medical Officer of Health was replaced by that of the Community Physician, on the staff of the District Management Team.
4. Health visitors and district nurses were removed from local authority staff to form 'primary care teams' attached to general practice. By this time, though general practitioners had defeated the intentions of the framers of the NHS Act 1946 by refusing to join health centres run by the local authorities, they had responded well to Government initiatives which enabled them to set up health centres for group practice under their own control. The pattern of GP care was therefore moving from that of a single doctor working alone to that of a team with support staff.

These changes were accompanied by an extensive retraining programme for senior hospital staff. This embodied a new management philosophy set out in what was known as the 'Grey Book',[14] largely the product of an American firm of management consultants, McKinsey and Co. It relied on currently popular concepts of consensus management and travelling leadership.

The lack of a clear management structure, and the cumbersome nature of a four-tier system soon defeated the innovators in the extended Hospital and Community services. In 1979, a Royal Commission reported that 'we need not be ashamed of our health service, and there are many aspects of which we can be justly proud'[15] but criticized the top-heavy administration, and the failure to make swift decisions. In 1980, in a further revision, Area Health Authorities were abolished, and District Health Authorities set up to make major policy decisions at the local level.[16]

III Reorganization of the local authority structure

The county and county borough structure had worked well since its inception in 1888, but the distribution of the population was changing. City populations had for the most part ceased to grow. There was talk of 'inner city decay' and 'exurbanisation'. Communications were vastly improved, and the distinction between town and country was no longer clear-cut. As Dr Hedley Marshall of INLOGOV, the Institute of Local Government Studies, noted, 'the defects in the eighty-year-old structure were becoming more apparent. Local government areas no longer corresponded to the settlement pattern. Nor was there consistency in size, population or financial resources... Overspill, changes in life styles, and particularly the advent of the motor car, made it impossible for local authorities to solve their problems within their own boundaries'.[17]

The Redcliffe-Maud Commission[18] recommended the abolition

Figure X Local Government areas, England, before 1 April 1974
Source: *Redcliffe-Maud Report*, p. 171, HMSO
For the use of this figure, the publisher acknowledges Her Majesty's Stationery Office.

of county boroughs, and the introduction of a new administrative framework. Their proposals were largely implemented in the Local Government Act of 1972. For most of the country, county councils took over the major responsibility of local government for rural and urban areas alike. In the major conurbations of

Figure XI Local Government areas, England, since 1 April 1974
Source: *Local Government Chronicle*, 17 November 1972
For the use of this figure, the publisher acknowledges the Local Government Chronicle.

Merseyside, Greater Manchester, West Yorkshire, South Yorkshire and the West Midlands, a two-tier system was established; metropolitan county councils took overall responsibility for strategic planning, police, passenger transport, and certain other matters best administered over a wide area, while metropolitan boroughs within their boundaries were responsible for such services as education, social and personal health services, and housing. This structure was similar to that in London, where the Greater London Council had been established in 1965 as a joint structure covering the work of the London Boroughs.

The distinction between metropolitan councils and metropolitan boroughs was not clear-cut, since there were joint powers in many areas of work, and a balance had to be worked out in practice. In addition, in both metropolitan and non-metropolitan counties, some powers, chiefly concerned with issues of housing, public health or environmental protection, were delegated to district or parish councils operating at lower levels.

The most controversial effects of the changes at the time were the redrawing of boundaries and the changing of some traditional shire titles. The East Riding of Yorkshire became part of an extended County of Humberside, Avon was interposed between the counties of Gloucester and Somerset, and Rutland, with a population of only 25,000, was absorbed into Leicestershire (though local loyalists have continued to resist the change, and Rutland still keeps its road signs on the A1); but the major effect was in the strength of the new metropolitan counties. As J. D. Stewart predicted, party political interests became much more pronounced in these large authorities – and in the 1973 elections, all the metropolitan counties, in addition to the Greater London Council, were Labour controlled.[19] Thus the Local Government Act of 1972 set the stage for the conflicts which were to take place between central and local government in the 1980s.

EPAs and CDPs

The Seebohm Committee had recommended that Social Services Departments should be 'community based'. Hospital Services became 'Hospital and Community Services' under the NHS reorganization Act of 1974. The theme of 'community' was also evident in two notable social experiments of the late 1960s and early 1970s, Educational Priority Areas and Community Development Projects. The EPA scheme owed much to the Plowden Report, *Children and Their Primary Schools*, published in 1966.[20] Lady Plowden and her colleagues were concerned with primary education as the most basic step in educational and social opportunity. They argued that 'equality of opportunity' was not enough. The main problems lay in the decaying areas of the inner cities. There were areas in which the children never had a chance to grasp the opportunities which were theoretically available to them. There were old 'board school' buildings dating from the days of the 1902 Education Act, with poor equipment and outdated books. In such schools, the turnover of teachers tended to be high, and few of them lived in the local community. Many pupils came from home backgrounds where education was neither understood nor valued. The Plowden Committee was much influenced by developments in the United States, where community work was developing rapidly in the inner cities, and 'Head Start' programmes offered special tuition to underprivileged children, particularly blacks and Puerto Ricans. The Plowden Report stressed the importance of nursery education – the origins of inequality start young. They asked for a policy of 'positive discrimination' for designated 'areas of disadvantage', and for local diagnosis of the needs and the possible achievements, rather than 'standard national formulae'. They recommended community schools, where parents could become involved in the educational process, and the school would be part of the locality.

As a result of these recommendations, a national experiment was set up, in which five Educational Priority Areas were designated, and special services set up in partnership with university departments of Education.[21] Much enthusiasm developed for 'community schools', in which parents and other adults could take part, and children would learn in the context of their own cultural group. The supporters of EPAs were keen that the experiments should be broadened into a national policy, but the money was never available for the findings to be applied nation-wide. Even if this could have been done, there were two sources of doubt: was it desirable to socialize children into the local area, when the population was increasingly geographically and socially mobile? And could the educational system alone really change society?

There were no more EPAs, and subsequent research has cast some doubt on the validity of the data.[22]

Under the Heath Conservative administration of 1970–1974, a very different approach to education emerged. The authors of *The Black Papers on Education*[23] alleged that state education was failing; that educational standards, measured in terms of the three Rs, had actually declined since the First World War; that 'permissive' educational practices resulted in 'a vacuum into which the worst features of the pop and drug world can enter'. They took the view that postgraduate training of teachers was unnecessary, that the school-leaving age should go back to 14, and that discipline and sound drilling in the fundamentals had been abandoned in the search for social egalitarianism.

The *Black Papers* were strongly opposed by many educationists, who found the arguments élitist and retrogressive, and the material highly inaccurate in detail.[24] Nevertheless, they were to have a long-term effect on the education system in influencing policy decisions in the 1980s.

In the early 1970s, the enthusiasm for social change moved from the Department of Education and Science to the Home Office, which sponsored an ambitious scheme for Community Development Projects. Twelve CDPs were set up in run-down areas in different parts of Britain. In each, an action team of community workers was appointed to attempt the revitalization of the area, and a research team was appointed to analyse the work of the action team and to report on the findings.

The CDP scheme was 'the brain-child of a remarkable civil servant, Derek Morrell'.[25] Alex Lyon, who was Minister of State at the Home Office at the time, described it in the following terms:

> Those projects ... were designed to put teams of articulate young people into areas where the population, though deprived, was inarticulate, to help those people to express their own sense of grievance, and to put pressure on the authority to do something about the situation. The teams have been successful in carrying out that task to the extent that many local councillors wish they did not exist.[26]

Between 1969 and 1975, £5 million was spent on CDP work. The articulate young people went to work with a will, setting up advice and opinion centres, tenants' groups, welfare rights centres, adventure playgrounds, leafletting, organizing protests, marching. CDP workers saw themselves as 'change agents'. They saw it as their task to 'fight the system', to oppose social control, to 'lead the march on the Town Hall'. The late 1960s were a time of social revolt, and CDP was in the forefront, with the cry of 'Power to the people'.

Martin Loney charts the story of the rise and fall of CDP.[27] The reasons for its fall were many. Derek Morrell, the gifted civil servant who might have steered it on manageable lines, died suddenly. The Home Office support thereafter was less than whole-hearted. Central Government increasingly withdrew, leaving the twelve action and research teams largely to their own devices. Most of the teams made no attempt to co-operate with the existing workers in their areas – local government councillors, social workers, voluntary organizations – in their enthusiasm for growth through conflict. As one of the more moderate research directors commented, 'A constrained, harassed and politically sensitive system does not welcome outside pressure which appears to raise conflict, increase sectionalism, add to the insatiable demand which outstrips resources, and generally threaten the representative system'.[28]

Councillors complained of 'long hair and earrings among project members'.[29] There was certainly a culture clash; but beyond that, and the disintegrating relationships with the local authorities, were more serious problems. CDP was set up to test whether an enthusiasm for public participation and a small input of resources could revitalize deprived areas. The answer which emerged in a flood of pamphlets and reports from all twelve areas was that the task was impossible. The problems were not local in origin. They derived from national problems – low incomes, unemployment, housing shortages, lack of economic opportunity. Some (though not all) of the teams became dominated by militant neo-Marxists, who saw political revolution as the only solution.[30]

If this development was unwelcome to a Conservative Government, it was equally unwelcome to their successors. It was a Labour Home Secretary, Merlyn Rees, who decided to end CDP funding in 1975, and there was no final evaluation of the work which had been done. In the United States, the great 'War on Poverty' had already ground to a halt. The world was changing.

The five EPAs and the twelve CDPs covered only small designated areas. Though there were lessons which could be drawn from both sets of experiments, no major changes resulted. The schemes were in fact little more than tokenism – a gesture to an expansionist philosophy which could no longer be sustained. The initiative passed to the Urban Aid funds, which concentrated on reviving industry in inner city areas rather than on stimulating public participation.

Conservative policy in the 1970s

The 'welfare consensus' held in the Conservative administration of 1970–1974 under the premiership of Edward Heath. Sir Keith Joseph, as Secretary of State for the Social Services,[31] was concerned to improve the services within the resources available. He was impressed by the arguments of the Child Poverty Action Group concerning the need to improve access and take-up of social security benefits, and initiated a campaign to ensure that all those who were entitled to benefits knew of their entitlement, and were encouraged to claim. Posters and new, readable leaflets written without jargon were sent to every post office, and leaders of local communities – councillors, doctors, teachers, clergy – were circularized and asked for their help in making the benefits known.

The Family Income Supplement scheme (FIS), introduced in 1970, provided extra money for families on low incomes – a means of improving benefits which had been advocated by some Fabians as well as by some members of the Conservative Party. Though other Fabians argued that this would depress wages, and advocated a minimum income scheme, the objection was (and remains) that this would price workers of limited capacity, such as some mentally and physically handicapped people, out of the employment market altogether.

Another Conservative innovation at this time was the Family Fund, a sum of money (now running into many millions of pounds) specially dedicated to the needs of families with handicapped children. It was decided that this fund should be administered through a charitable trust rather than through statutory channels, and the Joseph Rowntree Memorial Trust took on the considerable task of organizing it nationally. Though the Family Fund is not widely known by the general public, it is extensively used by professionals to provide for special needs – a car, a house extension, extra clothing or holidays – for hard pressed families.[32] In June 1972, Sir Keith Joseph promoted a major research initiative on 'Transmitted Deprivation'. According to the then Chairman of the Social Science Research Council, the aim was to call attention to 'the persistence of deprivation, despite general economic advance, and to the evidence that the same families tended to be deprived generation after generation'.[33]

At this time, theories about the 'culture of poverty' were much in vogue in the United States. It was postulated that poverty and deprivation were learned in childhood, and passed from one generation to the next. In Britain, a joint working party was set up between the Department of Education and Science and the SSRC, and an ambitious research programme was set up. In fact, the initial review of existing research by Rutter and Madge spelled out the inadequacy of the theory to meet the facts. In an exhaustive survey of research on economic status, housing, crime, psychological disorder, parenting behaviour, multiple problem families, the status of ethnic minorities and other issues, the authors pointed out that though there was much evidence of inequality in Britain, it was not only a matter of economic inequality; and that while there were 'continuities over time', these were by no means all due to familial influences. There were regional continuities, like the persistently high unemployment rate in Scotland, or the persistently high delinquency rate in London; and there were ethnic continuities, like the poor housing and employment status of many West Indian families.[34]

A major programme of social research was carried out over nearly ten years, and a final report summarized the findings.[35] These, though interesting and valuable to social scientists, did not answer the original question in the form in which it had been put. Sir Keith wanted a clear-cut answer which could be translated into positive terms for a targeted group of 'deprived' families. He did not want to be told that the question was a good deal more complicated than he had thought, and that the answer lay in an improvement in the social services as a whole. It may have been with this experience in mind that he insisted on changing the title of the Social Science Research Council to the Economic and Social Studies Research Council (on the grounds that social research was not 'scientific') and reduced its budget. As in the case of

Community Development Projects, social research workers had not come up with the answers which the Government of the day wanted. Some took the view that the Government had been asking the wrong questions.

A new round of cuts

If the economic crisis of the mid-1960s provided the first major rethinking of 'Welfare State' principles, the oil crisis of 1973 was to precipitate the second. The sudden increase in prices by the Middle Eastern oil producers had profound effects on the economies of most industrialized countries. According to Denis Healey, who was Labour Chancellor of the Exchequer at the time, the increase in oil prices added £2.5 billion to Britain's current account deficit, increased the cost of living by 10 per cent, and reduced the Gross Domestic Product by 5 per cent, all in a single year.[36]

Healey provides a thoughtful analysis of how Keynesian economic principles were breaking down: Keynesian theory ignored institutional factors, such as the power of the trade unions; and it started from an assumption of national economic self-sufficiency. The theory had worked well enough in the United States in the late 1930s (when it was the basis of Roosevelt's New Deal); but Britain in the 1970s had powerful trade unions, and over 30 per cent of the Gross Domestic Product was dependent on exports. Industrial stagnation had been assumed not to coexist with rampant inflation, but now Britain was suffering from both simultaneously. The international currency markets were in turmoil, production in Britain lagged behind that of powerful competitors. When the country's currency reserves were endangered, Healey was forced to ask the International Monetary Fund for a loan; but the IMF was American-dominated, and the United States was still opposed to socialism in Britain. The loan was granted – on condition that Britain made severe cuts in public sector expenditure. According to Healey, it was repaid before the Labour Government left office in 1979; but public confidence in Labour's ability to handle the economy had been badly shaken.[37]

'"Zero growth" . . . "times of economic stringency" . . . "given the financial situation" . . . "cutback" . . . "restraint". These were the key terms of 1975', began the editorial preface to the *Year Book of Social Policy in Britain 1975*. In the following year, the editors commented that 'The economic descent from affluence to poverty has been more devastating than ... seemed possible'.

So the days of the welfare consensus were numbered. The attacks of the New Right, which argued for the diminution or even the abolition of the welfare services, were gaining force in the second half of the 1970s, and a new and powerful ideology was to give them political legitimacy.

FOURTEEN
Social Policy in the 1980s

In the 1980s, productivity increased, home ownership increased, share ownership increased, income tax was slashed, and members of the public queued to acquire shares in public utilities – telecommunications, British Airways, gas, water. The average wage increased by more than inflation, and fortunes were made out of property. 'Popular capitalism' became the aim, and to some extent the reality.

But the 1980s also saw the massive growth of unemployment, and the reappearance of beggars on the city streets. It became fashionable once more to talk of 'the poor' as a single class, and of 'scroungers' and 'layabouts' who would not work. The numbers of homeless people rose. The numbers of bankruptcies and company liquidations soared,[1] public sector expenditure was sharply reduced, and schools, universities and hospitals struggled to maintain services.

This was a decade of astonishing and drastic change. A consensus of more than forty years' duration on the nature of social progress and the role of the state was abruptly broken, and fundamentally different principles of operation were employed. In order to place these developments in perspective, it is necessary to record the basic facts while avoiding the quite bitter political rhetoric which has been current both among those who supported the new policies and those who opposed them.

Breaking the consensus

Labour was still in power in the winter of 1978–1979 – typified by the Press as the 'Winter of Discontent'.[2] Attempts to control inflation were failing, and the Government's limitation of wage increases to five per cent produced a wave of strikes. Britain's industrial output fell, and many services were disrupted. The trade unions were flexing their 'industrial muscle', and strikers included not only the road transport workers, who demanded a pay rise of 25 per cent but also ambulance staff, water and sewerage staff, grave-diggers, roadmen, dustmen, and school caretakers, whose refusal to work had immediate public impact. Ironically enough, it was the action of these relatively poorly paid groups which created a revulsion against the power of the unions. As sick people were refused hospital admission, water supplies became polluted, bodies remained unburied, sacks of rubbish piled up in the streets and children were sent home, public alarm grew and became a major factor in Labour's electoral defeat in May 1979.

At the time, the changes did not seem momentous. The Conservative Party manifesto promised the control of inflation, curbs to the power of the trade unions, the maintenance of the Rule of Law, support of family life, and better health and education services. The new government had a parliamentary majority of only 55; but it was to stay in power throughout the decade and into the 1990s, and to reshape Britain in a new frame of reference – individualist rather than collectivist, stressing the values of self-help and enterprise rather than those of community and social concern.

Sooner or later, the welfarist philosophy had to be challenged and tested. As we have seen, economic factors were working against it as early as 1965, when it became apparent that public expectations were running ahead of public willingness to bear taxation, with consequent problems for politicians. Election promises had to be made to win an election; but it became increasingly difficult to redeem them as industrial growth slackened and international competition for markets became sharper.

The approach of the first Thatcher administration was pragmatic rather than ideological, but the general lines of argument were as follows:

1. Health and welfare services have a built-in tendency to expand, and limits must be set. In a 'Welfare State', Government is subject to constant pressure to expand particular services, and may be led into making promises which it cannot sustain. The

'Wenceslaus myth'[3] of the state as universal provider must be checked.

2. State services are inherently paternalistic, and place too much power in the hands of professionals such as doctors, teachers and social workers. Privatization is therefore in the public interest. A cash nexus between professional and customer (patient/student/ client) puts power and dignity back in the hands of the individual, by allowing freedom of choice.

3. Rewarding those who show greater enterprise will in time create a more prosperous state, to the benefit of all. This is known as the 'trickle-down' or 'echelon' effect.[4]

4. A genuinely free market will produce a state of spontaneous order or *catallaxy* in which regulation and planning are largely unnecessary, and the response to consumer demand is swift and efficient.[5]

5. Government may therefore largely withdraw from the arena of social policy, leaving consumers to make the decisions with a minimum of public service intervention.

The decline of welfare policies is more difficult to document than the development of welfare policies. The building up of the 'Welfare State' was a fairly orderly and planned process in which groups of experts made recommendations, parliamentary Bills were framed, Acts were passed and then subjected to scrutiny. The reversal has been finance-led. Until the third Thatcher administration (following the General Election of 1987) policy was framed less by Acts of Parliament than by budgetary allocations and drastic expenditure cuts. In the third term, however, a new legislative programme with far-reaching implications was introduced.

Employment and unemployment

The Conservative Party fought the 1979 General Election on a Saatchi and Saatchi campaign with the slogan 'Labour isn't working' and a poster showing a long dole queue. The figure for the registered unemployed then stood at 1.2 million. By the third quarter of 1984, the official figure was over 3 million, and the basis of calculation had been redrawn to exclude a further 300,000.[6] Adrian Sinfield, who has explored the social meaning of unemployment,[7] points out that these figures exclude many other people who are affected by unemployment: the people (mainly women and ethnic minorities) who lose heart and do not register, the early retired, the marginally disabled who would work if there were jobs available, the dependent wives and children. He also stresses that even short-term unemployment represents a severe financial blow – in the erosion of savings, in debt and postponed mortgage payments, in opportunities foregone and hardships endured, from which it may take years to recover. In all, unemployment in 1983 may have affected some eight million people – 20 per cent of the population. Over a million of these were long-term unemployed.

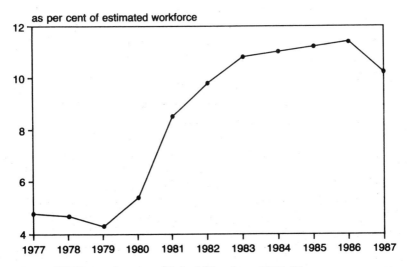

Figure XII Unemployment, United Kingdom, 1977–87
Source: *Annual Abstract of Statistics* 1989, table 6.6

The rationale for allowing unemployment to increase was that it was necessary to shake out industry, and produce a slimmer, more efficient work force; and that unemployment was the best weapon against inflation; but there was a heavy price to be paid in social distress, and the burdens fell unequally on the poorer sections of the population.

Unemployment was also a powerful weapon against the trade unions. The Employment Act of 1980 restricted picketing, which had led to some angry scenes in 1978–1979. The Employment Act of 1982 went further in outlawing political strikes, and – more drastically – rendering Union funds liable to confiscation in the case of support of unlawful action. The miners' strike of 1984 was a crucial test of political strength. The strikers were warned grimly that this time there would be 'no beer and sandwiches at Number 10' as under recent Labour Governments. The coal industry was overmanned, unprofitable pits had to be closed. There were alternative sources of energy – notably, cheap oil – and alternative sources of coal, which could be imported more cheaply from abroad. In the resultant industrial battle, Arthur Scargill and the leaders of the National Union of Mineworkers refused to condemn the use of violence, and lost the support of the Labour Party, while the Government enforced management's 'right to manage' by the deployment of huge police pickets. Law and order were restored at the cost of badly damaged industrial relations.[8]

After the peak of 1984, the number of registered unemployed began slowly to fall. At the end of the 1980s, it stood at 1.6 million – still substantially higher than at the start of the decade – and the threat of further inflation from a level nearing 8 per cent suggested that it might go higher still. Meanwhile, though unemployment benefit had been maintained without recourse to the kinds of drastic measures undertaken in the 1930s, a series of regulatory measures worsened the position of many unemployed people. The link between the rate of long-term benefits and earnings was abandoned in 1980, and that between short-term benefits and earnings in 1982. From 1984, it was announced that benefit would be paid fortnightly in arrears (a saving of £8.5 million).[9] The installation of wire grilles in Social Security offices testifies to the deterioration of relations between clients and officers.

So the power of organized labour was decisively broken, but there was a social cost to be paid. The record of the Conservative Governments of the 1980s will ultimately be judged on whether these measures were successful in restoring economic prosperity, and whether inflation could be held in check.

Local Government

One of the unanticipated effects of local government reorganization in 1974 had been to create powerful Labour dominated metropolitan councils.[10] After Labour's defeat in the General Election of 1979,

like the Greater London Council, these Labour controlled authorities became a target for Conservative attack. The Public Sector
Borowing Requirement was severely restricted, and the Rates Act
of 1984 introduced 'rate-capping', making it illegal for councils to
set rates above a prescribed level.

Some councils lurched to the Left – notably Liverpool, where
the 'Militant Tendency' gained control, high spending continued,
and the city was virtually bankrupt by 1986. Some councils in
desperation took extreme measures, such as selling and leasing
back their own town halls, or playing the stock market. Government speakers repeatedly attacked the minor activities of some
local authorities in supporting homosexual and lesbian organizations,
groups for single parents, Asians and blacks, as remote from the
interests of solid working-class opinion. The excesses of the so-
called 'loony Left' were certainly exaggerated, but they were
enough to provide a rationale for ending strong metropolitan
government. In 1986, the GLC and the metropolitan councils were
disbanded. The GLC, damaged by a judicial decision which
defeated its 'Fares Fair' campaign for flat-rate fares in the London
area, characteristically went out with a blaze of fireworks, and
London's County Hall, once the bastion of municipal socialism,
was put up for sale for commercial purposes.

There has been some public concern that a Government which is
avowedly non-interventionist has greatly weakened local government, with a consequent centralization of power. The Community
Charge Act 1989, which introduced the 'poll tax', may have
adverse effects on local government financing. The Act abolishes
domestic rates (based on house property values) and substitutes a
flat rate charge on individuals, which can vary from area to area
and year to year. There are some exemptions, such as people in
long-term hospital accommodation or nursing homes for the
elderly; but every other citizen will be liable to pay the charge.
Though there are reductions for students and unemployed people
and those on very low incomes, even they will have to pay 20 per
cent.

The stated aim is to make local government more responsive to
the wishes of the people: however, regressive taxation shifts the
burden from property owners to almost the whole of the adult
public, including young and elderly on small incomes, and some
people with no income at all. The tax will be very difficult to

collect (houses are static, people move) and local authorities have had to divert both manpower and money from other purposes to ensure efficient collection. Local authority assessments of community charge levels are in most cases considerably higher than Government estimates.

It is possible to argue that local government is unrepresentative, since the majority of the electorate do not bother to vote; or that local government is largely unnecessary as communications improve; or that local government is of minor importance if people have the money to arrange things for themselves. But the debate has not been argued on issues of principle: it has been concerned with expedient methods of raising money, rather than with constitutional rights and obligations.

The weakening of local authority power also weakens three of its core activities: housing, social services and education. Specific measures in these fields in the third term of the Thatcher administration have added to the responsibilities of local government without restoring its status. These will be discussed at later points in this chapter.

The National Health Service

The first moves of the new Conservative Government were aimed at administrative improvement. The cumbersome nature of the four-tier system introduced as a result of the 1974 reorganization soon defeated the innovators in the extended Health and Community Services. In 1982 in a limited revision, one tier was abolished – that of the Area Health Authority. Since then, the intention of Government has been to bring the efficiency of the business world into the National Health Service. In 1983, Sir Roy Griffiths, a Government adviser from Sainsbury's food chain was asked to examine the problems, and as a result of his report,[11] a clearer management structure was introduced to replace the consensus management of the 'Grey Book'. This followed the Government's belief that 'the duty of a manager is to manage'. At the District level, there is now a functional split, with separate managers for different kinds of service – Acute, Mental Illness, Elderly and so on. The responsibility is individual, not corporate, and includes a measure of budgetary control. The District General Manager is responsible for the whole service of a District, and is accountable to the Regional Manager. Some 'Griffiths Managers' were recruited from industry and commerce rather than from the ranks of Health Service administrators. Since their contracts are short-term (four years, renewable), they have an incentive to produce rapid results – perhaps at the cost of long-term planning in some cases.

Hospitals are encouraged to use privatized services where they can, putting such functions as laundry, rubbish collection and even catering out to tender. The White Paper *Working for Patients*[12] and the National Health Service and Community Care Act 1990 contain provisions for hospitals to opt out of the NHS, and to develop service on contract, and for general practitioners to handle their own budgets. These proposals have been strongly resisted by the medical profession.

Community Care and the Social Services

One way in which the Health Service has been able to save money is in the continued rundown of hospitals and homes for long-term care. The all-party House of Commons Social Services Committee produced a report in 1985[13] in which it drew attention to the results of this policy in a period in which the local authorities did not have the resources to provide alternative services.

The Social Services Committee took the view that there was 'a crisis in the community'. Mentally ill and mentally handicapped people were being discharged without proper after-care arrangements. There was a sharp increase in homelessness, in people inappropriately sent to prison, and in family stress as relatives desperately tried to cope with problems beyond their capacity. The report called unequivocally for government action and increased local expenditure.

In the following year, the Audit Commission for Local Authorities tackled the same theme in a report[14] which pointed out that even in financial terms, the situation needed remedial action. Local authorities, subject to financial restriction, could not deal with the needs. Neither could the Health Service. Two inadequate services were 'struggling along in parallel'. This situation made for 'perverse incentives': patients, particularly the elderly infirm, were being forced into the private sector. While this might be in accord with the current Government ethos, private sector Homes were being heavily supported out of public funds via the Social Security budget. The costs were soaring, and, since the private sector was almost exclusively residential in nature, it could hardly be described as 'care in the community'. Real community care could be achieved at very much lower cost in patients' own homes.

Sir Roy Griffiths was asked to make a second investigation in his capacity as Deputy Chairman of the NHS Management Committee. He tackled the task with characteristic thoroughness, and submitted a report towards the end of 1987.[15] This was subject to some delay in publication, and finally appeared without Government endorsement, accompanied only by the statement that the Government would put forward its own proposals in due course. These proposals did not become public until November 1989 – over eighteen months later.

Sir Roy's recommendations included the nomination of a minister of state 'clearly and publicly responsible for community care' – with, it could be assumed, an appropriate staff of civil servants; the transfer of community care for all the client groups involved to the local authorities; the provision of 50 per cent grants by central government, the grants to be earmarked for this specific purpose rather than forming part of the block grant; and the provision by the local authorities of 'clear packages of care' for individual clients which might be made up of elements from statutory, voluntary and private sector sources.

The Government response[16] was a weakened version of the original Griffiths plan. Accordingly, there will now be no community care section in the Department of Health (the title of Minister for Community Care was added to the responsibilities of an existing minister of state). Community care will be the responsibility of local authorities; but there will be no earmarked grants, though there was a promise of some special additional funding for the care of mentally ill people. Since there are no definitive statements on the degree of financial support from central government (the matter being left to the next round of allocations) the question of whether clear 'packages of care' can be devised for individual patients has been left largely unanswered. Local authorities, like District Health Authorities, and Housing Authorities, are to be managers of services bought in from other sources, rather than direct providers.

Community care responsibilities under the National Health

Service and Community Care Act 1990 devolve largely on local authority Social Services Departments, where social work staff must learn new managerial tasks, rather than working in face-to-face contact with clients. Social workers were one of the early targets of attack from the New Right, which saw them as typical of the 'Nanny State'. In 1979 and 1980, the columns of the *Daily Telegraph* were regularly occupied with contributions on this theme from Colin Brewer and June Lait, whose book *Can Social Work Survive?* strongly attacked the Seebohm Report and its consequences. The Local Authority Social Services Act was pronounced 'a foolish, unnecessary and extravagant measure', the Central Council for Education and Training in Social Work 'arguably superfluous' and Social Services Departments 'constructed on a false unity'.[17]

Social work in local authorities has undergone major changes in the 1980s. The Mental Health Act of 1983 introduced a strongly legal element into the work of 'approved social workers', giving them new powers and duties in relation to mentally ill and mentally handicapped people. Thereafter, a series of highly publicized cases – Jasmine Beckford, Tyra Henry, Beverley Lewis – in which young people in need of care had been abused or grossly neglected, led to a focus of attention on child abuse. The Children Act of 1989 proposes a new and complex set of provisions for the protection of children by the courts which places heavy new responsibilities on social workers, and further strengthens their connection with the courts.

Social work has not disappeared as a profession; but the cumulative effect of legislation has been to stress the social control element in care, to focus social workers' attention on statutory requirements relating to mental illness and child abuse, and to farm out much of the work of caring for the infirm elderly and disabled to other agencies. Social workers are now required to be inspectors, resource managers and budget holders. The emphasis of their work has been substantially shifted from the skills in human relations which traditionally formed the core of their discipline.

Local authority funds for staffing and retraining have been scarce. Though the Central Council for Education and Training in Social Work was encouraged by the Department of Health to develop an elaborate scheme for the reorganization and upgrading of the profession, central government backing for the scheme has been very limited. CCETSW estimated the costs at £50 million. The Government offer in 1988 was £1 million.[18]

Social Security

In financial terms, the Social Security system is easily the largest of the social services.[19] In 1985, it absorbed nearly 30 per cent of all public expenditure, and cost nearly three times as much as health and welfare and education combined. Some 22 different benefits cover a wide range of individual and family needs, and are administered by an army of nearly 90,000 staff. It is a system which affects a wide spectrum of the population; in 1982, 75 per cent of household units received some of their income from social security benefits, and 11 per cent received 90 per cent or more of their income from this source.

Government action in this field has been comparatively minor. There have been some improvements – a new disablement benefit, improvements in the take-up rate for FIS (now Family Credit) and Attendance Allowances, an extension of Mobility Allowance. Correspondingly, there have been moves to reduce the cost of other types of benefit. Mention has already been made of small changes designed to reduce the cost of unemployment benefit. Other minor savings in expenditure have been made by transferring the cost of the first eight weeks of sickness benefit to employers, paying child benefit four-weekly in arrears instead of weekly, cutting eligibility to housing benefit under the revised scheme introduced in 1984, and delaying upratings in benefit required to keep pace with inflation.[20] The Social Security Act of 1986, which involved new bases of calculation and set up the Social Fund, more than halved the amount of money available, and effectively cut the rate of benefit for many clients.[21] Under the operation of the Social Fund, Supplementary Benefit has been replaced by Income Support (subject to a much larger degree of discretion from cash-limited sources) and many 'one-off' payments which were previously made as grants are now given as repayable loans. Child benefit was frozen in 1987, 1988, 1989 and 1990 – equivalent to a cut of nearly one-third.

Despite these measures, the overall social security budget has continued to grow. The cost has been consistently higher than

Government estimates, and repeated attempts to target the money available more closely to the most needy groups have met with only limited success. This is partly because of demographic trends – the rise in the number of retirement pensioners has been much greater than the decline in the number of children; but also partly a result of Government policies. High unemployment rates, early retirement and the existence of very low paid jobs have been tolerated, if not encouraged, in order to keep down inflation, with consequent increases in the numbers claiming unemployment benefit, state pensions and Family Credit (formerly FIS). The Government's reluctance to subscribe to the European Community Social Charter stems in part from a belief that these measures are necessary in order to keep British industry competitive. Similarly, a rise in attendance allowance claims can be correlated with the reduction in residential care for the elderly and disabled: if the Government reduces one kind of benefit, it often finds itself providing another.

Perhaps the outstanding fact is that a Government which set its face against 'dependency' has been unable to reduce dependence on state benefits, and has in some ways been forced to increase provision in pursuance of its economic ends.

Housing

'The Conservatives projected a powerful image of a property-owning democracy through the creation of a "right to buy"'.[22] Mass home ownership, like mass share ownership, has been encouraged to give individuals a stake in the country, and to create popular capitalism. In the first two Thatcher administrations, this was achieved largely by restrictions on local authority funding (which forced local authorities to sell Council houses on terms favourable to sitting tenants) and by financial measures designed to keep the interest rate low, and hence facilitate mortgages. These measures substantially increased the demand for house purchase – with the result that property prices soared, demand further strengthened and a self-perpetuating spiral began. House prices in many areas doubled within a single year as the 'ripple effect' spread from the highly industrialized south-east to the Midlands, the West Country, East Anglia and further north. Fortunes were made, particularly by large commercial companies which could afford to acquire blocks of property, and on a smaller scale by people who could move from a high-cost area to a low-cost area, or who inherited property which could be turned into disposable income.[23] The result has been a further increase in inflation.

Between 1979 and 1987, home ownership increased from 55 to 64 per cent of housing tenure, while public sector housing starts dropped from 107,000 to 30,000 – mainly for special groups such as the elderly.[24] About one million Council houses were sold off, and these sales, coupled with the low number of housing starts, substantially restricted the availability of low-cost rented housing. A Department of the Environment survey published in 1985 estimated that the condition of public sector housing was deteriorating, 85 per cent being in need of repair and maintenance.[25]

In 1987, the Government issued a White Paper on Housing[26] which made clear the intention to continue the expansion of home ownership and incidentally of mortgage relief, repeatedly attacked by Labour as a subsidy to property owners. Steps would also be taken to 'put new life into the rented sector'. Local authorities would in future be 'enablers' rather than 'providers', and would be expected to provide 'businesslike financial frameworks' for the operation of Housing Action Trusts and other small-scale bodies. Public housing was seen 'as symptomatic of a wider malaise of dependence on the Welfare State, a weakening of the moral fibre of the working classes'.[27]

In 1989, the housing market, which had been buoyant throughout the 1980s, collapsed suddenly under the impact of two rapid rises in the interest rate. The belief which had fuelled home ownership was that 'house prices never go down'. By the end of 1989, 20 per cent reductions were being forecast for the London area. Building Society repossessions for non-payment of mortgage interest, which had stood at only 2,500 in 1979, rose to 21,000 in 1986.[28] Despite the efforts of the major building societies to keep interest charges down and to spread payments further into the future, the figures continued to rise until 1990.

There has been a growing disenchantment with home ownership as owners have come to terms with the costs and the risks involved. Though this is an immediate response to high interest rate levels, it seems unlikely that the massive property boom of the 1980s will be repeated. Meanwhile, rented accommodation was expensive (since many people let property they were unable to sell, and had to meet high mortgage payments) and the ability of local authorities to provide low-cost housing was considerably reduced.

Education

The somewhat exaggerated hopes of the 1960s that education would create a better society and enable each child to fulfil his or her own potential gave way in the 1980s to a profound disillusionment in which education is valued primarily for its relevance to future employment.

The setting up in 1982 of an extended Manpower Services Commission under Lord Young with a £2,000 million budget took many young people off the unemployment register. It coincided with a marked restriction of further education opportunities which local education authorities could no longer fund. Independent City Technology Colleges, supported by industry, are increasingly to prepare bright youngsters with a technological bent for a technological age.

In the school system, the message has been 'decentralize and diversify'. Private schools on traditional lines have enjoyed a new lease of life. Grammar schools have been preserved, and under the Education Reform Act 1988, schools may opt out of local authority control with 'grant-maintained' status. Many head teachers, like general practitioners and social workers, have become resource-holders and financial managers. The Education Reform Act also specifies a new centrally imposed curriculum which binds teachers to the conveying of skills and information on set subjects, and to complex assessment procedures.

The Higher Education sector has been at a particular disadvantage. Polytechnics, funded by local authorities until the creation of the Polytechnics and Colleges Funding Council in 1989, have shared in the general financial restriction of other local authority services. The universities, funded directly by Government through the University Grants Committee (now the Universities Funding Council), faced a more sudden reversal of conditions. In 1981, the Department of Education and Science gave them a month in which to plan 18 per cent cuts over three years.[29] Since the largest budget item was that of staff salaries, and most academic staff had security of tenure (finally abolished under the Education Reform Act) this was only made possible by the termination of temporary posts and early retirement, without regard to the nature or quality of teaching and research, or the effects on the teaching of individual subjects.

Since that time, there has been steady pressure to reduce the dependence of higher education institutions on central Government funding, and a marked swing away from the humanities and the social sciences (with the exception of Economics) towards Accounting, Business Management, Electronics and Computer Science. The Education (Student Loans) Act 1990 will require students to pay part of their own maintenance costs for the first time since the Butler Act of 1944 came into effect.

The impact of change

The first two Thatcher administrations adopted a cautious attitude to issues of social policy. Though financial measures were designed to limit the work of the public sector authorities and to promote the privatization of many of their activities, the only major changes by statute were those introduced by the Social Security Act of 1986, which were only just coming into effect at the time of the General Election of 1987. After that election, which gave the Government a majority of 102 in the House of Commons, the decision was taken at Cabinet level to embark on a major new legislative programme. The Education Reform Act 1988, the Children Act 1989 and the National Health Service and Community Care Act 1990 all embody the philosophy of diversification: the use of public authorities as managers rather than providers, a reduction in public sector services, and a shift to the private sector.

Public opinion polls have consistently shown that this programme does not carry popular support. Respondents not only want better health and social services, but say that they are prepared to pay for them through increased taxation. For instance, *British Social Attitudes*, an annual publication of some standing in the Social Policy field, includes questions on the attitudes of respondents to the health, education and social services. When respondents are asked whether they favour cutting taxes and reducing these services; keeping both taxes and services at the current level; or

increasing both taxes and services, responses for successive years
have been as follows:

	(per cent of all respondents)				
	1983	*1984*	*1985*	*1986*	*1987*
Reduce taxes/services	9	6	6	5	3
Maintain at present levels	54	50	43	44	42
Increase taxes/services	32	39	45	46	50

Table 14.1. *Responses to survey questions on paying for the social
services, 1983–7*
Source: British Social Attitudes 1987 p. 3, 1988/9 p. 96.

When questioned about priorities in public spending, respondents over the same five years have consistently placed the
National Health Service at the top of their list, with Education
second.

There is of course no guarantee that individuals will stand by
their expressed attitudes when the tax demands come in; and a
Government with an unpopular social policy might maintain its
position if the electorate continued to have confidence in its
foreign policy and its management of the economy; but there are
major causes for concern in the early 1990s. The most fundamental
of these are the current lack of official statistical information about
poverty and hardship, and the growing evidence that monetarist
policies, so far from benefitting the whole population, are creating
a permanent underclass.

One of the early actions of the new Government after the 1979
General Election was to abolish over 200 'quangos' or advisory
bodies, some of which possessed specialized expertise in dealing
with social problems. One of them was the Personal Social
Services Council, which was working on the development of the
local authority and voluntary social services. Another was the
standing Royal Commission on Income and Wealth, the Diamond
Commission, which had produced a series of major reports on the
distribution of wealth, and the persistence of the gap between the
rich and the poor.

Though successive Governments had used the Royal Commission
and the departmental or interdepartmental Committee of Inquiry
as major instruments of social policy, there were to be no further
fact-finding bodies of this kind. Hugo Young comments:

The Royal Commission and the departmental committee were traditional power-bases for middle-ground intellectuals. But no longer ... the idea passed into the museum of political dinosaurs. In a climate in which everything was political, detachment was held to be a chimera and objectivity a fraud, and the classes who claimed these virtues lost their foothold in public life.[30]

Regular official sources of statistical information became less helpful. The Civil Service Strike of 1981 was a preliminary to the disbanding of the Civil Service Department, and to substantial cuts in Civil Service staffing. A White Paper of 1981 endorsed a recommendation by Sir Derek (now Lord) Rayner, Chairman of Marks and Spencer, that official statistical services should be cut by 25 per cent. Sir Derek had laid down the principle that 'information should not be collected primarily for publication. It should be collected because Government needs it for its own business'.[31]

From that time on, Government statistical publications have become very expensive (the full set of volumes of the Rayner Report cost over £100 at 1981 prices) and in many cases have steadily yielded less and less information on social topics, though economic data have been maintained to the previous standard.

Concern among statisticians at the lack of accurate statistical information was expressed in October 1989 by Sir Claus Moser, former head of the Government Statistical Service, and Sir David Cox, former president of the Royal Statistical Society. Sir Claus and Sir David called for an independent body to monitor the Government's use of statistics, criticizing the conclusions of the Rayner Report. Sir Claus was reported as saying: 'Before the Rayner review, the purpose of the Government statistical service was to serve several masters – first and foremost ... the Government, but also industry, academics, the public, indeed the whole nation... What worries me is the effect of the cuts following Rayner on the overall accuracy of Government statistics'.[32] In the absence of official enquiries and accurate statistics, it is difficult to judge the severity of the hardship caused to the poorer members of society by the social policies of the 1980s. Yet this is a crucial issue in judging the success of those policies.

Kenneth Harris comments:

> There is no doubt that Britain's economic growth in the 1980s
> has been brought about at a cost. A cost of three million
> unemployed, a further five million living in poverty, and a
> widening difference between the rich and the poor, the north
> and the south. As in America, neo-Liberalism risks creating a
> permanent underclass, who are excluded from enjoying the
> freedoms that the rest of society can afford ... the cohesion
> conferred on Britain by the Welfare State may be forfeited.[33]

The existence of a sizeable underclass, if substantiated, would be a
serious blow to Hayek's 'trickle-down' philosophy, which assumes
that in time the whole of society will benefit from the wealth
created at the top. However, facts and figures are now relatively
hard to come by.

The *Black Report* of 1980 provided detailed evidence of inequalities in health between the Registrar-General's five social (or
occupational) classes: for instance, for both sexes, the risk of death
before retirement was two and a half times as great in Class V
(unskilled manual workers) as in Social Class I (professional and
managerial workers); sickness and medical consultation rates in
successive age-groups were consistently higher for Social Classes
IV and V. The Working Group sought explanations for the fact
that these differentials persisted in a period of increased purchasing
power and state provision of medical services. Explanations are
discussed primarily in terms of poverty, poor work conditions and
childhood deprivation, and a wide-ranging series of recommendations designed to help families and young children follow. Despite
the status of the report (Sir Douglas Black was Chief Scientist to
the DHSS at the time) and the considerable scholarship which
went into it, it was published with an official disclaimer from the
Conservative Secretary of State to the effect that it was 'quite
unrealistic', and distributed by the DHSS only in a photocopied
form. A Penguin edition with a foreword by Peter Townsend, who
was a member of the Working Group, had wide sales.[34]

The Brixton Riot of April 1981, which sparked off other riots,
notably in Toxteth, Liverpool, was analysed in a report from Lord
Scarman[35] in which he was at pains to make it clear that, though
there was an ethnic element, this was not primarily a race riot; and

that while the Rule of Law must be maintained, a more conciliatory attitude on the part of the police and better social
conditions in poverty-stricken urban areas with a large ethnic
population could help to prevent further outbreaks. Lord Scarman
concluded:

> The inner city is crucial for the future of the British nation. The
> inner cities are the testing ground where the character of Britain
> will be determined. This is because of their population mix,
> their high rate of unemployment and their substandard physical
> environment. Most importantly, our fellow citizens who live
> there see themselves at a disadvantage compared with the rest of
> us, and many of them attribute their disadvantage to racial
> prejudice. ... This brings me to what was, and is, my central
> contention – that we have to embark on social policies that will
> eradicate the multiple disadvantages that British blacks now
> suffer from ... we must tackle the crisis of the inner cities, not
> because we are frightened of conflict, but because we are all
> fired by conscience and a passion for justice.[36]

Two years later, the Archbishop of Canterbury set up his own
Commission on the problems of 'Urban Priority Areas' (UPAs),
a term which covered both the decaying areas of the inner
cities and some outlying areas of deprivation on local authority
estates. The members of the Archbishop's Commission included
two eminent sociologists, Professor A. H. Halsey of the University
of Oxford and Professor Ray Pahl of the University of Kent at
Canterbury. The first section of the report consisted of a closely
argued analysis of the problems of poverty and deprivation in
Britain:

> To describe UPAs is to write of squalor and dilapidation. Grey
> walls, littered streets, boarded-up windows, graffiti, demolition
> and debris are the drearily standard features.[37]

Using six social indicators of deprivation derived from previous
work by the Department of the Environment, the analysis built up
'an elaborate picture of inequality': of areas of an increasingly
affluent Britain where people lived on low wages in sub-standard
housing, where crime, vandalism and marriage breakdown were
rife, and where there was 'a general frailty of civil order':

The more recent history has been one of growing inequality – in life chances, income, housing, education, public services, and the general level of civic amenity.[38]

A particularly acute problem in urban areas is that of single homelessness. Shelter, the national charity, estimated at the end of 1989 that there were at least 400,000 homeless people, and other estimates have risen as high as two million, but there are no accurate figures.[39] This situation seems to be the result of the interaction of at least three different sets of factors – demographic, institutional and social security. The demographic factors relate to the increasing breakdown of family life: some young people literally have no home when parents divorce and remarry, and others may leave home as a result of physical or sexual abuse. Many older men become homeless when their own marriages break up. (This is largely a male problem: homeless single women are a comparative rarity).

Institutional factors relate to the rapid run-down of psychiatric hospitals and other residential accommodation by both the NHS and local authorities. Many single homeless people are suffering from chronic mental illness. Dr Malcolm Weller and his colleagues, who investigated the condition of destitute men briefly cared for by Crisis at Christmas over four years, writes:

> Many psychiatrically very ill people are living like feral children in the forest of the city, scavenging for garbage and subsisting from charitable handouts. This neglect is constantly before us – and yet we seem to be inured to the desperate plight of these vulnerable individuals.[40]

The social security factors relate to two different issues: one is a DHSS decision in 1988 to refuse benefit to young people between the ages of 16 and 18 who would not accept a place on an Employment Training Scheme. This has since been somewhat modified. The other issue is a long-standing one: in order to claim full Income Support, a homeless person has to have an address. In order to have an address, he has to have money. The comparatively few voluntary hostels – Salvation Army, Church Army and the rest – which will provide an address on trust are overcrowded, and seldom able to provide a bed for more than a few days. The private 'hotels' and lodging houses, which have increased in the past few years to make a profit out of this most basic of markets are often of very poor standard. At the beginning of the 1990s, there is at least the promise of more money for certain hard pressed groups. In the final weeks of 1989, additional financial allocations were announced for the young disabled, for the elderly infirm and for the single homeless. The Minister of Social Security began to show a more conciliatory attitude to clients; but a legal challenge sponsored by the Child Poverty Action Group on behalf of clients who had been refused Income Support because their local offices had exhausted their budgets met with only temporary success. A High Court judgement of February 1990[41] found the Government guidelines limiting payments from the Social Fund by budget restrictions on local Social Security offices 'unlawful'. The immediate Government response was to state that legislation would be introduced to make it lawful.

The gap between those who think that poverty is society's responsibility and those who think that it is the individual's responsibility does not seem to have narrowed.

Epilogue

In the jargon of the late twentieth century, this study has been about 'quality of life': the struggle out of the dark days of the 1830s to the age of the fifth-generation computer. We have made quantum leaps in technology. People live longer, have better health care and a minimum income, travel faster, and communicate across the world with ease. Stinking slums have been turned into brightly lit concrete jungles. Women have been freed from the annual pregnancy, and men from heavy labour which made them old at forty.

But the development of technology – from the first anaesthetics to open heart surgery, from Stephenson's Rocket to Concorde, from Rowland Hill's Penny Post to FAX, has not been matched by a comparable development in social insight. Old arguments and old dilemmas surface again, unresolved; old prejudices recur.

'Do you ever get the feeling that the world is going backwards?' asks John Mortimer's bewildered elderly cleric of his wife, 'It's as if we got tired of chugging on slowly, and put the whole engine into reverse. Back to the dole queues, and poverty being thought of as a shameful little secret, something respectable people don't get involved in'.[1]

The idea of a 'Welfare State' involved a belief in linear development: that we were 'progressing' in competence to manage our social life at roughly the same pace as we progressed in technical competence; and that we would presumably reach some ideal state of affairs where all the problems would be solved, and all the needs met. But there never was a 'Welfare State'. Beveridge rejected the term, preferring to talk of a Welfare Society, in which statutory and voluntary services would work in partnership. Richard Titmuss referred to the 'Welfare State' in quotation marks – a practice which has been followed in the present narrative. The vision of the late 1940s became tarnished on contact with reality. Changes in social policy in the 1980s have shaken a widely held faith in linear progress, and produced a number of conflicting speculations about the future development of the social services, loosely based on economic or political philosophy, or a philosophy of history. They may be summarized as follows:–

1. Britain was on the wrong track. The way forward lies in making citizens rich enough to make their own decisions, and pay for their own needs without the intervention of the state.

2. Britain was on the right track. The developments of the 1980s are simply a 'hiccup' in progress, and will soon be forgotten.

3. Capitalism is inherently unstable. Social services are a means of deflecting revolution, and their collapse will bring the collapse of capitalism nearer.

4. Society evolves through a process of thesis – antithesis – synthesis, and the next step will be a synthesis of 'Welfare State' and 'anti-Welfare State' thinking.

5. There are swings of the pendulum – from altruism to egoism, or from state monopoly to pluralism, or from community living to personal autonomy, and the pendulum will swing again. And again.

6. Civilizations rise and fall. Ours may be in a state of disintegration if it neglects moral values.

7. New patterns are emerging but are difficult to identify. The new interest in chaos theory as applied to human affairs may reflect an inability to make sense of the conflicts and confusions of social policies and social attitudes.

Chaos theory derives from propositions in physics and mathematics, and suggests that phenomena can be divided into those we can order and predict, and those which are apparently of a random nature.[2] But there may be more subtle patterns in seeming confusion if we can detect them. (A particularly unhelpful formulation for present purposes is that of the 'Butterfly Effect', which tells us that an event which seems of little importance today may be of overwhelming importance at some time in the future.)

None of this theorizing helps very much with the all-important question of *what happens next?* But this much can be said: though the future will contain some new elements (two of the more predictable are the move towards integration with Europe and the increasing threat of AIDS), it will not be entirely new. We will take with us our accumulated baggage: genetic endowment, concepts, habits of thought, training, experience; and the problems we face will not be entirely new either. There will still be questions of how to provide for the basic needs of all citizens – protection in childhood, a good education, a home, a job and the opportunity of family life, care in sickness or disability, help in adversity and support in old age. There will still be room for discussion on the appropriate balance between security and incentives, organization and freedom, planning and natural development, communal provision and personal responsibility.

Human beings are capable of being highly competitive, self-seeking and materialistic. They are also capable of an astonishing degree of co-operation, self-sacrifice and idealism.[3] But beyond the models of 'Economic Man' and 'Philanthropic Man', there is an increasing appreciation of the concept of the human race as problem-solving animals.[4] In this view, there are no 'ultimate solutions'. We progress by making mistakes, recognizing them and correcting them. This process requires a kind of intellectual humility, a willingness to be proved wrong, a capacity for growth through learning. A knowledge of the past can be constructively used – not to hamper change, but to inform it, and help in new choices. We can at least learn from our mistakes: from the long-lived hatred of the Poor Law, from Chadwick's experience of being right at the wrong time about public health measures, from the local distrust of centralizing policies, from the organizational problems of the voluntary services, from the conquest of the slums and the epidemic diseases, from the dreams and the visions and the failures. This is part of our heritage. We have no need to go on reinventing the wheel.

> Time present and time past
> Are both perhaps present in time future
> And time future contained in time past.[5]

APPENDIX I
Political Parties in Power
1830–1990

Note: where changes of government or leadership were frequent, this table has been slightly simplified.

	Prime Minister	*Ruling Party*	*Parliamentary Reform*
1830–32	Grey	Whig	Reform Act 1832
1832–34	Melbourne I	Whig	
1834–35	Peel I	Conservative	
1835–41	Melbourne II	Whig	
1841–46	Peel II	Conservative	
1846–52	Russell I	Whig	
1852	Derby–Disraeli I	Conservative	
1852–55	Aberdeen	Whig	
1855–58	Palmerston I	Whig	
1858–59	Derby–Disraeli II	Conservative	
1859–65	Palmerston II	Whig	
1865–66	Russell II	Whig	
1866–67	Derby/Disraeli III	Conservative	Reform Act 1867
1867–68	Disraeli I	Conservative	
1868–74	Gladstone I	Liberal	
1874–80	Disraeli II	Conservative	
1880–85	Gladstone II	Liberal	Manhood Suffrage 1884
1885–86	Salisbury I	Conservative	
1886	Gladstone III	Liberal	
1886–92	Salisbury II	Conservative	
1892–94	Gladstone IV	Liberal	
1894–95	Rosebery	Conservative	
1895–1902	Salisbury	Conservative	
1902–06	Balfour	Conservative	

1906–08	Campbell-Bannerman	Liberal
1908–16	Asquith	Liberal
1916–22	Lloyd George	Liberal . . . . Votes for Women 1918
1922–23	Bonar Law	Conservative
1923–24	Baldwin I	Conservative
1924	Macdonald I	Labour
1924–29	Baldwin II	Conservative . . . 'Flapper Vote' 1928
1929–31	Macdonald II	Labour
1931–35	Baldwin–Macdonald	National
1935–40	Baldwin IV	Conservative
1940–45	Churchill I	Coalition
1945–51	Attlee	Labour
1951–55	Churchill II	Conservative
1955–57	Eden	Conservative
1957–63	Macmillan	Conservative
1963–64	Douglas-Home	Conservative
1964–70	Wilson	Labour
1970–74	Heath	Conservative
1974–76	Wilson	Labour
1976–79	Callaghan	Labour
1979–83	Thatcher I	Conservative
1983–87	Thatcher II	Conservative
1987–	Thatcher III	Conservative

APPENDIX II
Biographical Notes

These brief notes are intended as an aid to reading the foregoing chapters. They are drawn in the main from the *Dictionary of National Biography (DNB)*, *Who's Who* and *Who Was Who*, which should be consulted for a fuller account. Individuals are listed by the name they were generally known by in their career, with later titles in parentheses.

Attlee, Clement Richard, (Earl Attlee) 1883–1967, Labour politician. Secretary, Toynbee Hall, Lecturer, Ruskin College Oxford and London School of Economics, MP, member of Coalition War Cabinet, 1940–45, Prime Minister 1945–1951.

Arnott, (Dr) Neil, 1788–1874, physician and public health reformer, worked with Chadwick and Southwood Smith (q.v.) on the Poor Law Commission and the General Board of Health. Physician extraordinary to Queen Victoria, 1837. FRS. 1838. Member of (General) Medical Council, 1854.

Barnardo, (Dr) Thomas John, 1845–1905, founder of Dr Barnardo's Homes. Missionary medical student, worked at the Ernest Street Ragged School, founded East End Juvenile Mission, developed Homes for destitute children. Licentiate of the Royal College of Surgeons, 1876, Fellow 1879.

Bentham, Jeremy, 1747–1832, founder of Utilitarianism and writer on jurisprudence, known for the principle of 'the greatest happiness of the greatest number' and the 'hedonistic calculus'. Promoter of the Panopticon (invented by his brother). Author of the *Introduction to the Principles of Morals and Legislation, Principles of Penal Law* and *the Constitutional Code*, among many other works.

Bevan, Aneurin, 1897–1960, Labour politician, former coal miner. Minister of Health, 1945–51, Minister of Labour and National Service, 1951, member of Tribune Group, resigned 1951.

Beveridge, (Sir) William, (Lord Beveridge), 1879–1963. Sub-warden of Toynbee Hall, first Chairman of the Employment Exchange Committee. Director, London School of Economics, 1919–1937, Master of University College, Oxford, 1937–1945. Sole signatory of the *Beveridge Report*, 1942, author of *Full Employment in a Free Society* and *Voluntary Action*.

Black, (Sir) Douglas, b. 1913, Chief Scientist, DHSS, 1973–1977. Chairman, Working Party on Inequalities in Health. Previously Professor of Medicine, University of Manchester.

Butler, R. A. (Lord Butler of Saffron Walden) 1902–80, Conservative politician. Minister of Education, 1940–1945, subsequently Chancellor of the Exchequer, Lord Privy Seal, Home Secretary, Foreign Secretary, Master of Trinity College Cambridge.

Booth, William, ('General Booth'), 1829–1912, founder of the Salvation Army. Methodist itinerant preacher, ran a Christian mission in Whitechapel. Salvation Army launched on military lines 1878 – *DNB* calls it 'a world-wide engine of revivalism'. Author of *In Darkest England*.

Bosanquet, Bernard, 1848–1928, Oxford philosopher and writer on Ethics. Editor of *Aspects of the Social Problem*, giving philosophical backing to the views of the Charity Organisation Society. Friend of C. S. Loch (q.v.).

Bosanquet, Helen, (née Dendy), wife of Bernard Bosanquet, supporter of the Charity Organisation Society, member of the Royal Commission on the Poor Laws, 1905–1909, author of *Social Work in London*.

Boyson, (Sir) Rhodes, b. 1925, Conservative politician, MP for Brent North. Joint author of the *Black Papers on Education*, author of *Down with the Poor*. Hobby (according to *Who's Who*), 'exciting the millenialist Left in education and politics'. Under-Secretary of State for Education, Minister of State, Social Security, Northern Ireland Office, and Local Government (Department of the Environment).

Castle, Barbara, (née Betts), b. 1910, Labour politician. MP for Blackburn, 1945–1979, Chairman of the Labour Party, 1958–1959, Minister of Overseas Development, Minister of Transport, Secretary of State for Employment, Secretary of State for the Social Services, MEP since 1979.

Chadwick, (Sir) Edwin, 1800–1889, senior civil servant. Poor law, factory and public health reformer. Secretary to Jeremy Bentham (q.v.), Assistant Poor Law Commissioner, 1832–1834, Secretary to the Poor Law Commission 1834–1848, Commissioner of the General Board of Health, 1848–1854, dismissed 1854.

Churchill, (Sir) Winston, 1908–1965, MP (Liberal), President of the Board of Trade, 1908–1910, Home Secretary, 1910–1911, (Conservative) Chancellor of the Exchequer, 1924–1929, First Lord of the

Admiralty 1939–1940, Prime Minister 1940–1945 and 1951–1955, Leader of the Opposition 1945–1951.

Cripps, (Sir) (Richard) Stafford, ('Austerity Cripps'), 1889–1952, Labour politician and lawyer. MP, Leader of the House of Commons and Minister of Aircraft Production in the Coalition Government in the Second World War, President of the Board of Trade, Chancellor of the Exchequer 1947–1950.

Crossman, R. H. S., 1907–1974, Labour politician. Fellow and Tutor of New College, Oxford, assistant editor *New Statesman and Nation,* MP, Minister of Housing and Local Government, Secretary of State for the Social Services, 1968–70.

Farr, William, 1807–1883, medical statistician. Compiler of Abstracts in the Registrar-General's Office, 1838–1879. President of the Statistical Society, 1871 and 1872. Author of *Vital Statistics.*

Fry, Elizabeth, 1780–1845, Quaker prison reformer. Wife of banker Joseph Fry. Formed association for improvement of female prisoners in Newgate Prison, 1817. Instituted an order of nursing sisters, some of whom went to the Crimea with Florence Nightingale (q.v.).

Galton, (Sir) Francis (1822–1911), biologist and founder of the Eugenics School, cousin of Charles Darwin. Worked on genetics, credited with the discovery of fingerprinting. Author of *Hereditary Genius.* General secretary of the British Association, 1863–1867, consulting editor of *Biometrika.*

Griffiths, (Sir) (Ernest) Roy, b. 1926. Deputy Chairman, Sainsbury's. Deputy Chairman, National Health Service Management Board since 1986.

Hall, (Sir) Benjamin, (Baron Llanover), 1802–1867. MP, opponent of the General Board of Health 1848–1854, when he represented the existing water and sewage authorities. Described in S. E. Finer's *Chadwick* as 'The prince of London rabble-rousers'. President of the reconstituted General Board of Health, 1854, Privy Councillor 1854, Chief Commissioner of Works, 1855–1858.

Halsey, A. H., b. 1923, Professor of Social and Administrative Studies, University of Oxford, 1978–90, Professorial Fellow of Nuffield College. Research publications on education and social class. Edited reports on Educational Priority Areas.

Hannington, Wal, 1896–1966, leader and organizer of the National Unemployed Workers' Committee Movement, member of the Central Committee of the Communist Party. Led hunger marches in the 1920s and 1930s. Author of *The Problem of the Distressed Areas, Ten Lean Years,* and *Unemployed Struggles 1919–1936.*

Healey, Denis, b. 1917, Labour politician. MP, Institute of Strategic Studies, Secretary of State for Defence, Chancellor of the Exchequer,

1974–1979, Chairman of the Interim Committee of the International Monetary Fund, 1977–1979.

Heath, Edward, b. 1916, Conservative politician, MP, Parliamentary Secretary to the Treasury and Government Chief Whip, 1955–1959, Lord Privy Seal, Secretary of State for Industry, Leader of the Opposition 1965–1970, Prime Minister 1970–1974.

Hill, Octavia, 1838–1912, housing reformer and supporter of the Charity Organisation Society. Managed property for John Ruskin and subsequently the Ecclesiastical Commissioners on the principle 'not alms, but a friend'. Member of the Royal Commission on the Poor Laws, 1905–1909. Co-founder of the National Trust.

Hyndman, Henry Mayes, 1842–1921, Socialist writer and propagandist, leader of the Social Democratic Federation (Marxist) until 1914. Responsible for the SDF social survey which attracted the attention of Charles Booth, and led to his own survey (q.v.).

Joseph, (Sir) Keith, (Lord Joseph), b. 1918, Conservative politician. Fellow of All Souls College, Oxford, Minister of Housing and Local Government, Secretary of State for Social Services, for Industry, for Education and Science.

Kay, James (afterwards Sir James Kay-Shuttleworth), 1804–1877. Medical practitioner, worked with Chadwick and Southwood Smith (q.v.) on the Poor Law Commission and the General Board of Health, subsequently moved into the field of popular education.

Keynes, John Maynard, (Lord Keynes), 1883–1946, Cambridge economist. Editor of the *Economic Journal,* Secretary of the Royal Economics Society, *A Treatise on Money,* 1930, *General Theory of Employment, Interest and Money,* 1936. Adviser to Government, involved in German reparations after The First World War, American Lend-Lease, Breton Woods agreement and setting up of the International Monetary Fund after The Second World War.

Lansbury, George, 1859–1940, Labour leader and politician. Member of Poplar Board of Poor Law Guardians, member, Royal Commission on the Poor Laws 1905–1909 (signatory to the Minority Report), MP for Poplar and later Bow, Christian pacifist, joint founder of the *Daily Herald.*

Lewis, (Sir) George Cornewall, 1806–1863, son of Thomas Frankland Lewis (q.v.), succeeded his father on the Poor Law Board, (1839–1847). Chancellor of the Exchequer, 1855–1858, Home Secretary, 1859–1861, Secretary of State for War, 1861–1863.

Lewis, (Sir) Thomas Frankland, 1780–1855, MP, Joint Secretary to the Treasury, 1827, Privy Councillor 1828, Treasurer of the Navy, 1830, Chairman of the Poor Law Commission, 1834–1838.

Livingstone, Ken, b. 1945, teacher, local government leader and Labour politician. Councillor, Lambeth and Camden Borough Councils, Leader of the Greater London Council 1981–1986, MP for Brent East since 1987. Author of *If voting changed anything, they'd abolish it,* 1987.

Lloyd George, David, (Earl Lloyd George of Dwyfor), 1889–1943, Liberal politician. MP, President of the Board of Trade 1906–1908, Chancellor of the Exchequer 1908–1911, Minister of Munitions, Prime Minister 1916–1923.

Loch, (Sir) Charles Stewart, 1849–1923. Secretary to the Council of the Charity Organisation Society, 1875–1914, strongly opposed to state intervention in welfare. Initiated the *Charities Register* and the *Charities Digest.* Member of the Royal Commission on the Poor Laws, 1905–1909; the Majority Report was largely his work.

Malthus, (Rev.) T. R., 1766–1834, mathematician and demographer. Fellow of Jesus College, Cambridge. Author of the *Essay on Population,* 1798, and subsequent revisions.

Mayhew, Henry, 1812–1887, journalist and sometime editor of *Punch.* Author of *London Labour and the London Poor.*

[Melbourne], William Lamb, (second Viscount Melbourne), 1779–1848, Whig politician. Irish Secretary, Home Secretary 1830–1834, Prime Minister 1834–1838, Leader of the Opposition 1838–1842.

More, Hannah, 1745–1833, writer and social reformer. Member of the 'Blue Stocking Society' of literary ladies, and of the Evangelical Clapham Sect. Organized schools and women's groups in the Cheddar Valley.

More, (Sir) Thomas, 1478–1535, lawyer, judge and humanist. Influenced by Erasmus and Colet. Under-Sheriff of London, 1510. Wrote *Utopia* while on a commercial mission to the Low Countries, 1516. Lord Chancellor of England, 1529, resigned 1532. Refused to assent to Henry VIII's Act of Supremacy. 1534. Executed 1535. Canonized by the Roman Catholic Church, 1935.

Moser, (Sir) Claus, b. 1922, Director, *The Economist,* Director, Central Statistical Office and Head of Government Statistical Services 1967–1978, President Royal Statistical Society, 1978–1980, Warden, Wadham College, Oxford.

Nicholls, (Sir) George, 1781–1865, Director, Birmingham Canal Navigations, Superintendent, Birmingham Branch of the Bank of England, Poor Law Commissioner 1834, Permanent Secretary of the Poor Law Board, 1848.

Nightingale, Florence, 1820–1910, reformer of hospital nursing. Visited the hospital at Kaiserwerth, near Dusseldorf, 1850 and 1851. Superintendent of the Hospital for Invalid Gentlewomen, Chandos Street, London. Expedition to the Scutari Hospital in the Crimea, 1854. Nightingale School and Home for Nurses, St Thomas's Hospital, founded, London, 1854.

Orwell, George (real name Eric Blair), 1903–1950, journalist and writer. Author of *Down and Out in Paris and London, The Road to Wigan Pier, Animal Farm.*

Powell, (John) Enoch, b. 1912, Conservative politician, (now Liberal Unionist). Professor of Greek in the University of Sydney, Australia, 1937–1939. Rose from Army rank of private to brigadier in the Second World War. MP 1950. Financial Secretary to the Treasury, 1957–1958, Minister of Health, 1960–1963. 'Rivers of Blood' speech on immigration, 1968.

Ricardo, David, 1772–1823, economist, MP, author of *Principles of Political Economy and Taxation,* in which he developed 'The Iron Law of Wages'. Colleague of T. R. Malthus (q.v.).

Senior, Nassau William, 1790–1844, economist and barrister. First Professor of Political Economy, University of Oxford, 1825. Worked with Edwin Chadwick (q.v.) on the Poor Law Commission of 1832–1834.

Scarman, Leslie, (Lord Scarman), b. 1911. Barrister, High Court judge, Lord Justice of Appeal. Chairman, Law Commission, President, Constitutional Reform Centre.

Seebohm, (Sir) Frederick, (Lord Seebohm), b. 1909. Chairman, Barclays Bank DCO, Chairman, Joseph Rowntree Memorial Trust, Chairman, Seebohm Committee, 1965–1988.

[Shaftesbury], Anthony Ashley Cooper, (7th Earl of Shaftesbury), 1801–1885, social reformer. MP (as Lord Ashley) until he succeeded his father in 1851. Involved in ragged schools, reform of lunacy laws and factory laws, conditions of juveniles (including chimney sweeps and juvenile offenders), lodging houses, housing for the poor, and many other voluntary and statutory movements. Lunacy Commissioner 1828–1884, member of the General Board of Health (with Edwin Chadwick) 1848–1854, prominent Evangelical.

Shaw-Lefevre, (Sir) John, 1797–1879, Under-Secretary to Edward Smith Stanley (afterwards Earl of Derby and Prime Minister), FRS. 1820, Poor Law Commissioner, 1834, Vice-Chancellor, University of London, 1842.

Simon, (Sir) John (pronounced 'Simone', he was of Huguenot stock), 1816–1904, sanitary reformer and public health specialist. First Medical Officer of Health for London, 1848, Medical Officer to the General Board of Health and the Medical Department of the Privy Council, 1848–1871, retired (under protest) following the setting up of the Local Government Board, 1877.

Smiles, Samuel, 1812–1899, medical practitioner and popular writer, lecturer to Mechanics' Institutes etc. Left medical practice 1845, secretary to the Leeds and Thirsk Railway, and then to the South-Eastern Railway. Author of *Self-Help, Duty, Thrift, Character,* and *The Lives of the Engineers.*

Smith,   (Dr) Thomas Southwood, 1788–1861, sanitary reformer and author of *A Treatise on Fever.* Medical adviser to the Poor Law Commission and the General Board of Health. Grandfather of Octavia Hill (q.v.).

Snow,   (Dr) John, medical pioneer, 1813–1858. Discovered water was contaminated by cholera (hence the episode of the Broad Street Pump) and introduced the scientific use of ether into English surgical practice.

Temple,   William, 1881–1944, Bishop of Manchester and Archbishop of Canterbury, Christian Socialist. Promoted the Life and Liberty Movement in the Church of England, and the Malvern Conference, 1942. Author of *Men without Work* and *Christianity and the Social Order* as well as of theological works.

Titmuss,   Richard Morris, 1907–1973, Professor of Social Administration, London School of Economics. Left school at 14, worked for 16 years for an insurance firm, and never took a degree (though he was awarded eleven honorary degrees). Author of *Problems of Social Policy in Wartime* (official history of the Second World War), *Essays on the 'Welfare State'*, *Commitment to Welfare*, *The Gift Relationship*, described in *DNB* as 'the high priest of the Welfare State'.

Townsend,   Peter, b. 1928. Professor of Social Policy, University of Bristol since 1982, formerly at the London School of Economics and University of Essex. Chairman, Child Poverty Action Group since 1969. Chairman, Disability Alliance since 1974. Author of many works on poverty, disability and old age, member of Government Working party on Inequalities in Health, joint editor of the *Black Report.*

Tuke,   William, 1732–1822, Quaker tea and coffee merchant, founder of the York Retreat for the humane treatment of the insane.

Walter,   John I, 1739–1812, founded *The Times* in 1788.

Walter,   John II (1776–1847), second son of John Walter I. MP, chief proprietor of *The Times,* High Tory opponent of the New Poor Law.

Walter,   John III (1818–1894), eldest son of John Walter II. MP, chief proprietor of *The Times,* High Tory opponent of the General Board of Health.

Webb,   Beatrice, (née Potter), 1858–1943, m. Sidney Webb, 1859–1947. The Webbs, who worked closely together, were Fabian reformers and social historians. They were involved in the foundation of the *New Statesman and Nation* and the London School of Economics, where they both lectured for many years. Beatrice was a member of the Royal Commission on the Poor Laws, 1905–1909, but Sidney apparently wrote the report. Sidney Webb became Baron Passfield in 1929 (under a Labour Government) but Beatrice refused the title. Many of their writings are listed in the Bibliography.

Wilson, Harold, (Lord Wilson of Rievaulx), b. 1916, Labour politician. Director of Economics and Statistics, Ministry of Fuel and Power, 1943–1945, President, Board of Trade, 1947–1951, Prime Minister 1964–1970, Leader of the Opposition 1963–1964 and 1970–1974.

Bibliography

All books published in London unless otherwise stated.

Abel-Smith, Brian, *A History of the Nursing Profession*, Heinemann, 1960.
—— *The Hospitals, 1800–1948*, Heinemann, 1964.
—— *Value for Money in Health Services: a comparative study*, Heinemann, 1976.
—— and Peter Townsend, *The Poor and the Poorest, Occasional Papers in Social Administration*, Bell, 1966.
Andover Union: Report of Select Committee of The Andover Union 1846. Parliamentary Papers 11, 22620.
Annual Abstract of Statistics, HMSO.
Archbishop's Commission on Urban Priority Areas, *Faith in the City: a call for action by the Church and the nation*, Church Publishing House, 1985.
Audit Commission for England and Wales, *Making a Reality of Community Care*, (HMSO, 1986).
Attlee, Clement, *As It Happened*, Heinemann, 1954.
Baldwin, Sally, Gillian Parker and Robert Walker (eds), *Social Security and Community Care*, Avebury, Gower, 1988.
[Barlow Report], Report of the Royal Commission on the Distribution of the Industrial Population, HMSO, Cmd. 6513, 1940.
Baxter, G. Wythen, *The Book of the Bastiles, or, the History of the Working of the New Poor Law*, Stephens, 1841.
Bean, Philip, John Ferris and David Whynes (eds), *In Defence of Welfare*, Tavistock Publications, 1985.
Bentham, Jeremy, *The Works of Jeremy Bentham*, edited by J. Bowring, Edinburgh, Tait, 1843.

Bevan, Aneurin, *In Place of Fear*, McGibbon and Kee, Quartet, 1976.
—— ('Celticus'), *Why Not Trust the Tories?*, Gollancz, 1944.
Beveridge, Janet, *Beveridge and his Plan*, Hodder and Stoughton, 1954.
[Beveridge Report], Report of the Committee on Social Insurance and Allied Services, HMSO, Cmd. 6404, 1942.
Beveridge, William, *Full Employment in a Free Society*, Allen and Unwin, 1944.
—— *Voluntary Action: a report on methods of social advance*, Allen and Unwin, 1948.
—— *Power and Influence*, Hodder and Stoughton, 1953.
[Black Report], Inequalities in Health, report of a Research Working Group, DHSS, 1980 (photocopy only. See also Townsend).
[Blanesburgh Report], Report of the Unemployment Insurance Committee, 2 vols., HMSO 1927.
Boddy, Martin, *The Building Societies*, Macmillan, 1980.
Bonham Carter, Violet, *Winston Churchill as I knew him*. Eyre and Spottiswoode, 1965.
Booth, Charles, *Life and Labour of the People of London*, Macmillan, 17 vols, 1889–1903.
Booth, William, *In Darkest England, or, The Way Out*, Salvation Army, 1890.
Bosanquet, Bernard (ed.), *Aspects of the Social Problem*, Macmillan, 1895.
Bosanquet, Helen, *Social Work in London*, Murray, 1914.
—— *The Poor Law Report of 1909*, Macmillan, 1912.
Bosanquet, Nicholas, *After the New Right*, Heinemann, 1983.
Bourdillon, A. F. C. (ed.), *The Voluntary Social Services: their place in the modern state*, Methuen, 1965.
Bowley, Marion, *Housing and the State*, Allen and Unwin, 1944.
Boyson, Rhodes, *Down with the Poor*, Churchill Press, 1971.
Bradshaw, Jonathan, *The Family Fund*, Routledge and Kegan Paul, 1980.
—— 'A defence of social security', in Philip Bean, John Ferris and David Whynes (eds), *A Defence of Welfare*, Tavistock Publications, 1985.
Brewer, Colin and June Lait, *Can Social Work Survive?*, Temple Smith, 1980.
Briggs, Asa, *Social Thought and Social Action: a study of the work of Seebohmn Rowntree, 1871–1954*, Longmans, 1961.
Bristol Corporation of the Poor, *Selected Records 1696–1834*, Bristol, Bristol Records Society Publications, 1932.
Brittan, Samuel, *The Role and Limits of Government: essays in political economy*, Temple Smith, 1983.
Broad, L., *Winston Churchill, 1874–1951*, Hutchinson, 1951.

Brown, Muriel and Nicola Madge, *Despite the Welfare State*, Heinemann, 1982.

Brown, Philip and Richard Sparks (eds), *Beyond Thatcherism: social policy, politics and society*, Open University Press, 1989.

Bruce, Maurice, *The Coming of the Welfare State*, Batsford, 1961.

Bruce, Maurice, (ed.), *The Rise of the Welfare State*, Weidenfeld and Nicolson, 1973.

Brundage, Anthony, The Making of the New Poor Law, Hutchinson, 1978.

Bulmer, Martin, *Royal Commissions and Departmental Committees of Inquiry the lessons of experience*, Royal Institute of Public Administration, 1983.

Burnett, John, *A Social History of Housing, 1815–1985*, Methuen, 1978.

Butterworth, Eric, 'Race Relations – the next step', (chapter 9) in *The Year Book of Social Policy, 1973*, Routledge and Kegan Paul, 1974.

Cartwright, Frederick F., *A Social History of Medicine*, Longmans 1977.

Castle, Barbara, *The Castle Diaries*, Weidenfeld and Nicholson, 1980.

Cecil, David, *Lord M.*, Constable 1954, reprinted in David Cecil, *Melbourne*, Book Club, 1972.

Chadwick, Edwin, *The Sanitary Condition of the Labouring Population of Great Britain*, with an introduction by M. W. Flinn, Edinburgh, Edinburgh University Press, 1965.

Child Poverty Action Group: Poverty Leaflets, Research Leaflets, Rights Leaflets.

Cleary, E. J., *The Building Society Movement*, Elek Books, 1965.

Clemens, Cyril, *The Man from Limehouse: Clement Attlee*, New York, Didier, 1946.

Cobbett, William, *Rural Rides*, London, A. Cobbett, 1853.

Cohen, Percy, *The British System of Social Insurance*, Allan, 1932.

—— *Unemployment Insurance and Assistance in Britain*, Harrap, 1938.

Cole, G. D. H. and Raymond Postgate, *The Common People*, Methuen 1948.

Cole, Margaret, *The Story of Fabian Socialism*, Heinemann, 1961, Mercury, 1963.

Cole, Margaret (ed.), *The Diaries of Beatrice Webb, 1924–1932*, Gollancz, 1945.

Cooney, E. W., 'High flats in local authority housing in England and Wales since 1945', in Anthony Sutcliffe (ed.), *Multi-Storey Housing: the British Working Class Experience*, Croom Helm, 1974.

Cooper, M. and Culyer, A. J., *The Price of Blood*, Hobart Papers 48, 1968.

Corina, Lewis, 'Community work and local authority decision-making', *Community Development Journal*, XI (3), 1976.

Cox, Brian and A. E. Dyson (eds), *The Black Papers on Education,* Davis Paynter, 1971.

Cox, Brian and Rhodes Boyson, *Black Paper 1975,* Dent, 1975.

Cronin, A. J., *The Stars look Down,* Gollancz, 1935.

—— *The Citadel,* Gollancz, 1937.

Crossman, R. H. S., *The Diaries of a Cabinet Minister,* 3 vols, Hamish Hamilton and Jonathan Cape, 1976, vol. II.

[Crowther Report], 15 to 18: Report of the Central Advisory Council for Education – England. 2 vols., HMSO, 1959.

Cullingworth, J. B., *Housing Needs and Planning Policy,* Routledge and Kegan Paul, 1960.

Dalton, Hugh, *High Tide and After: Memoirs,* 3 vols, Frederick Muller, 1962, vol. III.

Dant, Tim, 'Old, poor and at home', in Sally Baldwin, Gillian Parker and Robert Walker (eds), *Social Security and Community Care,* Avebury, Gower, 1988.

Department of Health; Department of Health and Social Security; see Health.

Dickens, Charles, *Oliver Twist,* Chapman and Hall, 1901.

Donnison, Jean, *Midwives and Medical Men,* Heinemann, 1977.

du Parcq, L., *Life of David Lloyd George,* Caxton, 1912.

Dunkley, Peter, *The Crisis of the Old Poor Law in England, 1795–1834* Garland, New York, 1982.

Eden, Frederick, *The State of the Poor,* 3 vols, 1797.

Education: for reports by the Ministry of Education and the Department of Education and Science: see under McNair, Norwood, Crowther, Newsom, Plowden, Robbins.

Educational Reconstruction, HMSO Cmd. 6458, 1943.

Employment Policy, HMSO Cmd. 6527, 1944.

Engels, F., *The Condition of the Working Class in England,* 1842, translated and edited by W. O. Henderson and W. H. Chaloner, Blackwell, Oxford, 1971.

Fabian Society publications:–

Bosanquet, Nicholas, *A New Deal for the Elderly,* Fabian Tracts 435, 1975.

Brooke, Rosalind, *Advice Centres in Welfare Rights,* Fabian Research Series 329, 1972.

Bull, David, *Action for Welfare Rights,* Fabian Research Series 288, 1970.

Castle, Barbara, *The NHS Revisited,* Fabian Tracts 440, 1976.

Crossman, R. H. S., *Paying for the Social Services* Fabian Tracts 399, 1969.

Draper, Peter et al., *The National Health Service: three views,* Fabian Research Series 287, 1970.

Lynes, Tony, *Welfare Rights,* Fabian Tracts 395, 1969.

Rendel, Margherita et al., *Equality for Women,* Fabian Research Series 268, 1968.

Sinfield, Adrian, *Which Way for Social Work?,* Fabian Tracts 393, 1969.

Townsend, Peter et al., *Social Services for All,* Fabian Tracts 382–5, 1968.

Townsend, Peter, *Why are the Many Poor?,* Fabian Tracts, 500, 1984.

Ferguson, Sheila, and Hilda Fitzgerald, *Studies in the Social Services, History of the Second World War,* United Kingdom Civil Series, HMSO, 1954.

Finer, S. E., *The Life and Times of Sir Edwin Chadwick,* Methuen, 1952.

Flinn, M. W., 'Introduction' to Edwin Chadwick, *The Sanitary Condition of the Labouring Population of Great Britain,* (1842), Edinburgh University Press, 1965.

Flinn, M. W., *Public Health Reform in Britain,* Macmillan, 1968.

Foot, Michael, *Aneurin Bevan,* McGibbon and Kee, 1962.

Fraser, Derek, *The Evolution of the British Welfare State,* Macmillan, 1973.

Frazer, William Mowll, *A History of English Public Health,* Ballière, Tindall and Cox, 1950.

Galton, Francis, *Hereditary Genius: an inquiry into its laws and consequences,* 1869, 2nd edition 1892.

Gilbert, Bentley B., *The Evolution of National Insurance in Britain: the origins of the welfare state,* Michael Joseph, 1966.

—— *British Social Policy, 1914–1939,* Batsford, 1970.

Gilbert, Martin, *Winston Churchill,* Heinemann, 1986, vol. VII.

Gittus, Elizabeth, *Flats, Families and the Under-Fives,* Routledge and Kegan Paul, 1960.

Gleick, James, *Chaos: making a new science,* Cardinal, 1987.

Gray, B. Kirkman, *A History of English Philanthropy,* King 1905.

Green Papers on the National Health Service, 1968 and 1970, see Health.

Greenwood, Walter, *Love on the Dole,* Jonathan Cape, 1933.

Gregg, Pauline, *The Welfare State,* Harrap, 1967.

[Gregory], *[Holman Gregory Report], Final Report of Royal Commission on Unemployment Insurance,* HMSO Cmd. 4185, 1932.

Griffiths, Sir Roy, see Health.

Grigg, John, *Lloyd George, The People's Champion,* Eyre Methuen, 1978.

Hall, Phoebe, *Reforming the Welfare,* Heinemann, 1976.

Halsey, A. H., *Educational Priority: report on a project sponsored by the Department of Education and Science and the Social Science Research Council,* HMSO, 1972, vol. 1, *EPA Problems and Policies.*

Hammond, J. L. and Barbara Hammond, *Lord Shaftesbury,* Constable, 1923.

—— *The Age of the Chartists,* Longmans Green, 1930.
—— *The Town Labourer 1760–1832,* 2 vols., Longmans Green, 1917, and Guild Books, 1949.
—— *The Village Labourer,* 2 vols., Longmans Green, 1911, and Guild Books 1948.
Hannington, Wal, *The Problem of the Distressed Areas,* Gollancz, 1937.
—— *Ten Lean Years,* Gollancz, 1940.
—— *Unemployed Struggles 1919–1936: My Life and Struggles,* Lawrence and Wishart, 1936, reprinted 1979.
Harris, Kenneth, *Thatcher,* Weidenfeld and Nicolson, 1988, and Fontana, 1989.
Hayek, F. A. von, *The Constitution of Liberty,* Routledge and Kegan Paul, 1960. See also Institute of Economic Affairs for other Hayek titles.
Healey, Denis, *The Time of my Life,* Michael Joseph, 1989.
Health (National Health Service): Ministry of Health (1918–67), Department of Health and Social Security (DHSS) (1967–88), Department of Health from 1988:
Ministry of Health, *A National Health Service,* HMSO, Cmd. 6502, 1944.
—— *Enquiry into the Cost of the National Health Service,* HMSO, Cmd. 9663, 1956 (The *Guillebaud Report*).
—— *A Hospital Plan for England and Wales,* HMSO, Cmd. 1604, 1962.
—— *Health and Welfare: the development of community care,* HMSO, Cmnd. 1973, 1963.
—— *Administrative Structure of Medical and Related Services in England and Wales,* (First Green Paper), HMSO 1968.
Department of Health and Social Security, *The future Structure of the National Health Service,* (Second Green Paper), HMSO, 1970.
—— *National Health Service Reorganisation: Consultative Document,* (White Paper), HMSO 1971.
—— *Management Arrangements for the Reorganised National Health Service,* (The 'Grey Book'), HMSO, 1972.
—— *Report of Royal Commission on the National Health Service,* (the *Merrison Report*), HMSO Cmnd. 7615, 1979.
—— *Patients First,* (White Paper), HMSO, 1979.
—— *Report of the National Health Service Management Committee,* chairman, Sir Roy Griffiths (the first *Griffiths Report,* HMSO, 1983.
Department of Health, *Community Care: agenda for action,* (the second *Griffiths Report*), HMSO, 1988.
—— *Caring for People: community care in the next decade and beyond,* HMSO, Cm. 849, 1989.
Heasman, Kathleen, *Evangelicals in Action,* Bles, 1962.

Hobart Papers, see Institute of Economic Affairs.

Hobsbawm, E. J. and George Rudé, *Captain Swing,* New York, Pantheon Books, 1968.

Hodder, Edwin, *The Life and Work of the Seventh Earl of Shaftesbury,* 3 vols., Cassell, 1886.

Holman, Gregory, see Gregory.

Holman, Robert A., *Poverty,* Robertson, 1978.

Holyoake, George Jacob, *The Rochdale Pioneers,* Allen and Unwin, 10th edition, 1983.

House of Commons, *Second report of the Social Services Committee, Session 1984–5, Community Care* vol. I, (HMSO, 1985).

Housing: the Government's Proposals, HMSO, Cmd. 214, 1987.

Howard, Christian, 'Women and the professions', (chapter 7) in *The Year Book of Social Policy, 1973,* Routledge and Kegan Paul, 1974.

Hyndman, F. D., *Record of an Adventurous Life,* Macmillan, 1911.

Institute of Economic Affairs:–

Burton, John et al., *Keynes' General Theory 50 Years On,* Hobart Papers 26, 1986.

Cooper, Michael and A. J. Culyer, *The Price of Blood,* Hobart Papers 48, 1968.

Ferns, Henry Stanley, *Towards an Independent University,* Occasional Papers 25, 1969.

Friedman, Milton, *Unemployment versus Inflation? An Evaluation of the Phillips Curve,* Occasional papers 44, 1975.

Hanson, C. G., *Trade Unions: a century of privilege,* Occasional papers 38, 1973.

Harris, Ralph (Lord Harris), *Beyond the Welfare State: an economic, political and moral critique of indiscriminate state welfare,* Occasional Papers 77, 1988.

Hayek, F. A. von, *Economic Freedom and Representative Government,* Occasional Papers 39, 1973.

—— *Full Employment at Any Price?,* Occasional Papers 45, 1975.

Houghton, Douglas, *Paying for the Social Services,* Occasional Papers 16, 1967.

Jewkes, John et al., *Economics, Business and Government,* Occasional Papers 8, 1966.

Lees, D. S. et al., *Monopoly or Choice in Health Services?* Occasional Papers 3, 1964.

Lees, D. S., *Health Through Choice,* Hobart Papers 14, 1961.

Prest, A. R., *Financing University Education: a study of university fees and loans to students in Great Britain,* Occasional Papers 12, 1966.

Seldon, Arthur and Hamish Gray, *Universal or Selective Social Benefits?,* Research Monographs 8, 1967.

Seldon, Arthur, *After the NHS,* Occasional papers 21, 1968.

—— *Wither the Welfare State,* Occasional Papers 60, 1981.

[Interment], *Supplementary Report on the result of a Special Inquiry into the Practice of Interment in Towns,* Parliamentary Papers, 1843, XII.

Jennings, Ivor (ed.), *The Poor Law Code,* Knight, 1930.

Jewkes, John and Sylvia Jewkes, *The Genesis of the National Health Service,* Oxford, Blackwell, 1961.

Jones, Kathleen, *The Teaching of Social Studies in British Universities,* Occasional Papers in Social Administration no. 12, Bell, 1965.

—— *The Compassionate Society,* SPCK, 1966.

—— *A History of the Mental Health Services,* Routledge and Kegan Paul, 1972.

—— *Eileen Younghusband: a biography,* Bedford Square Press, 1984.

Jones, Kathleen, John Brown, and Jonathan Bradshaw, *Issues in Social Policy,* Routledge and Kegan Paul, 1978, revised edition 1984.

Jordan, Bill, *Poor Parents,* Routledge and Kegan Paul, 1974.

Joseph, (Sir) Keith, 'A summary of some Conservative strategies', in *The Year Book of Social Policy in Britain,* Routledge and Kegan Paul, 1972.

Kay, James (Sir James Kay Shuttleworth), *The Moral and Physical Condition of the Working Classes Employed in the Cotton Manufacture in Manchester,* Ridgway, 1832.

Keynes, J. Maynard, *A General Theory of Unemployment, Interest and Money,* Macmillan, 1936.

Klein, Rudolph and Michael O'Higgins, *The Future of Welfare,* Blackwell, 1985.

Lambert, Royston, *Sir John Simon, 1816–1904 and English Social Administration,* McGibbon and Kee, 1963.

Lewes, C. L., *Dr Southwood Smith: a retrospect,* Edinburgh, 1899.

Lewis, Peter, *George Orwell: the road to 1984,* Heinemann, 1981.

Lewis, R. A., *Edwin Chadwick and the Public Health Movement,* Longmans Green, 1952.

Lister, Ruth, *Welfare Benefits,* Sweet and Maxwell, 1981.

Little, Alan, 'The Race Relations Act, 1976', (chapter 7) in *The Year Book of Social Policy, 1976,* Routledge and Kegan Paul, 1977.

Local Government, Report of Royal Commission, 1969; see *Redcliff-Maud Report.*

Loch, C. S., *Charity Organisation,* Swan Sonnenschein, 1905.

Lodge, Paul, 'Education', (chapter 1) in Paul Wilding (ed.), *In Defence of the Welfare State,* Manchester, Manchester University Press, 1986.

Loney, Martin, *Community Against Government,* Heinemann, 1983.

Longford, Elizabeth, *Victoria R.I.,* Weidenfeld and Nicolson, 1964.

Lowe, Stuart, 'Home ownership and capital accumulation', in Maria Brenton and Clare Ungerson, *Social Policy Review 1990,* Longmans, 1990.

—— *Housing*, Longman's Social Policy Today Series, 1985.

Lynes, Tony, *The Penguin Guide to Supplementary Benefits*, Penguin Books, 1972.

Mack, Mary P., *A Bentham Reader*, New York, Pegasus, 1969.

—— *Jeremy Bentham, An odyssey of ideas, 1748–1792*, Heinemann 1962, vol. I.

MacCleary, G. F., *The Maternity and Child Welfare Movement*, King, 1935.

MacLeod, Iain and Enoch Powell, *The Social Services – Needs and Means*, Conservative Political Centre, 1954.

[McNair Report], *The Supply, Recruitment and Training of Teachers and Youth Leaders*, HMSO, 1944.

Malthus, T. R., *An Essay on the Principle of Population*, 1st edition 1798, edited by Anthony Flew, Penguin, 1970.

Marshall, Hedley, 'An introduction to reorganisation', (chapter 1) in *The Year Book of Social Policy in Britain, 1973*, Routledge and Kegan Paul, 1974.

Marshall, T. H., *Social Policy*, Hutchinson, 1965, revised edition 1967.

—— *The Right to Welfare*, Heineman, 1981.

Martineau, Harriet, *Harriet Martineau's Autobiography* 2 vols, Smith, Elder, 1877.

Mayhew, Henry, *London Labour and the London Poor* 1851. Originally issued in weekly parts in the *Morning Chronicle*. Peter Quennell's edited versions are *Mayhew's London*, Pilot Press, 1949; *London's Underworld*, Kimber, 1950; and *Mayhew's Characters*, Kimber 1951.

Mearns, Andrew, *The Bitter Cry of Outcast London*, 1883, reprint edited by Anthony S. Wohl, Leicester University Press, 1970. (The Victorian Library).

Medical Services Review Committee, see Porritt.

Merrison Report, see Health (National Health Service), Report of Royal Commission.

Ministry of Health, see Health.

Monk, Sarah and Mark Kleinman, 'Housing', in Philip Brown and Richard Sparks (eds), *Beyond Thatcherism*, Open University Press, 1989.

Morgan, Kenneth O., *Labour in Power, 1945–51*, Oxford, Clarendon Press, 1984.

More, Thomas, *Utopia*, 1516. Edited by Paul Turner, Penguin, 1965.

Mortimer, John, *Paradise Postponed*, Viking, 1985, Penguin, 1986.

National Health Service: see Health.

Newsholme, Arthur, *Fifty Years in Public Health*, Allen and Unwin, 1935.

[Newsom Report], *Half Our Future: Report of the Central Advisory Council for Education – England*, HMSO, 1963.

[Norwood Report], *Curriculum and examination: Report of the Committee*

of the Secondary Schools Examination Council, HMSO, Cmd. 6502, 1943.

Orwell, George, *Down and out in Paris and London*, Gollancz, 1933, Penguin, 1940.

—— *The Road to Wigan Pier*, Gollancz 1937, Penguin, 1962.

Owen, David, *English Philanthropy, 1660–1960*, Oxford University Press, 1965.

Owen, Robert, *The Life of Robert Owen, by himself*, with an introduction by John Butt, Knight, London, 1971.

Pakenham, Elizabeth, see Longford.

[Parker-Morris Report], Central Housing Advisory Committee, *Homes for Today and Tomorrow*, 1961.

Pearson, Geoffrey, *The Deviant Imagination*, Macmillan, 1975.

Peden, G. C., *British Economic and Social Policy: Lloyd George to Margaret Thatcher*, Philip Allen, 1985.

Pelling, Margaret, *Cholera, Fever and English Medicine*, Oxford University Press, 1978.

Pinker, Robert A., *The Idea of Welfare*, Heineman, 1979.

Plant, Raymond, 'The very idea of a welfare state', in Philip Bean, John Ferris and David Whynes (eds) *In Defence of Welfare*, Tavistock Publications, 1985.

[Plowden Report], *Children and their Primary Schools: report of the Central Advisory Council for Education (England)*, HMSO, vol. 1, 1966, vol. 2, 1967.

Political and Economic Planning (PEP.), *Report on the British Social Services* published by PEP., June 1937.

—— *Report on the British Health Services*, PEP December, 1937.

[Poor Laws], *Report of H.M. Commission for enquiring into the administration and practical operation of the Poor Laws*, 1834, 1 vol. plus 11 vols of evidence.

—— *Report of Royal Commission on the Poor Laws and the Relief of Distress*, 1 vol. plus 37 vols of evidence, HMSO, Cmd. 4499, 1909.

—— *Break Up the Poor Law and Abolish the Workhouse*, Minority Report of the Royal Commission, 1909, published separately by the Fabian Society, 1909.

Popper, Karl, *Unended Quest: an intellectual autobiography*, Fontana, 1976.

[Porritt Report], *A Review of Medical Services in Great Britain*, Medical Services Review Committee, Social Assay, 1963.

[Redcliff-Maud Report], *Report of the Royal Commission on Local Government*, 3 vols, HMSO Cmnd. 4040–1, 1969.

Ricardo, David, *The Principles of Political Economy and Taxation*, 1817. Edited by W. Fellner, Homewood, Illinois, Irwin, 1963.

Ringen, Stein, *The Possibility of Politics: a study in the political economy of the Welfare State*, Oxford, Clarendon Press, 1987.

Robbins Report, *Higher Education,* Cmnd. 2154, 1963.

Roberts, David, *Victorian Origins of the British Welfare State,* Connecticut, Yale University Press, 1960.

Rodgers, Barbara, and June Stevenson, *A New Portrait of Social Work,* Heinemann, 1973.

Ross, J. Stirling, *The National Health Service in Great Britain,* Oxford University Press, 1956.

Rowland, Peter, *The Last Liberal Governments:* vol. 1, *The Promised Land 1905–10,* Barrie and Cresset, 1965; vol. 2, *Unfinished Business 1911–18* Barrie and Jenkins, 1971.

Rowntree, B. Seebohm, *Poverty: a study of town life,* Macmillan, 1901.

—— *Poverty and Progress,* Longmans Green, 1941.

Rutter, Michael and Nicola Madge, *Cycles of Transmitted Deprivation,* Heinemann, 1976.

Seear, Nancy, 'Equal opportunities for men and women', (chapter 8) in *The Year Book of Social Policy in Britain, 1973,* Routledge and Kegan Paul, 1974.

[Scarman, Leslie (Lord)], *The Brixton Disorders, 10–12 April 1981, report of an inquiry by Lord Scarman,* HMSO, Cmd. 8427, 1981.

[Scott Report], Report of the Committee on Land Utilisation in Rural Areas, HMSO, Cmd. 6378, 1942.

[Seebohm Report], Report of the Committee on Local Authority and Allied Social Services, HMSO, Cmd. 3703, 1968.

Simey, T. S., *Charles Booth, Social Scientist,* Oxford, Oxford University Press, 1960.

Simon, John, *English Sanitary Institutions,* Cassell, 1890.

Sinfield, Adrian, *What Unemployment Means,* Robertson, 1981.

Smellie, K. B., *A History of Local Government,* Unwin, 1968.

Smiles, Aileen, *Samuel Smiles and his Surroundings,* Hale, 1956.

Smiles, Samuel, *Self-Help,* Murray, 1859.

—— *Character,* Murray, 1871.

—— *Thrift,* Murray, 1875.

—— *Duty,* Murray, 1880.

Smith, Adam, *The Wealth of Nations,* 1776. Available in modern editions.

Smith, Cecil Woodham, see Woodham Smith.

Smith, Francis Barrymore, *The People's Health, 1830–1890,* Croom Helm, 1979.

—— *Florence Nightingale: reputation and power,* Croom Helm, 1982.

Smith, Jef, 'Top jobs in the Social Services', in *The Year Book of Social Policy in Britain, 1971,* Routledge and Kegan Paul, 1972.

Smith, Thomas Southwood, *A Treatise on Fever,* London, 1830.

Social Affairs Unit:–
Anderson, Digby, (ed.), *Full Circle? Bringing up children in the post-permissive society,* 1988.
Anderson, Digby (ed.), *Breaking the Spell of the Welfare State: strategies for reducing public expenditure,* 1981.
O'Keefe, Dennis, *The Wayward Curriculum: a cause for parents' concern?,* 1986.
Social Insurance, Part I, HMSO, Cmd. 6550, 1944.
Social Insurance Part II: industrial injuries, HMSO, Cmd. 6551, 1944.
Stocks, Mary D., *Eleanor Rathbone: a biography,* Gollancz, 1949.
Strachey, Lytton, and Roger Fulford, *The Greville Memoirs,* Macmillan, 1938.
Sutcliffe, Anthony (ed.), *Multi-Storey Housing: the British working-class experience,* Croom Helm, 1974.
Taylor, A. J. P., *English History 1914–1945,* Oxford University Press, 1965, Pelican, 1975, reprinted 1987.
Tebbit, Norman, *Upwardly Mobile,* Futura, 1989.
Thane, Pat, *The Foundations of the Welfare State,* Longmans, 1982.
Thompson, Flora, *Lark Rise,* Oxford University Press, 1939.
Tivey, Leonard and Anthony Wright, *Party Ideology in Britain,* Routledge, 1989.
Titmuss, R. M., *Commitment to Welfare,* Allen and Unwin, 1968.
—— *Essays on 'The Welfare State',* Allen and Unwin, 1958.
—— *Problems of Social Policy,* Official History of the Second World War, United Kingdom Civil Series, HMSO, 1950.
—— *The Gift Relationship,* Allen and Unwin, 1970.
Townsend, Peter, *The Last Refuge,* Routledge and Kegan Paul, 1963.
—— *The Social Minority,* Allen Lane, 1972.
Townsend, Peter, and Brian Abel-Smith, *The Poor and the Poorest,* Occasional Papers in Social Administration, Bedford Square Press, 1966.
Townsend, Peter and Nick Davidson (eds), *Inequalities in Health: the Black Report,* Penguin, 1982.
Twining, Louisa, *Recollections of Workhouse Management and Visiting,* Kegan Paul, 1880.
[Uthwatt Report], Report of the Expert Committee on Compensation and Betterment, HMSO, Cmd. 6386, 1942.
Walton, Ronald, *Women in Social Work,* Routledge and Kegan Paul, 1975.
Webb, Beatrice, *My Apprenticeship,* Longmans Green, 1929.
—— *Our Partnership,* edited by B. Drake and M. Cole, Longmans Green, 1948.

Webb, Sidney and Beatrice Webb, *The Consumers' Co-operative Movement*, Longmans Green, 1921, revised edition, 1930.

—— *English Poor Law History*, Longmans Green, vol. 1, 1910, vol. 2, 1929.

—— *English Poor Law Policy*, Longmans Green, 1910.

—— *A History of Trade Unionism*, Longmans Green, 1894.

Weller, Malcolm, R.I. Tobiansky, D. Hollander and S. Ibrahim, 'Psychosis and destitution at Christmas', *Lancet* (1989) 23/30 December, 335 (8680).

Wickwar, Bernard, *The Social Services: an historical survey*, Cobden Sanderson, 1936.

Wilding, Paul (ed.), *In Defence of the Welfare State*, Manchester, Manchester University Press, 1986.

Willcocks, A. J., *The Creation of the National Health Service*, Routledge and Kegan Paul, 1967.

Wohl, Anthony S., *Endangered Lives: public health in Victorian Britain*, Methuen, 1984.

Wolff, Henry W., *People's Banks: a record of social and economic success*, King, 3rd edition, 1910.

Woodham Smith, Cecil, *Florence Nightingale, 1820–1910*, Constable 1950.

Young, Hugo, *One of Us: a biography of Margaret Thatcher*, Macmillan, 1989.

[Younghusband, Eileen], *Report on the Employment and Training of Social Workers*, Carnegie United Kingdom Trust, 1947.

—— *Second Report on the Employment and Training of Social Workers*, Carnegie United Kingdom Trust, 1951.

Younghusband, E., *Social Work in Britain, 1950–75*, 2 vols, Allen and Unwin, 1978.

[Younghusband Report], Report of Working Party on Social Workers in the Local Authority Health and Welfare Services, HMSO, 1959.

Notes and Sources

Introduction

1. A. J. P. Taylor, *English History 1914–1945,* (1965), (Penguin, 1987), p. 729.

Chapter 1

1. Sidney and Beatrice Webb, *English Poor Law Policy,* (1910), p. 1.
2. Thomas More, *Utopia,* 1516, Book I. (edited by Paul Turner, 1965, Penguin), p. 47.
3. J. L. and Barbara Hammond, *The Village Labourer,* vol. 1, (1911), Guild Books, 1948.
4. Hammond, op. cit., p. 39.
5. Hammond, op. cit., p. 93.
6. Elizabeth Longford, *Victoria R. I.,* (1964), p. 154.
7. Bristol Corporation of the Poor, *Selected Records, 1696–1834,* (Bristol Records Society Publications, 1932).
8. Adam Smith, *The Wealth of Nations,* (1776). Modern editions are available.
9. P. Dunkley, *The Crisis of the Old Poor Law in England,* (New York, 1982), p. 99, quoting a letter from Nassau Senior to Lord Brougham, 14 September 1832.
10. Ibid.
11. T. R. Malthus, *An Essay on the Principle of Population,* (1798). The extracts following in the text are taken from pp. 11, 16–17, 204 and 139.
12. H. Martineau, *Harriet Martineau's Autobiography,* (1877), vol. I, pp. 209–11. The blue stockings, learned and literary women of the late

eighteenth and nineteenth century, took their name from the Blue
Stocking Society founded in London about 1750. The name indicated
that they wore their everyday clothes, despising fashionable dress.
13. D. Ricardo, *The Principles of Political Economy and Taxation*,
(1817), edited by W. Fellner, (Homewood, Illinois, Richard D. Irwin,
1963), p. 52.
14. Mary P. Mack, *Jeremy Bentham, An odyssey of ideas, 1748–1792*,
(1962), vol. I.
15. Ibid.
16. J. Bentham, 'Leading Principles of a Constitutional Code for Any
State', *The Pamphleteer* no. 44, reprinted in J. Bowring (ed.), *The
Works of Jeremy Bentham*, (Edinburgh, 1843),p. 1n.
17. David Roberts, *Victorian Origins of the British Welfare State*,
(Connecticut, 1960).

Sources

The best account of the operation of the Old Poor Law is Nassau Senior's,
in the *Report of H.M. Commission for enquiring into the Administration
and Practical Operation of the Poor Laws, 1834*. The description of the
subject in chapter 1 is largely drawn from this source.

The Webbs' *English Poor Law History* has an exhaustive account of
Poor Law practice from mediaeval times, but is perhaps more appropriate
for consultation than for solid reading. Their *English Poor Law Policy*
does not deal with the situation before 1834.

Good secondary texts on the Old Poor Law are Peter Dunkley, *The
Crisis of the Old Poor Law in England* and the works of J. L. and Barbara
Hammonds, of *The Town Labourer, The Village Labourer* and *The Age of
the Chartists*. The last of these is concerned primarily with conditions in
the 1840s, but has interesting material on the situation before the Poor
Law Amendment Act.

Malthus and Ricardo should be read in the original: both write
concisely and with some passion, and their works are available in a
number of different editions. According to the Dictionary of National
Biography, they were close friends and colleagues. Readers will find many
overlaps in their ideas on what should be done to reform the Poor Laws.
Malthus originally published the *Essay on Population* as a pamphlet. He
revised and added to it on a number of occasions. The Pelican Classics
edition (ed. Anthony Flew) has a useful introduction.

Mary Mack's *Jeremy Bentham, vol. 1: an odyssey of ideas 1748–1792* is a
luminous and interesting account of a complex subject, and her *A
Bentham Reader* is probably the best introduction to Bentham's many
texts.

Chapter 2

1. E. J. Hobsbawm and George Rudé, *Captain Swing*, (New York, 1968).
2. William Cobbett, *Rural Rides*, (1830) 1853 edition, p. 559.
3. Anthony Brundage, *The Making of the New Poor Law*, (1978), pp. 22–4.
4. Brundage, op. cit., p. 182.
5. S. E. Finer, *Life and Times of Sir Edwin Chadwick*, (1952), pp. 43–4 nn, 75.
6. David Cecil, *Melbourne*, (Book Club, 1972), p. 305.
7. Brundage, op. cit., pp. 56, 67.
8. Finer, op. cit., pp. 109–11.
9. Finer, op. cit., p. 111.
10. *Report of the Select Committee of the House of Commons to enquire into the Andover Union, Parliamentary Papers* (1846), 11, 22620.
11. Brundage, op. cit., p. 101.
12. Brundage, op. cit., p. 95.
13. J. L. and Barbara Hammond, *The Age of the Chartists, 1832–54,* (1930), p. 72.
14. Finer, op. cit., p. 83.
15. Brundage, op. cit., p. 95.
16. G. Wythen Baxter, *The Book of the Bastiles, or the History of the Working of the New Poor Law*, (1841), p. 320. The quotations in the following paragraphs are taken from the same source.
17. Charles Dickens, *Oliver Twist*, (Chapman and Hall, 1901), p. 9.
18. Dickens, op. cit., p. 11.
19. *Bradford Argus*, 27 June, 1837.
20. *Parliamentary Debates (Hansard), House of Commons*, LVI, 377, Benjamin D'Israeli, 8 February 1841.
21. Brundage, op. cit., p. 153.
22. Wythen Baxter, op. cit., p. 4.

Sources

The Poor Law Report of 1834 records in considerable detail both the Commission's mode of operation and the rationale for its conclusions. Wythen Baxter's *Book of the Bastiles*, published in 1841, provides a rich source of anti-Poor Law sentiment, ranging from invective to considered protest.

Most people have read *Oliver Twist*. It is worth re-reading the first chapter with the knowledge that it was written early in the implementation of the New Poor Law, at a time when the deterrent policy was shocking public opinion. Dickens was a journalist, and he wrote to

238   The Making of Social Policy in Britain

deadlines. If the first chapters of *Oliver Twist* were published in February 1837, they were probably written only weeks or days before. John Walter II's invective in his leaders in *The Times* is worth reading. *The Times* has an excellent index, which makes referencing easy. Of the secondary sourses, Professor S. E. Finer's *The Life and Times of Sir Edwin Chadwick* is a major contribution to understanding this remarkable man, using many fresh documentary sources. The first half of the book deals largely with Chadwick's intellectual background, the Poor Law Commission and Report, his experiences at Somerset House, and his massive unpopularity, as he was blamed (to some extent unjustly, in view of his lack of authority) for the rigours of the New Poor Law.

Anthony Brundage's *The Making of the New Poor Law* is a clear and cogent analysis of the policy process, based on original research.

Chapter 3

1. James Kay, *The Moral and Physical Condition of the Working Classes Employed in the Cotton Manufacture in Manchester,* (1832).
2. James Kay and Neil Arnott, *Fever in the Metropolis,* (1836).
3. M. W. Flinn, Introduction to Edwin Chadwick, *The Sanitary Condition of the Labouring Population of Great Britain,* (1842), (Edinburgh University Press, 1965), p. 4.
4. Flinn, op. cit., p. 8.
5. T. Southwood Smith, *A Treatise on Fever,* (1830), p. 204.
6. Flinn, op. cit., p. 27.
7. S. E. Finer, *Life and Times of Sir Edwin Chadwick,* (1965), p. 125.
8. *Tenth Annual Report of the Registrar-General's Office,* (1847), p. xvii.
9. Finer, op. cit., p. 221.
10. Flinn, op. cit., p. 51.
11. Chadwick, op. cit., p. 246.
12. Finer, op. cit., p. 234, quoting a letter from Chadwick to Major Graham, 1843.
13. Flinn, op. cit., p. 13.
14. Chadwick, op. cit., p. 256.
15. Chadwick, op. cit., p. 92.
16. Chadwick, op. cit., p. 91.
17. Chadwick, op. cit., p. 339.
18. Chadwick, op. cit., p. 423.
19. Chadwick, op. cit., p. 203.
20. Chadwick, op. cit., pp. 421–5.
21. D. Roberts, *Victorian Origins of the British Welfare State,* (1960), p. 71.
22. Finer, op. cit., p. 293.

23. Quoted by David Roberts, op. cit., p. 96.
24. Roberts, op. cit., p. 77.
25. *Supplementary Report on the result of a Special Inquiry into the Practice of Interment in Towns,* Parliamentary Papers, (1843), XII.
26. R. A. Lewis, *Edwin Chadwick and the Public Health Movement,* 1952, p. 201.
27. *Lancet,* (1849) 2:21, 9 July and (1849) 2: 159–60, 11 August.
28. Finer, op. cit., p. 341. See also Chadwick, op. cit., pp 148–9.
29. Southwood Smith, op. cit., pp. 348–9.
30. Finer, op. cit., p. 298.
31. C. L. Lewes, *Dr Southwood Smith.* (1899), p. 77.
32. R. A. Lewis, op. cit., p. 190.
33. *The Times,* 1 Oct. 1849.
34. Finer, op. cit., p. 479.
35. A. Newsholme, *Fifty Years in Public Health,* (1935), p. 93. See also W. M. Frazer, *A History of English Public Health,* (1950), pp. 66–7.
36. Finer, op. cit., p. 509.

Sources

The most important primary source is the *Sanitary Report* of 1842 – a remarkable document in its command of the subject and the thoroughness of its approach. The *Supplementary Report on Interments* completes a grim picture of the problems of over-population and under-regulation in crowded city centres. Contemporary comment on the General Board of Health in 1853–1854, particularly from John Walter III in *The Times* and Thomas Wakley in the *Lancet,* makes lively reading.

The echoes of conflict can be perceived even in the secondary accounts. Finer's *Life and Times of Sir Edwin Chadwick* gives an excellent account of Chadwick's own outstanding contribution to the public health services and the work of the sanitary engineers, but perhaps underplays the contribution of the medical profession. For instance, Finer does not mention the incident of the Broad Street Pump, which may be taken as effective proof of the claims of the specific contagionists. Medical histories, on the other hand, are mainly written by public health doctors, who tend to stress the achievements of their own profession, to the detriment of Chadwick and the sanitary engineers. Sir Arthur Newsholme's *Fifty Years in Public Health* covers the years roughly from 1860 to 1909, but includes some of the earlier background, such as the contribution of Kay, Arnott and Southwood Smith, and the work of John Snow, William Farr and John Simon. Sir Arthur was sometime Chief Medical Officer to the Local Government Board, but the book, despite its title, is not based on his own professional experiences, as he was born in

1857. Dr William Mowll Frazer's *History of English Public Health* is a more modern account of the same period written by the Medical Officer of Health for Liverpool. Of the recent sources, M. W. Flinn's introduction to his edition of the *Sanitary Report* is a comparatively brief but concise account of the issues. Margaret Pelling's *Cholera, Fever and English Medicine* and Frances B. Smith's *The People's Health, 1830–1890* are good on the medical issues, but less concerned with administrative and political problems. Anthony S. Wohl's *Endangered Lives: public health in Victorian Britain* is highly descriptive social history.

David Roberts' *Victorian Origins of the British Welfare State* provides some new insights into the ideas of the reformers, and the ways in which they were translated into administrative systems, particularly in respect of the issue of centralization and the powers of the inspectors.

It has not been possible to include a chapter on the companion developments in Factory Reform, in which Chadwick and Ashley (Shaftesbury) again played leading parts, together with Michael Sadler, Richard Oastler and John Fielden. The appointment of the first factory inspectors in 1833, the struggle to end child labour and protect women, the Mines Act of 1842, the campaign for the 'Ten Hours Bill' and the successive Factory Acts of 1847, 1853, 1867, 1874 and 1878 are well chronicled by Fraser (*The Evolution of the British Welfare State*, chapter 1), and by Finer and the Hammonds in their biographies of Chadwick and Shaftesbury. As Fraser notes (p. 26), 'the factory movement disappeared in the 1850s, with great success to its credit'.

Chapter 4

1. W. Beveridge, *Voluntary Action*, (1948), p. 9.
2. Derek Fraser, *The Evolution of the British Welfare State*, (1973), p. 115.
3. Kathleen Jones, *The Compassionate Society*, pp. 59–62.
4. E. Hodder, *The Life and Work of the Seventh Earl of Shaftesbury*, (1886), vol. II, pp. 367–9.
5. Kathleen Heasman, *Evangelicals in Action*, (1962).
6. J. L. and Barbara Hammond, *Lord Shaftesbury*, (1923), p. 233.
7. See Geoffrey Pearson, *The Deviant Imagination*, (1975).
8. Lytton Strachey and Roger Fulford (eds), *The Greville Memoirs*, 1938, vol. VI, pp. 52–3.
9. Hammon, op. cit., p. 233.
10. C. Woodham Smith, *Florence Nightingale, 1820–1910*, (1950), p. 149.
11. Derek Fraser, op. cit., p. 121.
12. David Owen, *English Philanthropy, 1660–1960*, (1965), p. 218.

13. Goschen Minute of 20 November 1969. See S. and B. Webb, *English Poor Law Policy*, (1910), pp. 144–6.
14. Owen, op. cit., p. 221.
15. Owen, op. cit., p. 243.
16. Beveridge, op. cit., pp. 21–117, from which this brief account of friendly societies is largely drawn.
17. E. J. Cleary, *The Building Society Movement*, (1965), pp. 10–11.
18. Martin Boddy, *The Building Societies*, (1980), p. 8.
19. G. D. H. Cole and Raymond Postgate, *The Common People*, (1948), pp. 638–9.
20. Henry W. Wolff, *People's Banks*, 3rd edition, (1910), p. 2.
21. G. J. Holyoake, *The Rochdale Pioneers*, 10th edition, (1893), pp. 2, 10.
22. Beveridge, op. cit., p. 57.
23. Samuel Smiles, *Self-Help*, (1859), p. 1.
24. Smiles, *Self-Help*, p. 269.
25. *Dictionary of National Biography*, (1917).
26. Samuel Smiles, *Thrift*, (1875), p. 37.
27. Smiles, *Thrift*, p. 183.

Sources

In general, conservative writers tend to stress the importance of the philanthropic movement, while liberal writers tend to emphasize the friendly societies, and socialist writers the trade union and co-operative movements. Smiles is rarely mentioned in modern texts, though the views he represents have enjoyed a resurgence in recent years.

The standard scholarly accounts of philanthropy are B. Kirkman Gray's *History of English Philanthropy* and David Owen's *English Philanthropy 1660–1960*. Kirkman Gray's book, published in 1905, has a period flavour. Owen's account has a sharper analytical edge, and represents a more modern view of the subject, though a spread of 300 years is rather long for a single volume.

The Dictionary of National Biography (D.N.B.) provides a quick source of reference about individual philanthrophists, and there are specialized biographies available in most libraries of those whose work is well-known.

There are two main accounts of the work of the Charity Organisation Society: Charles Loch's *Charity Organisation* and Helen Bosanquet's *Social Work in London*. The subject is further considered in Chapter Seven.

Lord Beveridge's *Voluntary Action* is somewhat patchy, and gives the appearance of having been written in a hurry by a busy man. It was written five or six years after the Beveridge Report, when the 'Welfare

State' legislation was at last coming into effect, and Beveridge was much involved with the voluntary social services. He deals fairly briefly with philanthropy. 'A Chapter of Pioneers' gives potted biographies of twenty-seven individuals he considers worthy of note – some well known and some lesser known. As might be expected, his main enthusiasm is reserved for the friendly societies, which were the forerunners of the social security system. Beveridge wrote with the advantage of a long practical involvement with the friendly societies, and an affection for curious bodies like the Total Abstinence Sons of the Phoenix Society.

Sidney and Beatrice Webb made major studies of the Socialist mutual aid movements – *A History of Trade Unionism* and *The Consumers' Co-operative Movement*. G. D. H. Cole's account of Mutual Aid in the symposium edited by A. F. C. Bourdillon, *The Voluntary Social Services*, also stresses the contribution made by these movements. The symposium, undertaken for the Nuffield College Social Reconstruction Survey in the final years of the Second World War, has many interesting sidelights on the development of the voluntary services.

The most lively account of the co-operative movement is George Jacob Holyoake's *The Rochdale Pioneers*. According to the Webbs, Holyoake was himself one of the Co-operative pioneers in the Owenite tradition – disappointed when the plans for 'a multiplication of self-governing workshops' failed and only the consumers' movement was left. Holyoake's book attracted international attention, and was translated into several European languages, including Hungarian.

There is a good deal of literature on building societies, including individual histories of some of the major societies. A useful and comparatively recent text is Martin Boddy's *The Building Societies*, published in 1980.

H. J. Hamilton's *Savings and Savings Institutions* and Henry Wolff's *The People's Banks* cover common ground, but Hamilton emphasizes the social effects of the movement, while Wolff is more concerned with its economic success.

The works of Samuel Smiles make fairly repetitive reading, but *Self-Help* at least should be encountered in the original. There are still many copies in circulation. The only full-length biography of Smiles appears to be one written by a relative, Aileen Smiles, entitled *Samuel Smiles and his Surroundings*.

Chapter 5

1. H. Mayhew, *London Labour and the London Poor: a cyclopaedia of those that will work, those that cannot work and those that will not work,* (1851), no. 1, pp. 2–4, 'Of Wandering tribes in General'. The

modern versions are Peter Quennell (ed.), *Mayhew's London*, (Pilot Press, 1949), *London's Underworld*, (Kimber, 1950), and *Mayhew's Characters*, (Kimber, 1951).
2. Ibid.
3. William Booth, *In Darkest England, or The Way Out*, (1890), pp. 11–12.
4. F. D. Hyndman, *Record of an Adventurous Life*, (1911), pp. 330–2.
5. Hyndman, op. cit., p. 322.
6. Hyndman, op. cit., p. 330–1.
7. Beatrice Webb, *My Apprenticeship*, (1929), p. 219.
8. Charles Booth, *Life and Labour of the People of London*, (1892), vol. II, p. 21.
9. Charles Booth, op. cit., (1903), vol. XVII, p. 216. The allusion is to the Book of Ezekiel, chapter 37, verses 1–10.
10. Simey, T. S., *Charles Booth, Social Scientist*, (1960), Appendix IV, p. 278.
11. B. Seebohm Rowntree, *Poverty – A Study of Town Life*, (1901), p. 305.
12. Asa Briggs, *Social Thought and Social Action: a study of the work of Seebohm Rowntree*, (1961), p. 37.
13. Peter Townsend, *The Social Minority*, (1973), pp. 25–32.
14. Robert Holman, *Poverty*, (1978), pp. 8–13.
15. Briggs, op. cit., p. 38.
16. Briggs, op. cit., p. 37.

Sources

The main sources referred to in the text are readily available. Mayhew's *London Labour and the London Poor* was originally published in penny copies, and achieved book form in 1851. The modern editions unfortunately omit the interesting theories about the 'wandering hordes'. General Booth's *In Darkest England* sold 70,000 copies in the first year of publication, but has not been reprinted since 1890.

Charles Booth's *Life and Labour of the People of London* runs to seventeen volumes, of which the first four may be the most rewarding for general readers to consult. His biographer, T. S. Simey (later Lord Simey of Toxteth), was Charles Booth Professor of Social Science in the University of Liverpool.

Seebohm Rowntree's *Poverty – A Study of Town Life* was originally published in 1901, reprinted in 1902, came out in a cheap edition in 1922, and reached a further revised edition in 1922. Asa Briggs (later Lord Briggs) devotes only one chapter of his life of Rowntree to the first Poverty Study, but provides some useful comparisons with Rowntree's later work: *Poverty and Progress* (1936) and *Poverty and the Welfare State* (with G. R. Lavers, 1951), together with a complete bibliography of Rowntree's writings.

A good modern analysis of the argument about absolute and relative poverty can be found in Stein Ringen's *The Possibility of Politics: a study in the political economy of the Welfare State*, 1987, chapter 7.

Chapter 6

1. Brian Abel-Smith, *A History of the Nursing Profession*, (1960), p. 40. See also W. M. Frazer, *A History of English Public Health*, (1950), pp. 86–8.
2. Louisa Twining, *Recollections of Workhouse Management and Visiting*, (1880), pp. 69–70.
3. Twining, op. cit., pp. 64, 65.
4. *D.N.B.* (Entry for Professor Nassau Senior. His daughter-in-law was not accorded a separate entry).
5. W. M. Frazer, op. cit., pp. 161–87.
6. John Simon, *English Sanitary Institutions*, (1890), p. 232.
7. Simon, op. cit., pp. 355–6.
8. Simon, op. cit., p. 389.
9. K. B. Smellie, *A History of Local Government*, (1968), p. 60.
10. Smellie, op. cit., p. 60.
11. Smellie, op. cit., p. 68.
12. David Owen, *English Philanthropy, 1660–1960*, (1965), p. 242.
13. G. F. MacCleary, *The Maternity and Child Welfare Movement*, (1935).
14. A. Newsholme, *Fifty Years in English Public Health*, (1935), pp. 55–6.
15. Jean Donnison, *Midwives and Medical Men*, (1977).

Sources

The story of the Medical Officers of Health and their departments does not appear to have greatly engaged the interest of recent scholars. Medical Officers of Health ceased to exist in 1975, when most of the public health responsibilities of the local authority were transferred to the Community Medicine Department of the District Health Authority. By that time, the main public health problems had been conquered. This example of a self-eliminating profession would have pleased Jeremy Bentham.

Sir John Simon and Sir Arthur Newsholme were both public health doctors, though their accounts relate more to central government policy than to local government. Dr McCleary, whose *Maternity and Child Welfare in Great Britain* is the basic source on maternity and child welfare, was Medical Officer of Health for Battersea, and much involved in the movement. Dr W. M. Frazer was Medical Officer of Health for Liverpool, and his *History of English Public Health* is a good foundation. F. F. Cartwright's *A Social History of Medicine* and M. W. Flinn's *Public Health Reform in Britain* tell the story from varying approaches.

Brian Abel-Smith's *The Hospitals, 1800–1948* and *A History of the Nursing Profession* provide a well-documented account of the complementary developments in hospital medicine in the same period.

Developments in the Mental Health Services have been chronicled elsewhere (Kathleen Jones, *A History of the Mental Health Services*). K. B. Smellie's *History of Local Government* is a standard work which puts all the pieces of a somewhat fragmented subject together.

Jean Donnison's *Midwives and Medical Men* is a case-study in gender politics, and in the emergence of the first of the professions 'ancillary to medicine'. Midwives achieved nationally recognized status in 1902, and general nurses (State Registered Nurses) not until 1918.

Chapter 7

1. David Owen, *English Philanthropy 1660–1960*, (1965), p. 218.
2. Owen, op. cit., p. 224.
3. Helen Dendy, in B. Bosanquet (ed.), *Aspects of the Social Problem*, (1895), pp. 167–8.
4. C. S. Loch, *Charity Organisation*, (1905).
5. Margaret Cole, *The Story of Fabian Socialism*, (1961), (Mercury, 1963), p. 138.
6. Beatrice Webb, *My Apprenticeship*, (1929), p. 195.
7. Cole, *The Story of Fabian Socialism*, p. 18.
8. Cole, *The Story of Fabian Socialism*, p. 69.
9. Beatrice Webb, *Our Partnership*, edited by B. Drake and M. Cole, (1948), p. 329.
10. Webb, *Our Partnership*, p. 377.
11. Webb, *Our Partnership*, p. 392.
12. *Report of the Royal Commission on the Poor Laws and the Relief of Distress, 1909*, HMSO. Cmd. 4499, 1909, vol. 1, pp. 102–3.
13. Cole, *The Story of Fabian Socialism*, p. 138.
14. *Poor Law Report, 1909*, evidence, vol. 18, pp. 38–9.
15. *Poor Law Report, 1909*, evidence, vol. 18, p. 61.
16. Webb, *Our Partnership*, p. 419.
17. Helen Bosanquet, *The Poor Law Report of 1909*, (1912).
18. Margaret Cole, *Beatrice Webb*, (1961), (Mercury, 1961), p. 109.

19. W. Ivor Jennings, editor's introduction to *The Poor Law Code*, (1930).

Sources

The main sources for the work of the Royal Commission on the Poor Laws of 1905–1909 are the Majority and Minority Reports. As indicated in the text of Chapter seven, these should be read with care, and with some knowledge of the personal and ideological conflicts involved.

Beatrice Webb's *Our Partnership* devotes most of Chapter VII to extracts from her diaries relating to the Commission's work. *The Diaries of Beatrice Webb*, edited by Margaret Cole, are separately published.

Margaret Cole's *The Story of Fabian Socialism* is the standard account of the Fabian movement before 1960. This is always pro-Fabian, but not always pro-Webb. In particular, Mrs Cole contends that the 'real partnership' was 'Sidney and Bernard' (Bernard Shaw), rather than 'Sidney and Beatrice'. Though Sidney Webb and G. B. S. did work together on a number of occasions, the evidence of the Webbs' joint work is really too strong to sustain this view.

The COS view of the debate is given in Helen Bosanquet's *The Poor Law Report of 1909*, which studiously avoids any suggestion of controversy or disagreement, and does not mention the Fabians. Though all 34 volumes of the appendices are meticulously listed, the Minority Report is ignored.

Maurice Bruce's edited volume of primary source material, *The Rise of the Welfare State*, includes in Chapter seven a comparison of the Majority and Minority Reports, but this is somewhat misleading.

Chapter 8

1. Derek Fraser, *The Evolution of the British Welfare State*, (1973), p. 136.
2. Flora Thompson, *Lark Rise*, (1939), p. 100.
3. Beatrice Webb, *Our Partnership*, (1948), pp. 417–8.
4. L. Broad, *Winston Churchill, 1874–1951*, (1951), p. 60.
5. Quoted in Maurice Bruce, *The Rise of the Welfare State*, (1961), pp. 127–8.
6. Violet Bonham Carter, *Winston Churchill as I knew him*, (1965), p. 135.
7. J. Grigg, *Lloyd George, The People's Champion*, (1978), p. 163.
8. Quoted in Fraser, op. cit., p. 151.
9. Quoted in du Parcq, *Life of David Lloyd George*, (1912), pp. 562–3.
10. *Parliamentary Debates (Hansard), House of Commons*, XXV 644, Rt. Hon. Lloyd George, 4 May, 1911.
11. Grigg, op. cit., p. 347; du Parcq, op. cit., p. 581.

Sources

The fullest academic accounts are Bentley Gilbert's *The Evolution of National Insurance in Britain* and Peter Rowland's *The Last Liberal Governments*, vol. 1, *The Promised Land* and vol. 2, *Unfinished Business*. Derek Fraser (*The Evolution of the Welfare State*) has a good chapter on the Liberal reforms, which includes original, if pro-Labour, comment. Lloyd George's biographies devote a considerable amount of space to the National Insurance Act. Lloyd George's speeches in the House of Commons, particularly on the Old Age Pensions Bill and the National Insurance Bill, are a classic mixture of social conviction and rhetoric.

This period in Winston Churchill's life is not well covered by his biographers, to whom the evidence of early Radicalism often seems something of an embarrassment in the career of a great Conservative Prime Minister. But Churchill's later career in any case tends to overshadow this interesting period in his life.

Maurice Bruce's edited volume of primary source material, *The Rise of The Welfare State,* has some well-chosen extracts on this period in Chapter seven 'Turning Away from the Poor Law'.

Chapter 9

1. A. J. P. Taylor, *English History 1914–1945,* revised edition (1970), p. 313.
2. Wal Hannington, *Unemployed Struggles 1919–1936,* (1936), reprinted 1979, p. 80–81.
3. Hannington, op. cit., p. 167.
4. Hannington, op. cit., pp. 276–7.
5. George Orwell, *The Road to Wigan Pier,* (1937) (Penguin, 1961), p. 16.
6. Orwell, op. cit., pp. 76–7.
7. *Report of the Unemployment Insurance Committee,* chairman, Lord Blanesburgh, *(Blanesburgh Report),* HMSO, 1928, para. 16.
8. Beveridge Papers, quoted in Fraser, *The Evolution of the British Welfare State,* (1973), p. 177.
9. *Report of the Royal Commission on Unemployment Insurance,* chairman, Judge Holman Gregory, *(Holman Gregory Report),* HMSO, Cmd. 4185, 1932, paras. 196–7.
10. *Holman Gregory Report* para. 258.
11. Orwell, op. cit., pp. 79–80.
12. Wal Hannington, *The Problem of the Distressed Areas,* (1937), p. 21.
13. *Parliamentary Debates (Hansard), House of Commons,* vol. 265, col. 1868, Rt Hon. David Lloyd George, 6 Dec., 1934.
14. Hannington, *The Problem of the Distressed Areas,* p. 24.

15. Fraser, *The Evolution of the British Welfare State*, p. 183.
16. Bernard Wickwar, *The Social Services: an historical survey*, (1936).
17. B. Seebohm Rowntree, *Poverty and Progress*, (1941), p.v.
18. Rowntree, op. cit., pp. 478–92.
19. Rowntree, op. cit., p. 114.
20. Rowntree, op. cit., pp. 468–9.
21. *Report on the British Social Services*, PEP, June 1937, p. 169.
22. *Report on the British Health Services*, PEP, December 1937, p. 387.
23. *Report on the British Health Services*, PEP, p. 393.
24. *Report on the British Health Services*, PEP, p. 414.

Sources

The PEP reports give a balanced picture, based on original research, of the services in the mid-1930s. Sharper and briefer, is Appendix B to the Beveridge Report (*Social Insurance and Allied Services*, HMSO, Cmd. 6404, 1942) which contains Beveridge's own summary of the gaps and anomalies in the insurance system.

Wal Hannington's account of the hunger marches has a remarkable immediacy and simplicity. George Orwell's *The Road to Wigan Pier* and *Down and Out in Paris and London* are more journalistic – the first deals with individual squalor rather than family poverty, and the latter is concerned with single homelessness – a situation in which men genuinely seeking work were treated as vagrants.

Among novels of the period, Walter Greenwood's *Love on the Dole*, which describes the impact of unemployment on a working-class family in a small Lancashire town, and A. J. Cronin's *The Stars Look Down*, based on a mining community in Tyneside, are particularly impressive. Cronin's *The Citadel* is a health service classic, describing the contrasts between a 'panel' practice in South Wales and private medical practice in a fashionable area of London. Both the Cronin books were made into films which are fairly faithful to the originals.

Of the secondary accounts, Bentley Gilbert's *British Social Policy 1914–1939* is both full and detailed, with less immediacy but more objectivity than the primary accounts.

Chapter 10

1. Richard M. Titmuss, *Problems of Social Policy*, Official History of the Second World War, United Kingdom Civil Series, (HMSO, 1950), p. 506.
2. Derek Fraser, *The Evolution of the British Welfare State*, (1973), p. 195.

3. Arthur Marwick, *Britain in the Century of Total War*, (1968) (Penguin, 1970), p. 304.
4. Pauline Gregg, *The Welfare State*, (1967), p. 31.
5. Fraser, op. cit., p. 206.
6. *Report of the Inter-Departmental Committee on Social Insurance and Allied Services* (the *Beveridge Report*) HMSO, 1942, Cmd. 6404, para. 40.
7. *Beveridge Report* paras 303–9.
8. *Beveridge Report*, para. 310.
9. *Beveridge Report*, para. 311.
10. At this time (before the general introduction of the antibiotics, developed in the early 1940s) the normal period of confinement for childbirth was 2–3 weeks, and most babies were born at home because of shortage of hospital accommodation.
11. *Beveridge Report* paras 410–43.
12. See Mary Stocks, *Eleanor Rathbone: a biography*, (1949).
13. War Cabinet Papers no. 18 of 1943, quoted in Martin Gilbert, *Winston Churchill*, (1986), vol. VII, p. 292.
14. War Cabinet Papers no. 65 of 1943, quoted Gilbert, op. cit., p. 293.
15. Lord Beveridge (William H. Beveridge), *Power and Influence*, (1953), p. 332.
16. Beveridge, *Power and Influence*, p. 323.
17. Beveridge, *Power and Influence*, pp. 329–31.
18. Beveridge, *Power and Influence*, p. 325.
19. Fraser, op. cit., p. 203.

Sources

There are many sources of information on the Second World War, including autobiographies of the main participants. Contemporary films (many of them made with the support of the Ministry of Information to raise public morale and assist the war effort) tend to perpetuate the functional myths of war-time rather than representing reality. Arthur Marwick's *Britain in the Century of Total War*, which formed part of an Open University course on war, is detailed and balanced. A. J. P. Taylor's *English History 1914–45* is good on the general background, but more concerned with military and political events than with their social consequences.

Richard Titmuss's *Social Policy in Wartime* is a detailed and well written study of his three chosen subjects – evacuation, care of the homeless, and the Emergency Medical Service – but since it is part of an official history, it tends, unlike his later works, to be somewhat bland. Sheila Ferguson and Hilda Fitzgerald's *Studies in the Social Services* is another volume in the same series, which deals with maternity and child welfare.

The *Beveridge Report* contains much detail about the insurance proposals. General readers may find it useful to start from the principles indicated in the footnotes above, and then to extend their reading by use of the index. It is a document to be consulted rather than read from cover to cover. The story of Beveridge's relations with Government after the publication of the report are treated both in his *Power and Influence* and in his wife's account (Janet Beveridge, *Beveridge and His Plan*).

Despite the problems of publishing in wartime (shortage of paper, lack of printers and typesetters, and a disrupted distribution system) many pamphlets were published commenting on the Government proposals from differing political points of view. Unfortunately, the quality of paper and binding was so poor that most of them have not survived, though collections of Army Bureau of Current Affairs (ABCA) pamphlets, which give a very lively picture of the debates, are still found to be in some major libraries.

The Nuffield College Social Reconstruction Survey, *The Voluntary Social Services* edited by A. F. C. Bourdillon, published in 1945, is a valuable summary of academic opinion on voluntary organizations at the end of the war.

Chapter 11

1. Hugh Dalton, *High Tide and After, Memoirs,* (1962), vol. III, p. 3.
2. Cyril Clemens, *The man from Limehouse: Clement Attlee,* (New York, 1946), p. 94.
3. Clement Attlee, *As It Happened,* (1954), p. 163.
4. *Social Insurance, Part 1,* HMSO, Cmd. 6550, September 1944. *Social Insurance Part II (Industrial Injuries)* HMSO, Cmd. 6551, September 1944.
5. *A National Health Service* HMSO, Cmd. 6502, February 1944.
6. Michael Foot, *Aneurin Bevan,* (1962), vol. I, p. 16.
7. Aneurin Bevan, *In Place of Fear,* (1952), (Quartet, 1976), pp. 98–101.
8. *Employment Policy,* HMSO Cmd. 6527, May 1944.
9. *The Supply, Recruitment and Training of Teachers and Youth Leaders,* (the *McNair Report*) (HMSO, 1944).
10. *Curriculum and Examination: Report of the Committee of the Secondary Schools Examination Council,* (the *Norwood Report*), HMSO, Cmd. 6502, 1943.
11. *Educational Reconstruction,* HMSO, Cmd. 6458, 1943.
12. The school leaving age was raised to 15 in 1947 and to 16 in 1972.

13. Pauline Gregg, *The Welfare State*, (1967), p. 194.
14. *Report of the Royal Commission on the Distribution of the Industrial Population*, (the *Barlow Report*), HMSO, Cmd. 6513, 1940.
15. *Report of the Committee on Land Utilisation in Rural Areas*, (the *Scott Report*), HMSO, Cmd. 6378, 1942.
16. *Report of the Expert Committee on Compensation and Betterment* (the *Uthwatt Report*), HMSO, Cmd. 6386, 1942.

Sources

The best sources for this period are the White Papers and Government Reports which have been noted above. House of Commons Debates are a good source for the views of individual politicians, but it was a period of much rhetoric, and the speeches add little to the debates which had already taken place across the country in the preceding years.

Biographies or autobiographies of Labour politicians tend to be disappointing. There is polemic, on the lines of Aneurin Bevan's *Why Not Trust the Tories?* There is quiet and reflective autobiography on the lines of Lord Attlee's unassuming *As it Happened*. But the major interest of both participants and commentators is in the nationalization of public utilities, which was still controversial, rather than in the social programme, which it was assumed represented a national consensus. It is also necessary to remember that the Attlee Government of 1945–1950 had other things on its mind – the ending of the war with Japan, the changeover from war to peace conditions, the settlement with Germany, the economic situation, the withdrawal from Palestine when the state of Israel was set up, the withdrawal from India and other parts of the Empire. As a result, there is surprisingly little about the new welfare system. The literature comes before and after the legislative changes, not while they were in progress.

The curious title of Cyril Clemens' life of Clement Attlee, *The Man from Limehouse*, results from the fact that Clemens, an American, had already written a life of President Truman entitled *The Man from Missouri*. Limehouse was Clement Attlee's constituency as a member of the House of Commons, but he was not 'from Limehouse' in the sense that Truman was 'from Missouri'.

Pauline Gregg's *The Welfare State* is more concerned with nationalization policies than with the social legislation of the period, though chapters 3 and 4 give lively accounts of the setting up of the social security system and the National Health Service. Derek Fraser's *The Evolution of the British Welfare State* covers the main legislation, but omits Town and Country Planning.

Arthur Willcocks' *The Creation of the National Health Service* is a valuable case-study in social policy, originally written as the author's Ph.D. thesis in the mid-1950s. The subject matter was then considered so controversial that publishers were unwilling to take a risk on it, and it was not published until 1967, when the controversy appeared to have died down.

Sir James Stirling Ross's *The National Health Service in Great Britain*, (1952), is a factual and fairly unexciting account of its subject, but it has one lyrical passage in which the author compares the events of the Appointed Day for the operation of the National Insurance Act, the National Assistance Act and the National Health Service Act (5 July 1948) to the opening of a gigantic bank vault. All the tumblers, it seemed, were falling into place at last.

Chapter 12

1. The Rt. Hon. Barbara Castle, television interview, BBC1, 28 September 1989.
2. Kathleen Jones, *The Teaching of Social Studies in British Universities, Occasional Papers in Social Administration*, (1964), chapter IV, *passim*.
3. Kenneth O. Morgan, *Labour in Power, 1945–51*, (Oxford, 1984), p. 161.
4. *Enquiry into the Cost of the National Health Service – the Report of the Guillebaud Committee*, HMSO, Cmd. 9663, 1956.
5. 'The Social Services – Needs and Means': analysis by two Conservative MPs, *The Times*, 17 January 1952, and editorial in the same edition.
6. Iain MacLeod and Enoch Powell, *The Social Services – Needs and Means*, (Conservative Political Centre, 1954).
7. John Jewkes and Sylvia Jewkes, *The Genesis of the National Health Service*, (Oxford, 1961).
8. D. S. Lees, *Health Through Choice*, (Institute of Economic Affairs, 1961).
9. R. M. Titmuss, *Commitment to Welfare*, (1968) chapter XVII, pp. 247–62.
10. Titmuss, op. cit., pp. 263–8.
11. Brian Abel-Smith, *Value for Money in Health Services: a comparative study*, (1976), p. 122.
12. *A Hospital Plan for England and Wales*, HMSO, Cmd. 1604, 1962.
13. Titmuss, op. cit., chapter IX, pp. 104.
14. *Health and Welfare: the development of community care*, HMSO, Cmd. 1973, 1963.
15. Stuart Lowe, *Housing*, 1985, p. 11.
16. P. Dunleavy, *The Politics of Mass Housing in Britain, 1945–75*, (Oxford, 1981), p. 39.

17. J. Burnett, *A Social History of Housing 1815–1985*, 2nd edition, (1978), p. 282.
18. Morgan, op. cit., p. 175.
19. *15 to 18, Report of the Central Advisory Council on Education, England* (the *Crowther Report*), 2 vols, HMSO, 1959.
20. *Half Our Future, Report of the Central Advisory Council on Education, England*, (the *Newsom Report*), (HMSO, 1963).
21. *Higher Education, Report of the Royal Commission on Higher Education* (the *Robbins Report*), HMSO, Cmd. 2154, 1963.
22. T. H. Marshall, *Social Policy*, (1965), revised edition, (1967), p. 182.
23. See introduction to Barbara Rodgers and June Stevenson, *A New Portrait of Social Work*, (1973).
24. Eileen Younghusband, *Report on the Employment and Training of Social Workers*, (Carnegie United Kingdom Trust, 1947); Eileen Younghusband, *Second Report on the Employment and Training of Social Workers*, (Carnegie United Kingdom Trust, 1951).
25. Kathleen Jones, *Eileen Younghusband: a biography*, (1984), chapters VII–IX, pp. 49–83.
26. *Report of the Working Party on Social Workers in the Local Authority Health and Welfare Services* (the *Younghusband Report*), (HMSO, 1959).
27. T. H. Marshall, op. cit., p. 97.
28. Kenneth Harris, *Thatcher*, (1988), (Fontana, 1989), pp. 12–13, 23–38, 290–3.

Sources

This was a great period for Government reports of all kinds. The members of Commissions, committees and working parties were experts, and in many cases they were given finance for their own research and enquiries. Major reports have been mentioned in the text and referenced above. The Newsom research (published in volume 2 of the Report) is a classic. The Robbins research involved an extensive statistical analysis of population trends and patterns of higher education.

Richard Titmuss's *The Gift Relationship*, referred to in Chapter 13, contains the developed version of his philosophy. Throughout the 1960s, the Institute of Economic Affairs produced a series of Hobart Papers under the editorship of Arthur Seldon which were to have a major effect in advancing a free market approach to the health and social services.

Sources on Housing for this period include John Burnett's *A Social History of Housing, 1815–1985*, P. Dunleavy's *The Politics of Mass Housing in Britain, 1945–75*, J. B. Cullingworth's *Housing Needs and*

Planning Policy, Anthony Sutcliffe (ed.), *Multi-Storey Living: the British Experience* and Elizabeth Gittus' *Flats, Families and the Under-Fives.* The Parker-Morris Report, *Homes for Today and Tomorrow,* is of particular interest in proposing what became known as 'Parker-Morris standards' for house building. Housing can also be studied from life: any large town will provide ample evidence of the mistakes of the post-war period, the adverse features of tower blocks and the constricted life of hastily developed estates.

Eileen Younghusband's *Social Work in Britain, 1950–75* is a meticulous record of the development of social work, though on the dull side. (Dame Eileen, as she became in 1964, often referred to it as 'the Albatross': it was a work of duty rather than pleasure.) The present writer's *Eileen Younghusband: a biography* is an attempt to show the human side of the process.

T. H. Marshall's *Social Policy* sums up the development of the subject in the first half of the twentieth century in less than a hundred pages, with a distinct preference for the quantifiable aspects, such as social insurance. The second half of the book, on 'Social policy at mid-century' is now of historical interest. Marshall's last book, *Social Welfare and the Citizen* contains a full exposition of his theories of citizenship which may have implications for future development. See John Ferris, Citizenship and the crisis in the Welfare State, in Philip Bean, John Ferris and David Whynes, *In Defence of Welfare,* chapter 3, *passim.*

Chapter 13

1. R. H. S. Crossman, *The Diaries of a Cabinet Minister,* (1976), vol. 2, p. 13.
2. Eric Butterworth, 'Race Relations: the next step', (chapter 9) in *The Year Book of Social Policy in Britain, 1973,* (1974). Note: this series ended in 1989, to be replaced by the *Social Policy Review.*
3. Crossman, *Diaries,* vol. 2, p. 20n.
4. Crossman, *Diaries,* vol. 2, pp. 28–9.
5. Alan Little, 'The Race Relations Act, 1976', (chapter 7) in *The Year Book of Social Policy in Britain, 1973.*
6. See Christian Howard, 'Women and the professions' (chapter 7) and Nancy Seear, 'Equal opportunities for men and women' (chapter 8) in *The Year Book of Social Policy in Britain, 1973.*
7. Peter Townsend and Brian Abel-Smith, *The Poor and the Poorest, Occasional Papers in Social Administration,* (1966).
8. Kathleen Jones, John Brown and J. R. Bradshaw, *Issues in Social Policy,* (1978), revised edition (1984), chapter 3, *passim.*
9. *Social Services for All?* Fabian Tracts 382–4, (1968).

10. *Report of the Committee on Personal and Allied Social Services,* (the *Seebohm Report*), HMSO, Cmd. 3703, 1968.
11. Op. cit. paras 581–663.
12. Medical Services Review Committee, *A Review of Medical Services in Great Britain* (the *Porritt Report*), (Social Assay, 1963).
13. The first Green Paper: *The Administrative Structure of Medical and Related Services in England and Wales* (1968).
    The second Green Paper: *The Future Structure of the National Health Service* (1970).
    The White Paper: *National Health Service Reorganisation: a Consultative Document,* (1971).
    All these documents were published by H.M. Stationery Office.
14. *Management Arrangements for the Reorganised National Health Service* (The 'Grey Book'), (HMSO, 1972).
15. *Report of the Royal Commission on the National Health Service,* HMSO Cmnd. 7615, 1979 (The *Merrison Report*), para. 3.23, p. 27.
16. White Paper *Patients First,* (HMSO, 1979).
17. Hedley Marshall, 'An introduction to reorganisation', in *The Year Book of Social Policy in Britain 1973,* Part I: The Reform of Local Government, p. 4.
18. *Report of the Royal Commission on Local Government,* (the *Redcliffe Maud Report*), 3 vols, HMSO, Cmd. 4040–1, 1969.
19. J. D. Stewart, 'The politics of local government reorganisation', in *The Year Book of Social Policy in Britain, 1973,* p. 23.
20. *Children and their Primary Schools: Report of the Central Advisory Council for Education (England)* (the *Plowden Report*) 2 vols, (HMSO, 1966 and 1967).
21. A. H. Halsey (ed.), *Educational Priority: Report on a Project sponsored by the Department of Education and Science and the Social Science Research Council,* (HMSO, 1972), vol: 1, *EPA Problems and Policies.*
22. H. Acland in Martin Bulmer (ed.), *Social Research and Royal Commissions of Inquiry: the lessons of experience,* (1983).
23. Brian Cox and A. E. Dyson (eds), *The Black Papers on Education,* Davis-Paynter, 1971; Brian Cox and Rhodes Boyson (eds), *Black Paper 1975,* 1975.
24. Paul Lodge, 'Education', in Paul Wilding (ed.), *In Defence of the Welfare State,* (1986), pp. 22–3.
25. *Parliamentary Debates (Hansard), House of Commons,* vol. 195, cd. 776, The Rt. Hon. James Callaghan (Prime Minister), 14 July 1977.
26. Quoted by Martin Loney, *Community Against Government,* (1983), p. 183.
27. Loney, op. cit.

28. Lewis Corina, 'Community Work and Local Authority Decision-making', *Community Development Journal* (1976) 11, (3), pp. 179–80.
29. Loney, op. cit., p. 145.
30. For comment see Loney, op. cit., pp. 65–7; Jones, Brown and Bradshaw, op. cit., pp. 170–3.
31. 'Secretary of State for the Social Services' was the somewhat misleading title given to the minister in charge of the Department of Health and Social Security (DHSS) from 1967 to 1988.
32. J. R. Bradshaw, *The Family Fund: an initiative in social policy*, (1980).
33. R. C. O. Matthews' preface to Michael Rutter and Nicola Madge, *Cycles of Transmitted Deprivation*, (1976).
34. Rutter and Madge, op. cit., pp. 302–28.
35. Muriel Brown and Nicola Madge, *Despite the Welfare State*, (1982).
36. Denis Healey, *The Time of my Life*, (1989), pp. 378–9.
37. Healey, op. cit., p. 434.

Sources

This chapter covers very recent history, and since it deals with a period of ideological conflict, only the lapse of time will make dispassionate analysis possible. However, no period is better supplied with primary material – reports of Royal Commissions and Government Committees, White Papers, Green Papers, research reports and pamphlets were published in profusion.

The journal *New Society* (which has now merged with the *New Statesman*) provided a weekly analysis of events. In the 1970s, it was devoted very largely to social policy issues, though it later veered towards the more sensational aspects of sociology.

The Year Book of Social Policy in Britain provides analyses by politicians and academics of current issues during the period covered by this chapter.

Fabian Tracts and other publications of the Fabian Society provide an important source of left-wing analysis in the 1960s and 1970s. The Fabian Society has continued to act as the research arm of the Labour Party.

CPAG publications include the *Poverty Leaflets, Poverty Pamphlets, Rights Guides, Rights Leaflets* and the *Welfare Rights Bulletin*. The Low Pay Unit produced its own series of research reports on families with low incomes.

The Institute of Economic Affairs produced over 300 pamphlets between 1964 and 1970, of which the Hobart Papers were probably the most influential. Most of these follow the approach of the New Right. Some are described as representing a Liberal approach – but 'Liberal' is used in a sense which would have been recognized by Lord Melbourne and Nassau Senior rather than David Steel and Alan Beith. The IEA has also produced *Progress Reports, Occasional Papers* and *Lectures. Full Employment at Any Price?* by F. A. von Hayek (no. 45 of The 1975 Occasional Papers series) is of particular significance in analysing the economic basis of monetarist thinking.

Phoebe Hall's *Reforming the Welfare* is a good introduction to the Seebohm reforms. Ronald Walton's *Women in Social Work,* describes the changes which took place when men began to take over many of the senior posts which had previously been filled by women.

The research reports of the EPA Projects are summarized in A. H. Halsey's *E.P.A. Problems and Policies.* Five volumes of research material were also published. The CDP Projects are summarized and listed in Martin Loney's *Community Against Government* and the Transmitted Deprivation Projects in Brown and Madge, *Despite the Welfare State.*

The Central Council for Education and Training in Social Work (CCETSW) has issued a number of influential reports on the nature of social work, and recruitment and training issues.

Biographies, autobiographies and memoirs of leading politicians of the period, such as Enoch Powell, James Callaghan, Barbara Castle, Denis Healey, Harold Wilson and R. H. S. Crossman provide much information on how and why particular policies were followed. Edward Heath is reported to be writing his memoirs. But much of the official material, being covered by the 30-year rule, will not be available for consultation until early next century.

The full force of opposition to 'Welfare State' policies comes out most clearly in the *Black Papers on Education* (Cox and Dyson, Cox and Boyson), in Rhodes Boyson's *Down with the Poor,* in which he compares the British public to battery hens, imprisoned by the bonds of Socialist thinking, and in *Breaking the Spell of the Welfare State,* by Digby Anderson, June Lait and David Marsland, which argues for major cuts in social work and education.

Chapter 14

1. *Annual Abstract of Statistics 1988,* p. 302, table 17.27, *'England and Wales:* Bankruptcies': 1979, 3, 158; 1986, 6, 682; p. 303, table 17.31, 'Company liquidations': 1979, 8,567; 1986, 18,930.
2. K. Harris, *Thatcher,* Weidenfeld and Nicolson, 1988, also Fontana, 1989, pp. 101–6.
3. The phrase is attributed to Samuel Brittan. See Raymond Plant, 'The very idea of a Welfare State' in Philip Bean, John Ferris and David Whynes, *In Defence of Welfare,* (1986), p. 7.

4. Raymond Plant, op. cit., pp. 5–6, quoting F. A. von Hayek, *The Constitution of Liberty*, (1960), p. 44.
5. Plant, op. cit., pp. 14–15.
6. *Annual Abstract of Statistics, 1988*, table 6.8, p. 116. (unemployment figures).
7. Adrian Sinfield, *What Unemployment Means*, (Oxford, 1981).
8. K. Harris, op. cit., pp. 215–17, 224–36.
9. J. Bradshaw, 'A Defence of Social Security', in Bean, Ferris and Whynes, op. cit., pp. 231–2.
10. See section 1 of *The Year Book of Social Policy in Britain, 1973*.
11. Department of Health and Social Security, *Report of the National Health Service Management Committee*, chairman, Sir Roy Griffiths, (HMSO, 1983), (the first *Griffiths Report*).
12. *Working for Patients, Contracts for Health Services: Operational Principles*, (HMSO, 1989).
13. House of Commons, *Second Report of the Social Services Committee 1984–5*: Community Care with special reference to adult mentally ill and mentally handicapped people, vol. 1, (HMSO, 1985).
14. Audit Commission for England and Wales, *Making a Reality of Community Care*, (HMSO, 1986).
15. Community Care: agenda for action, a report to the Secretary of State for Social Services by Sir Roy Griffiths (HMSO, 1988). (The second *Griffiths Report*).
16. *Caring for People: community care in the next decade and beyond*, HMSO, Cm. 849, 1989.
17. Colin Brewer and June Lait, *Can Social Work Survive?*, (1980), pp. 51, 48, 33.
18. *Social Work Today*, (1988) xix, 37: 6–7.
19. Jonathan Bradshaw, in Bean, Ferris and Whynes, op. cit., pp. 228–9.
20. Ibid.
21. Tim Dant, 'Old, poor and at home: social security and elderly people in the community', in Sally Baldwin, Gillian Parker and Robert W. Walker (eds), *Social Security and Community Care*, (Avebury, 1988), pp. 74–5.
22. Sarah Monk and Mark Kleinman, 'Housing', in Philip Brown and Richard Sparks (eds), *Beyond Thatcherism*, (1989), p. 121.
23. Stuart Lowe, 'Home Ownership and Capital Accumulation', in Maria Brenton and Clare Ungerson (eds), *Social Policy Review, 1990*, 1990.
24. Monk and Kleinman, op. cit., p. 127.
25. Monk and Kleinman, op. cit., p. 128.
26. *Housing: the Government's Proposals*, HMSO Cmnd. 214, 1987.
27. Monk and Kleinman, op. cit., p. 123.

28. Council of Mortgage Lenders: *Independent,* 15 September 1990.
29. Hugo Young, *One of Us,* (1989), p. 414.
30. Young, op. cit., p. 413.
31. *Government Statistical Services,* HMSO Cmnd. 8236, 1981, Annexe 2, para. 17.
32. Reported in *The Independent,* 9 October 1989.
33. Harris, *Thatcher,* p. 291.
34. *Inequalities in Health, Report of a Research Working Group,* chairman Sir Douglas Black, DHSS, 1980 (photocopy in quarto only). Published as, Peter Townsend and Nick Davidson (eds), *Inequalities in Health: the Black Report,* (1982).
35. *The Brixton Disorders, 10–12 April 1981, report of an inquiry by Lord Scarman,* HMSO Cmnd, 8427, 1981.
36. Preface to the *Scarman Report.*
37. *Faith in the City: a call for action by the Church and the Nation,* Report of the Archbishop's Commission on Urban Priority Areas, (1985), para 1.34, p. 18.
38. *Faith in the City,* para. 1.44, p. 22.
39. Sheila McKechnie, Director of Shelter, in a television interview Channel 4 News, 12 December 1989.
40. Malcolm Weller, R. I. Tobiansky et al., 'Psychosis and destitution at Christmas', *The Lancet,* (1989) 23/30 December, 335 (8680): 1509–11.
41. Regina v. Social Security Fund Inspector, ex parte Sherwin and ex parte Roberts, Queen's Bench Divisional Court (Lord Justice Woolf and Mr Justice Pill) 21 February 1990.

Sources

For this most recent period, sources tend to be very scattered – which is why there are so many footnotes. As the text suggests, official sources, so plentiful in the 1970s, have been less than adequate. The two principal biographies of Margaret Thatcher, while necessarily focussing on one personality, do contain helpful references to such major events as the 'Winter of Discontent', the ending of consensus politics, the battle with the trade unions and the miners' strike, and the conflict with the left-wing local authorities. The pamphlet publications of the Institute of Economic Affairs and the Fabian Society, so plentiful in the 1970s, are now relatively sparse.

The Acts of Parliament of 1988–1990 and the explanatory papers are worth reading: commentaries will no doubt appear in due course, but many of the new proposals will not take full effect and be susceptible of analysis until the mid-1990s. For the present, we are largely dependent on press comment and television documentaries.

Nicholas Bosanquet's *After the New Right,* Brown and Sparks' *Beyond Thatcherism,* Paul Wilding's *In Defence of the Welfare State* and Bean, Ferris and Whynes' *In Defence of Welfare* are useful collections of papers by academic writers in social policy, containing interim analyses of policies in the 1980s, and some speculations on the possible directions of change in the 1990s.

Epilogue

1. John Mortimer, *Paradise Postponed,* (1985) (Penguin, 1986), p. 363.
2. James Gleick, *Chaos: making a new science,* (1987).
3. See R. A. Pinker, *The Idea of Welfare,* (1979), especially chapters 1, 5 and 12.
4. Karl Popper, *Unended Quest: an intellectual autobiography,* (1976).
5. T. S. Eliot, *The Four Quartets,* I 'Burnt Norton', (1936).

Index

Absolute poverty, 67–8
Acts of Settlement, 2
'African Parallel', 57–9
Age Concern, 120
Agricultural labourers, 4
AIDS, 95, 211
Alexander, Mrs. Cecil, 44
Althorp, Lord, 16–17
Altruism, 43
Andover Scandal, 24, 69
Anti-Poor Law movement, 20–23
Army Bureau of Current Affairs, 131, 133
Arnott, Dr. Neil, 25
Ashley, Lord, see Shaftesbury
Asquith, Herbert, 95, 97, 98, 99
Assistance Board, 123, 138
Attlee, Clement, 122, 135–6, 148–9
Audit Commission for Local Authorities, Report, 195–6

Barlow Report, 145–6, 147, 156, 157
Barnardo, Dr. Thomas, 44, 48
Baths and Wash-houses Act, 1846, 34
Baxter, G. Wythen, 22–3
Book of the Bastiles, 22–3
Bentham, Jeremy, 10–12, 14, 15, 17, 24, 25, 33, 50, 52

Bevan, Aneurin, 139, 140–1, 143, 151–2, 153, 156
Beveridge, William, x, 42, 53, 97, 119, 125–133, 152, 153
Beveridge Report, 125–33
Bevin, Ernest, 122
Blanesburgh, 109–10
Births, Deaths and Marriages, registration of, 27, 57
Birth-rate 32–3, 77–79, 134–5, 156, 170
Bismarck, 99
Black Papers on Education, 182
Black Report on Inequalities in Health, 205
Blomfield, Bishop, 14, 17, 28
Boards of Governors, 14
Boards of Guardians, 48, 69–71, 88, 91
Boer War recruits, 77
Book of the Bastiles, 22–3
Booth, Charles, ix, 60–3, 66, 67, 77, 83, 87, 97, 108–9, 129
Booth, General William, 44, 45, 59–60
Bosanquet, Helen, 82, 83–4, 87
Bradford Argus, 22
Brewer, Colin, 197
Broad Street Pump, 40
Bridewells, 2
Briggs, Asa, 68

British Corporation of the Poor, 6
British Association, 27
British Association of Social
   Workers, 174
British Social Attitudes, 202–3
Brixton Riot, 205–6
Brougham, Lord, 7–8
Brown Plan, 140
Bruce, Maurice, ix
Brundage, Anthony, 15
Building societies, 51
Butler, R. A., 122, 144–5
Butterfly Effect, 210

Carey's Workhouse, 6
Cash nexus, 164, 190
Castle, Barbara, 149–50
Catallaxy, 190
Cecil, David, 15–16
Cemeteries, 36–7, 39, 189
Central Council for Education and
   Training in Social Work, 174–5,
   197–8
Centralization, 12, 14, 19, 21–2, 35,
   36, 41, 72–3, 193
Chaos theory, 210
Chadwick, Edwin, 14–19, 20, 23,
   24, 25–40, 57, 72–3
Charity Organisation Society, 44,
   47–9, 67, 76–7, 90, 91, 94, 111
Chartist Movement, 46–7
Child Benefit, see Family
   Allowance
Child Poverty Action Group,
   168–9, 184, 208
Children Act 1908, 96
Children Act, 1989, 197, 202
Children's Allowances, 129
Cholera, 25, 26, 28, 37, 40, 72
Christianity and the Social Order,
   122
Churchill, Winston S., 98–9, 100,
   122, 130–1, 134–5, 149, 150, 152
Citizens' rights, 164
Classification, see workhouse
   classification
Coalition Government, 1940–5,
   122, 133, 143

Cobbett, William, 14, 15, 22
Cole, Margaret and G. D. H. ix,
   51
Combination Acts, 50
Coming of the Welfare State, ix
Communist Party, 107–8
Community care, 154–6
Community charge, 193
Community Development
   Projects, 182–4
Comprehensive schools, 159
Consensus politics, welfare
   consensus, x, 150, 164–5, 184,
   186–7, 188
Conservative policy, 66, 82, 112,
   122, 130–1, 153, 154–6, 159, 162,
   166, 173, 182, 184–6, 189–208
'Consumption' (tuberculosis), 26
'Conviction politics', 165
Co-operative Movement, 52
Corn Laws, 5
County Council Act, 1888, 74–5
Cripps, Stafford, 150
Cronin, A. J., 107
Crossman, R. H. S., 166, 167
Crowther Report, 160
Culture of poverty, 185

Darkest England, In, 59–60
Diamond Commission (Royal
   Commission on Income and
   Wealth), 203
'Deserving' and 'undeserving',
   47–8, 74, 91, 94, 114–5, 188
Dickens, Charles, 21
Disabled Persons Employment
   Act, 1944, 133
Disraeli, Benjamin, 22
Distressed Areas, see Special
   Areas
Dorchester labourers, 16, 18, 50

Economic and Social Studies
   Research Council, 185–6
Economic distress, recession, 4–5,
   104–9, 143, 186–7
Education, 76, 95, 133, 143–5,
   158–62

Education Act 1902 (Balfour's Act), 95
Education Act, 1944, (Butler Act) 133, 143–5, 158, 202
Education (Administrative Provisions) Act 1907, 96
Education (Provision of Meals) Act, 1906, 96–7
Education Reform Act 1988, 201, 202
Educational Priority Areas, 180–1
Educational Reconstruction 1943, 145
Egg-shaped sewer, 28
Eleven plus examination, 144–5, 159
Emergency Medical Service, 120, 121, 124
Employment, see Unemployment, Full Employment
Employment Act, 1980, 191
Employment Act 1982, 191–2
Employment Training Schemes, 201, 207
Enclosure movement, 3–4
'End of ideology', 164–5
Essay on the Principles of Population, 8–11
Equal Opportunities Commission, 168
Evacuation, 120, 121, 122
Evangelicals in Action, 45
Evolution of the Welfare State, ix, 43, 95, 113, 123
Executive Councils, 142–3
Expenditure cuts, 1970s, 186–7

Fabian Society, 85–6, 89, 90, 93, 168, 170, 171
Facts for Socialists, 86
Faith in the City, 206
'Fares Fair', 193, Family Allowances, 133, 136, 168
Family Credit, 198, 199, see Family Income Supplement
Family Fund, 184–5
Farr, Dr. William, 27–8, 38, 71
Family Allowances, 129, 136

Family Income Supplement, 5–6, 184, 198
Finer, S. E., 15, 34, 38
'Five Giants' (Beveridge), 126, 134, 136–47
Foundations of the Welfare State, ix
Fraser, Derek, ix, 43, 95, 113, 123
Friendly societies, 49–50, 101, 102
Fry, Elizabeth, 45
Full Employment, 129, 131, 143, 151
Funeral grant, 129
Further education, 160

Gaitskell, Hugh, 151
Galton, Francis, 59–60
Geddes Axe, 105
General Board of Health, 35–41
General practice, 142–3
General Strike, 1926, 104–7, 109
General Theory of Unemployment, Interest and Money, 113
German insurance schemes, 99
Gilbert's Act, 7
Gregg, Pauline, 123, 145
Goschen Minute, 47–8, 74, 91, 114–5
Greater London Council, 180, 193
'Greatest happiness' principle, 11
'Grey Book', 177, 194
Griffiths, Roy, 194–5, 196
Guillebaud Committee, 152

Hall, Sir Benjamin, 40, 41
Halsey, A. H., 206
Hammond, J. L. and Barbara, 3–4, 19
Hannington, Wal, 107–8, 112
Hayek, F. A. von, 205
Health insurance, 101–3
Health of Towns movement, 33–4
Health services, 118–9, 129, 194–5, see also National Health Service
Health Through Choice, 153
Health visiting, 79

Health Vistors' and Social
  Workers' Training Act, 1962, 164
Healy, Denis, 186
Heasman, Kathleen, 45
Heath, Edward, 166, 182
Hedonistic calculus, 11, 15
Hereditary Genius, 59–60
Hill, Octavia, 44, 82, 84–5
Hobsbawm, Eric, 13
Holman, Gregory, 109–11, 112
Holman, Robert, 67
Hospital Plan, 154–5
Home ownership, 199–201
Homelessness, 188, 195, 207–8
House of Commons, Report of
  Social Services Committee, 195
Household Means Test, 111, 123
Housing Act 1949, 156–7
Housing market, 200–1
Housing societies, 50–1
Housing legislation, 76, 156–7
Human Needs Diet, 67
Hunger Marches, 107–8
Hutchinson Bequest, 86
Hyndman, F. A., 60–1

'Impotent poor', 7, 92
Income and Wealth, Royal
  Commission on, 203
Infant mortality rate, 78–9
INLOGOV, 177–8
Inner city, see Urban Priority
  Areas
Inspectorates, 14, 23, 33, 36
Institute of Economic Affairs, 153,
  169–70
Insurance, see Health Insurance,
  Unemployment Insurance,
  National Insurance
'Iron law of wages', 10

Jewkes, John 152–3
Jones, Agnes, 69, 70
Joseph, Sir Keith, 184–6
Justices of the peace, see
  magistrates

Kay, Dr. James, 25

Keynes, Maynard, 113–4, 131, 143,
  186
Khaki Election, 122, 123, 133

Labour Exchanges Act 1908, 97,
  101
Labour Party policy, 94, 95, 110,
  122–3, 133, 135–8, 148, 134, 148,
  149–52, 159, 162, 166, 170, 173,
  180, 183, 186–7, 192, 193
Labour rate, see 'Rate on aid of
  wages'
Laissez-faire, 7, 12, 32, 190
Lait, June, 197
Landowners, 2, 3–4
Lansbury, George, 86, 88, 90
Lark Rise, 98
Less eligibility, 15, 17, 19
Law Centres, 169
'Layabouts', 188
Lend-lease , cessation of, 148–9
Lewis, Thomas Frankland, 17–18,
  19
Lewis, George Cornewall, 18
Liberal party policy, 1, 13, 15–16,
  24, 66, 67, 95–103, 112
*Life and Labour of the People of
  London*, ix, 61–3
Life chances, 31
Lloyd George, David, 95–102,
  112
Local authorities, 74–81, 139, 142,
  154, 158, 172–5, 177–180, 192–4,
  195–8, 199–202
Local Authority Social Services
  Act, 1970, 173
Local authority Social Services
  Departments, 172–5, 197–8
Local boards of health, 35, 41
Local Government Act, 1929, 114
Local Government Act, 1972,
  179–80
Local Government Board, 73–4, 92
Loch, C. S., 67, 82–3, 87, see also
  Charity Organisation Society.
'Logic of the will', 12
*London Labour and the London
  Poor*, 57–9

London School of Economics, 86, 135, 162–3, 164
Loney, Martin, 183
Low Pay Unit, 169
Lyon, Alex, 182

Mack, Mary, 11
MacLeod, Iain, 152, 164
Magistrates, 2, 12
Majority Report (Poor Laws, 1909) 90–1, 94, 114
Malthus, T. H., Malthusian theory, 8–10, 17, 19, 32, 66, 77
Married women workers, 105, 128, 136
Marshall, T. H., 162, 164–5
Martineau, Harriet, 10
Marwick, Arthur, 123
Maternity and Child Welfare, 77–80
Maternity benefits, 136
Mayhew, Henry, 57–9, 60
Means Tests, 111, 123, 152, 171
Medical Department of the Privy Council, 41, 71–3
Medical Officers of Health, 34, 74, 173, 177
Medical profession, medical practice, 37–9, 41, 79, 152
Medical Qualifications Act, 41
Melbourne, Lord, 1, 5, 15–16
Mental Health Act, 1983, 197
Miasmatic theory, 38–9, 40, 41
Midwives, 79–80
Militant Tendency, 193
Milk depots, 79
Mill, John Stuart, 29–30
Millbank Penitentiary, 11–12
Miners, 105–7, 192
'Ministry of all the Talents, 1806, 1
Minority Report, (Poor Laws, 1909) 90, 91–4, 135
More, Hannah, 50
More, Sir Thomas, 3
Morpeth, 35, 37, 40
Morrell, Derek, 182, 183
Morrison, Herbert, 122
Mortality rates, 30, 31–3, 71, 78–9

Mortimer, John, 208
Moser, Claus, 204
Mutual aid, 42, 49–53, 56
My Apprenticeship, 85–6

National Assistance Act, 1948, 138–9, 142
National Assistance Board, 138–9
National Health Service 96, 129, 140–3, 151–6, 175–7, 194–5, see also Health Services
National Health Service Act 1946, 140–3
National Health Service and Community Care Act, 1990, 195, 196–7, 202
National Health Service Reorganisation Act, 1974, 175–7
National Institute of Social Work, 163
National Insurance Act 1911, 100–103, 126
National Insurance Act 1946, 136, 138, 139, 151
National Unemployed Workers' Movement, 107–8
Nationalization, 143, denationalization, 188
New Poor Law, 14–24
New Right, 165, 169, 187, 197
New Towns, 147, 157–8
Newsom Report, 160–1
Nicholls, George, 17
Nightingale, Florence, 43–4, 45, 47, 69, 79
'Ninepence for fourpence', 102
Nuisances Removal Act, 1846, 34

Oil Crisis, 186
Old Age Pensions, 96, 97–9, 101, 105, 111, 114, 116
Old Poor Law, 1–7, 10
Oliver Twist, 21
Orwell, George, 108–9, 111
Our Partnership, 86–7
Outdoor relief, 14–15, 18, 23, 69, 89, 91, 114
Overseers of the poor, 2

Owen, Robert, 51–2

Pahl, Ray, 206
Parish labour, 6
Panopticon, 12, 15
People's Banks, 50, 51
Philanthropy, 42–9, 56
'People's Budget', 1909, 99–100
Personal Social Services, 172–5
Physical Deterioration, Committee on, 77–9
Pleasure-pain principle, 11
Plowden Report, 181
Political and Economic Planning (PEP), 117–9
Poll tax, see Community Charge
Polytechnics, 161–2, 201–2
Poor and the Poorest, 168
Poor Law Act, 1930, 94, 114–5
Poor Law administration, 69–71, 81, 111, 117–8
Poor Law Amendment Act, 1834, x, xi, 13–24
Poor Law Amendment Bill, 1834, voting, 16
Poor Law Board, 1848–71, 24, 73
Poor Law Commission, 1834–48, 16–20, 23–4
Poor Law Commission, 1832–4, 7, 13–14
Poor Law Commissioners, appointment of, 16
Poor Law, decline of, 110–11, 114–5, 123, 138, 139
Poor Law Report, 1834, 14–15
Poor Laws, Royal Commission on, 1905–9, 82–94, 164
Poor Laws, Select Committee on, 1837, 23
Population increase, 4–5, 26
Population, Essay on the Principles of, 8–11
Positive discrimination, 181
Poverty – A Study of Town Life, xi, 63–8, 77, 97, 99
Poverty, definitions of, 63, 65–6, 67–8
Poverty Cycle, 66

Poverty Line, 63, 65, 67, 117
Poverty Surveys, 60–68, 115–9
Powell, Enoch, 152, 164, 167
Power and Influence, 131
Prescription charges, 152
Primary and secondary poverty, see Poverty Line
Prince Consort, 31
Privatization, 190, 195–6, 199, 200, 201, 202
Probation of Offenders Act, 1908, 96
Public Assistance, see Poor Law
Public expenditure, x, 188
Public Health Act 1848, 35
Public Health Act, 1875, 74

Quakers, 45
Queen Victoria, 4–5, 31, 54
Quetelet, Dr., 29

Race relations, 166–8, 191
Rayner, Derek, 204
'Rate in aid of wages', 5–6
Rathbone, Eleanor, 129
Rearmament, 114
Redcliffe-Maud Report, 178–9
Reddin, Mike, 171
Rees, Merlyn, 183
Reform Act, 1832, 1, 7
Regional Hospital Boards, 141
Regional Health Authorities, 175–7
Relative poverty, 67–8
Religious influences, 44, 45–6
Residential care, 139
Retirement pensions, 127, 128, 136
Ricardo, David, 10
Rich man in his castle, 44
'Right to buy', 199
'Ripple effect', 199
'Rivers of Blood, speech, 167
Roberts, David, 12
Roberts, Sam, 20–21
Robbins Report, 161
Roe, John, 28
Rose, George, 49
Roundsman system, 6

Rowntree, B. Seebohm, xi, 63–8, 77, 97, 99, 115–7, 129
Royal Commission on the Poor Laws, 1909, ix, 82–94, 100
Royal Commissions, 203–4
Royal Statistical Society, 60
Rudé, George, 13
Rule of Law, 189, 205
Rutter, M. and Nicola Madge, 185

Saatchi and Saatchi, 190
Salvation Army, 48, see General Booth
Sanitary engineers, 28, 33, 34, 36, 39, 41
Sanitary Act, 1866, 41, 71
Sanitary Report 1842, 28–33
Scargill, Arthur, 192
School meals, 76–7
Scarman, Leslie, 205
Scott Report, 146, 147, 156, 157
Schultz, Trudi, 67
'Scroungers', 188
Seebohm Report, 172–5
Self-eliminating mechanism, 11, 33
Self-Help, 42, 53–6, 189
Senior, Nassau 7–8, 14, 15, 16
Senior, Mrs. Nassau John, 71
Select Committee on the Poor Laws, 1816–17, 7
Select Committee on the Poor Laws, 1824, 7
Selectivity, 171
Serota, Lady, 175
'Setting the poor to work', 6
Settlement, Laws of, 2, 8, 15
Sewage system, 28, 29, 30, 31, 33, 40
Shaftesbury, 7th Earl, 35, 40, 44–5, 46, 47
Shaw-Lefevre, J. G., 17
Sickness benefit, see Health Insurance
Simey, T. S., 63
Simon, Dr. John, 34, 40, 71–3, 74
Sinfield, Adrian, 190–1
Single mothers, 89
Smart, William, 87, 88–89

Smiles, Samuel, 42, 53–6
Smith, Adam, 7
Snow, Dr. John, 40
Social control, 43, 46–7
Social Democratic Federation, 60
Social engineering, 151
Social Fund, 198, 208
Social Insurance, 125–30, 136–8, 151, 184, 198–9, 207, see also National Insurance
Social Policy and Administration, 150–1
Social reconstruction, 122, 125, 148
Social Science Association, 57
Social Science Research Council, 185–6
Social Security, see Social Insurance
Social Security Act 1986, 198, 202
Social workers, 162–4, 172–5, 197–8
Southwood Smith, Dr. T., 25, 34, 37, 38, 45
Special Areas, 112–3, 114, 117, 121
Specific contagion, theory of, 38–9, 71–2
Speenhamland System, 6
Statistical Society of London, 27, 57
Statistical techniques, 27, 29, 31, 57, 71, 137
Statistics, inadequacy of, 60, 204
Survey techniques, 14, 29, 61, 63, 64–6, 67–8
'Swing Riots', 13–14

Taylor, A. J. P., ix, 106
Temple, Archbishop William, 122
The Stars Look Down, 107
Thane, Pat, ix
Thatcher, Margaret, 165, 189–90, 194, 202
Thompson, Flora, 98
Titmuss, R. M., 121, 153, 155
Tolpuddle Martyrs, 16, 18, 50
Tory governments before 1830, 1
Town and Country Planning Act, 1947, 147, 156

Townsend, Peter, 67, 205, and Brian Abel-Smith, 168, 171
Trade cycle, 92, 104, 109, 113–4, 143
Trade unions, 13, 49, 50, 104–7, 186, 189, 190–2
'Transmitted Deprivation' 185
Transport improvements, effect of, 75–6
'Trickle down' philosophy, 190, 205
Tuberculosis, 26, 72
Tuke, William, 45
Twining, Louisa, 69–71
Typhus, typhoid fever, 26, 28, 31, 70, 72

'Uncrowned Kings of Somerset House', 17
Underclass, 205–7
Unemployed Struggles, 1919–36, 107–8
Unemployment, 105–14, 116, 121, 143, 190–2, see also Full Employment.
Unemployment Assistance Act, 111
Unemployment Assistance Board, 111, 115, 117–8, 123, 136
Unemployment insurance, 101–3, 104–14, 127, 129–30, 136
Universality, 171
Universities, 161, 201–2
University Grants Committee/ Universities Funding Council, 201
Urban Priority Areas, 206–7
Uthwatt Report, 145, 147
Utilitarianism, 10–12, 28, 33, see Bentham

Vagrancy laws, 2
Victorian Origins of the British Welfare State, 12
Victorian Philanthropy, 42–49, 56

'Vital statistics', 27, 41
Voluntary services, voluntary action, 42–56, 139, 171

Wall Street crash, 1931, 105
Walter, John Walter II, 21–2, 23
Walter, John Walter III, 39, 40
War and social policy, 121–5
Water supply, 33, 39, 40, 188
Webb, Beatrice, ix, 61, 85–90, 91–4, 97, 100, 135
Webb, Sidney, ix, 91–4, 97, 100, 135
Welfare consensus, see Consensus politics
Welfare Rights, 169
'Welfare State', x, xii, 94, 122, 125, 133, 147–8, 162, 169, 189–90, 209–10
Weller, Malcolm, 207
'Wenceslaus myth', 190
Whigs, 1, see Liberals
'White Paper Chase', 132
Wickwar, Bernard, 115
Widows Orphans and Old Age Pensions Act, 1925, 114, 128
Widows' Pensions, 127, 128
Willinck Plan, 140
Wilson, Harold, 166
'Winter of Discontent', 188–9
Workers' Educational Association, 132
Workhouses, 6, 14–15
Workhouse classification 15, 19–20, 70
Workhouse conditions, 20, 69–71
Workhouse diets, 19, 20, 24
Workshouse staff, 69–71
Workhouse Test, 7, 15
Workhouse Unions, Union workhouses, 7, 15, 19, 20
Workhouse Visiting, 69–71

Younghusband, Eileen, *Younghusband Report*, 162–4, 174